The Ramayana

Other books in this series

The Mahabharata

In Worship of Shiva

Hymns of Guru Nanak

The Ramayana

Lakshmi Lal

Illustrations by

Badri Narayan

Orient Longman

ORIENT LONGMAN LIMITED

Registered Office
3-6-272 Himayatnagar, Hyderabad 500 029

Other Offices
Kamani Marg, Ballard Estate, Bombay 400 038
17 Chittaranjan Avenue, Calcutta 700 072
160 Anna Salai, Madras 600 002
1/24 Asaf Ali Road, New Delhi 110 002
80/1 Mahatma Gandhi Road, Bangalore 560 001
3-6-272 Himayatnagar, Hyderabad 500 029
City Centre Ashok, Govind Mitra Road, Patna 800 004
House No. 28/31, 15 Ashok Marg, Lucknow 226 001
S.C. Goswami Road, Panbazar, Guwahati 781 001
Plot No. 365, Sahid Nagar, Bhubaneswar 751 007

Reprinted 1989, 1991, 1994

ISBN 0 86131 805 6

Book Design: Orient Longman

Phototypeset in Galliard by Phoenix Phototype Setters
Nariman Point, Bombay 400 021

Text printed in India at Hitech Printing Services,
Mazgaon, Bombay 400 010

Colour printing in India at Krishna Art Printery,
Byculla, Bombay 400 027

Published by Orient Longman Limited,
Kamani Marg, Ballard Estate, Bombay 400 038

Table of Contents

Colour Plates

Preface

There is a special need to retell the Ramayana in English, for the days of the East-West divide are over, and there is scope for mutual East-West enrichment. A global cultural reservoir is no longer a dream. Cross-cultural exchanges build up spiritual strengths so necessary to counter the flood of materialism that we could so easily drown in. English links worldwide and is an ideal language to convey universal concepts. It is fresh, porous and breathing, with a vocabulary that soaks in and holds virtually any idea.

In the writing of this particular Ramayana, two things exercised my mind—the relevance of this ancient work to the contemporary reader and the devising of a style that would convey its essence with a minimum loss of flavour. A high-flown, scriptural, archaic idiom, sprinkled with the gold-dust of antiquity, would have been an obvious way out. It might also have drained the Ramayana of its vigour and vitality. Intuitively, therefore I decided to be led by Valmiki's vivid and colourful imagery and retained throughout the parallels, the symbols, the anecdotes of the original Sanskrit. In the process, I stretched, even at times twisted and turned the English language into accommodating the rich and often heavy burden of Indian metaphor—the English of this volume is, in places, as the Queen would never speak it. But it held, and the contemporaneity of the Ramayana, its flesh-and-blood quality, its sap, strained through. All this, of course, arose out of my decision to read the original Sanskrit and not depend on translations, however faithful, literal and painstaking.

And here, I would like to thank my teacher Dr. G.H. Godbole for reading the Sanskrit Ramayana with me and lighting up the spaces in between with his wide knowledge of ancient Indian texts. I acknowledge his expert guidance with gratitude and reverence.

LAKSHMI LAL

Bombay
April, 1987

*To my mother
who taught me how to read
between the lines*

Introduction to the Text

The Ramayana, like anything to do with ancient India, is difficult to date precisely. It is a tangled skein of history, myth, legend, time, place and circumstance and unravels only to reveal that no piece of literature remains untouched in the oral tradition. Whatever was composed and recited grew and gathered accretions.

The Ramayana is largely the work of a single author, Valmiki, generally believed to have been a contemporary of its hero, Rama. The poem consists of 24,000 verses, divided into seven cantos. It tells us, quite simply, in the bardic style of epic lore, and in a distinctive metre, the story of Rama, prince and later, king of Kosala.

The central figure, Rama, is human, then superhuman and finally divine—divinity settling like a thin layer on a core of superhumanity. This describes the poetic journey of Rama through the verses of the Valmiki Ramayana with its accepted additions and interpolations. Subsequently, given a few more centuries of time, we have the full-blown and devoutly worshipped Rama of today, bathed in the many-splendoured visions of the saint-poets and composers of India—Kamban, Tulasidasa, Tyagaraja and many others.

Linguistic and historical research, aided by geographical, floral and faunal scrutiny, has enabled scholars to arrive at a reasonable set of surmises regarding the dates and provenance of the Ramayana. According to some scholars the earliest portions, which roughly take in Cantos II to VI, and which form the core, date back to 3000 B.C. Some, and these are quite a few, ascribe it to 1500 or 1400 B.C. And there are others who are more cautious and place the core between 500 and 400 B.C. with additions and interpolations continuing right up to the seventh century A.D., when, as it were, the Ramayana crossed the seas to South-East Asia.

The scene of action spreads from the north-west, over north-central and north-east India, going right down to the south—though Lanka could have been, at one time, a place in central India. The identification of it with present-day Sri Lanka is considered by some to be a later happening—a large body of water, perhaps a lake, turned, through interpolations, into an uncrossable ocean and Lanka itself became a full-fledged island with a fortified capital city. Time and place have therefore undergone shifts along with the enlargement of the Ramayana from the original 12,000 verses of Valmiki to the 24,000 verses that we have today.

It is possible to plot the course of the Ramayana material starting from its early existence as cycles of ballads centred round the cities of Ayodhya, Kishkindha and Lanka. Taking a cautious view, we can say that this would be around 500 B.C. These were then transmuted and composed into the Ramayana by Valmiki. Additions such as descriptions of cities, mention of certain geographical areas and boundaries came in later, urban sketches perhaps drawing heavily from Indo-Roman contacts.This stage could be anywhere from 300 B.C. to A.D. 100. The latest additions are those pertaining to the deification of Rama. These are the supernatural and mythical portions of the Balakanda and the Uttarakanda — the first and last cantos of the Ramayana as we have it today. This takes us up to A.D. 200. Also around this time this large and unwieldy body of verse was divided and structured into seven cantos. H.D. Sankalia tidies all this up into a neat summation when he says: 'The Ramayana as we have it today, seems to depict the socio-political conditions of India between the fourth century B.C. and the second century A.D.' This spread covers and explains the contradictions and anachronisms, which in places are quite startling, if not glaring.

Having cleared the historical path to the epic, we would do well to be guided by its legendary and mythical signposts —for here, in a way, lies the truth of the Ramayana, the secret of its survival. It collects, shapes and then enshrines a corpus of ethical and moral ideals pertaining to statesmanship, to human conduct and behaviour and to human relationships. King, country and family, held together by bonds of right rather than might, make up the subject matter of the Ramayana.

The Ramayana is exemplary in the literal sense of the word, and is therefore at times beyond the reach of human understanding or the scope of human endeavour. Rama is an ideal, perhaps an impossible ideal. He frequently persuades his family and associates into attempting the impossible. He himself, by implication and most often by demonstration, achieves the impossible. He is unbending in attitudes that he strikes dramatically and with a finality that staggers the imagination. He is a lesson in that most obsessive of ancient Indian preoccupations—dharma, rule of law and order in the life of a human being, the personal destiny that each one has to discover and then largely follow, but partly shape. The Ramayana is in that sense a compendium of object lessons in morality, a treatise of high thinking. It is the Indian book of values, in which dharma, the code, is all.

Comparisons are odious but unavoidable. It would be true to say that the Mahabharata, our second and later epic, is a panoramic view of life as it is, sprawling and inevitable, and the Ramayana a view of life as it should and could be. It is a model that stretches the human being to limits that draw upon the superhuman and divine in him. Rama lives at high moral pressure and his expectations for those nearest and dearest to him border on the unreasonable. To live with Rama is to live in a world of superhuman goals that one is expected to strain after life-long, without let, without give.

In this context one must remember that the Ramayana is set in the Treta Yuga, the second of the four ages that form the current time-cycle. The age of innocence, the Satayuga, had begun to acquire a slight tarnish as it turned into the Treta, and perhaps Valmiki set out to remind people of the goodness that held sway in an age not long gone by — and still largely prevalent. The later additions underline this and incorporate the idea of a divine incarnation sent down to set things right. As we know, by the time of the Mahabharata, the state of world affairs had escalated and assumed the nature of a crisis — as always, a moral crisis. Dharma had virtually capsized, for in the Mahabharata we are in the Dvapara Yuga, the third of the four ages, having travelled a long way from the Satayuga. Krishna had to resort to drastic measures, for soon it would be Kali Yuga, the fourth and final age, followed by total devastation.

In the Ramayana, there is a moral fervour fuelled by hope. In the Mahabharata, and specifically in the Gita, there is despair and utter confusion, a loss of faith and a darkening of the mind. Arjuna, warrior-hero and superman, lays down arms. He is faint with dread as cherished values blur and dissolve in his bewildered mind. There is no corresponding sketch of helplessness in the Ramayana. Hope and confidence run high in those battling for right, dharma. Equally, a sense of defeat pervades the opposite camp. The guidelines are clear, and the goals too. Consequently, there is a pristine purity, a daylight clarity in the story of Rama. It is as yet an unpolluted stream of thought and feeling wedded to the Vedic way of life, superstition and rites. Running parallel to this is the insistence on austerity.The crystal clarity of the inner life, fired by spiritual fervour and stoked with spiritual exercises, is exemplified by the sages. Rama draws sustenance from their way of life—excessive, obsessive. The victory of Rama over Ravana was a victory for the inner life. Ravana's vast resources, even though they included a great measure of penance and austerity, were directed not by dharma, but by a desire to dispense with dharma, even overcome it. Nowhere in Valmiki is there a glorification of Ravana. Even those closest to him do not absolve him of blame. The lines, or rather battle lines, between good and evil are drawn clearly.

To contemporary minds, working out their destinies in the Kali Yuga, the fourth and last of the ages in the current time cycle, the Ramayana might seem uncompromising in its pursuit of dharma. We move in the lengthening shadows of a moral twilight and before us looms the darkness of dead and dying values. We clutch at the straw of amorality that excuses and condones the evil in ourselves and others. We live uneasy lives, shutting out the blinding glare of truth, the searchlight of morality. Our world is an area of grey, slipping into darkness. But the story of Rama can still fascinate, still grip. For one thing, it is widespread and inescapable. Poetry, song and drama will work their magic and the seeds of Valmiki's vision will take fresh and repeated root. It is one of India's hidden weapons, performing unseen wonders, providing unknown strengths. It is cultural inputs such as the Ramayana that make the Indian illiterate, for instance, so wisely different from his unlettered brethren elsewhere in the world.

The Ramayana of Valmiki has been a seed bed and inexhaustible resource for many other Ramayanas, each well known in its own right. There are Ramayanas in all the major Indian languages, and Buddhist and Jain Ramayanas, too. Special mention must be made of the 'Kamba Ramayanam'

in Tamil written in the twelfth century and Tulasidasa's 'Ramacharitmanas' in Avadhi, written in the sixteenth century. Kamban and Tulasi are highly revered cult figures of the *bhakti* movement, the cult of devotion that earlier produced ecstatics and mystics like the Vaishnavite Alwars and the Shaivite Nayanmars of the South, and much later, saint-poets and composers like Tyagaraja. These inspired *bhaktas* or devotees were instrumental in completing and perfecting the process of deification that Rama began to undergo a few centuries after Valmiki.

LAKSHMI LAL

Prologue to the Epic

In the twilit hush of a forest hermitage, thick with trees and heavy with incense and meditation, by the light of a moon that played over dying ritual fires, two friends sat talking—Valmiki, chieftain-turned-sage, and Narada, the wandering bard and seer.

Narada, vina in hand, played to the beat of time past, present and future. He ranged freely over all three worlds, treading paths aerial, terrestrial and subterranean, taking all creation in his stride. He was mischief-maker, gossip and good-natured spy, all in one; beloved, respected and feared. He gathered and spread news, linking the universe with his storehouse of knowledge, information and rumour. Especially, he brought to the present, to the here and now, a perception sharpened by his unique and god-given gifts of hindsight and foreknowledge.

Valmiki had been musing on a vision of the ideal man. 'Is there,' he said, turning hopefully to his widely travelled companion, 'could there be, in all the three worlds, a man larger than life yet human? One who is an acknowledged hero, true to his word, firm in his vows, learned, eloquent and charming? A man patient as the earth and slow to anger—yet when roused, capable of striking terror into the gods themselves? Tell me, is there such a one?'

'Indeed there is,' replied Narada without the slightest hesitation. His face lit up with the memory of a rare experience. 'He is Rama of Ayodhya, strong, learned, of high principles, protector of the weak, destroyer of the oppressor.'

His fingers idling over his beloved vina, striking an occasional note, Narada gave Valmiki a glowing account of the life, times and deeds of Rama.

The jewel of the Ikshvaku clan, Rama spent his days on earth battling with all his might for dharma or righteousness. He fought with the fabled strength of his broad awesome shoulders, his long and sinewy arms, his blessed armoury of divine weapons; with all his training and all his skills. But most of all, he fought with the valour of spiritual strength, confident that right would always win over might and good triumph over evil.

Valmiki sat absorbed in the wonder of Narada's tale, his whole being suffused with the joy of discovery, his imagination fired. When Narada left, he rose gently, not wanting to disturb or dispel the splendid vision that stayed with him, keeping steady pace with his faltering, seeking steps. On the banks of the river Tamasa, he felt its presence; nor did it leave him as he plunged into the limpid waters or wandered the nearby forests in a blessed mood of high expectation.

It was in such a state of mind that he chanced to see a pair of mating birds, lost to the world as they perched with wings outspread, encircled in their bonds of love and desire.

All at once there was a bird-cry of agony. A hunter's arrow, swift and deadly, felled the male bird. The female rent the air with her piercing lament. Valmiki snapped out of his reverie and caught himself responding to the creature's distress with a loudly uttered curse. 'O hunter, may you never find rest or shelter for the sin of killing this bird who was in the throes of unfulfilled desire.'

It was a curse with a difference, a spontaneous outburst that had touched a poetic vein, sparking off a metric pattern—the original elegiac verse. Valmiki named it 'shloka'; literally, 'born of sorrow'.

The sage was both puzzled and perplexed, for sad though he was, and full of pity, he experienced a strange sense of fulfilment. He ordered his faithful disciple, Bharadwaja, to commit the verse immediately to memory.

Back at the hermitage Valmiki, entranced, drifted into the still waters of contemplation. The god Brahma, the Creator, soon appeared. As the sage waited on him, dutifully performing the rites of welcome, the memory of the verse returned and with it, afresh, the pain of the grieving bird. Valmiki recited the verse aloud in the presence of the divine Patriarch.

Brahma, giver of boons, smiled. He uttered the blessing that, above all, Valmiki craved to hear: 'Let this rhythmic phrase grow into poetry. Lodged in you, let it tell the story of Rama. As long as mountains stand on earth and rivers flow, this story will be remembered. So long, too, will you live in the higher regions. Such is my will and pleasure—and such your destiny.'

The Creator vanished. Valmiki's disciples, caught up in the magic of that moment, repeated the verse again and yet again, their joy rising higher with each chant, their souls astir with the birth of poetry. And the mystery awakened in Valmiki too, releasing in him the very fount of poesy, as the story of Rama, the Ramayana, Adikavya, the original poetic composition, our first and foremost poem, flowed like the waters of life unleashed.

sense of well-being prevailed. The men were brave; the women chaste. All was indeed well with the kingdom of Kosala.

As the sun spreads light and life with his circle of bright rays, so did Dasharatha and his band of lustrous ministers nurture their subjects and promote their welfare.

Happy in the stability of his kingdom, Dasharatha turned his thoughts to the question of the succession, for he had no sons. Summoning his council of ministers and priests, he announced his intention to perform the Ashwamedha, the traditional horse sacrifice, and his desire for a son who would be his heir.

Vasishtha and the others agreed with the king's plan. First, they advised, a suitable site should be chosen; they recommended to the king a place on the north bank of the Sarayu.

Preparations began. Kings and learned men were invited, the sacrificial site cleared, rich canopies raised, the sacrificial pit dug. Dasharatha issued the final instructions: 'Let loose the sacrificial horse to wander at will for a year. Follow him closely. Guard him well so that if and when he is captured and my power challenged, we are fully prepared.'

The rites proceeded smoothly with no hindrance. The year turned from one spring to the next, and the horse returned with never a challenge from prince or lord. The golden sacrificial pit, where the mystic fire blazed concealed from sight, was shaped like an eagle with wings outspread and set with precious gems. The priest tethered the horse, and with it three hundred other animals, all ready for the sacrifice.

Dasharatha's chief queen, Kausalya, in a solemn ceremony, severed the horse's head, and dutifully kept watch all night as custom demanded. In the morning the king, helped by the priests, trimmed the fat off the flesh for the ritual cooking and inhaled the sacred aroma for the prescribed length of time. For thus would he shed the burden of sin clinging to his corporeal self. More rituals followed as the sacrifice drew to a close.

Dasharatha, brimming with happiness at its completion, offered his whole kingdom to the officiating priests, such was his generosity. When they declined, he gave them gifts instead, gold and silver coins and cows in tens and thousands. But the king was not wholly content. His immediate object seemed no nearer fruition—the birth of sons, among them an heir for Kosala.

Responding to the king's unspoken thoughts, the chief priest then performed a special sacrifice. This was the Putrakameshti, prescribed for the begetting of children.

In the heavens, Vishnu the Preserver, driven by his own mysterious purposes, had chosen Dasharatha to father four sons, each of whom would be a part of his divine self. On earth, from the roaring fire of Dasharatha's sacrifice, to the sound of drumbeats, rose a being with a smouldering face, his burnished skin glowing in the firelight. He was clad all in red, and held out a golden pot with a silver lid, full of sweetened milk and rice.

'I come from the Creator,' he said, 'to give you this life-giving brew. Feed it to your wives and they will mother heirs to Kosala.'

Touching the vessel to his head in reverent thanks, Dasharatha went to his

queens in the inner apartments. He gave a portion each to Kausalya, Sumitra and Kaikeyi, and a second and last helping to Sumitra. The queens consumed the sacred offering, and their prayers and hopes turned within them into seeds of future warrior kings.

In course of time, the queens gave birth to four sons. Kausalya bore the eldest, Rama, a shining infant, a beautiful child who gladdened people by his mere presence. Kaikeyi's son, Bharata, was bold and full of grace. Sumitra had twins—Lakshmana and Shatrughna. They were quick-tempered, ever ready to meet a challenge or to start a fight.

And far from Ayodhya, in the forest regions, there was born at the same time a band of exceptional monkeys claiming lineage from the divinities—

Vali from Indra, chief of the gods; Sugriva from Surya, the sun god; Nila from Agni, god of fire; Sushena from Varuna, god of the waters; and Hanuman from Vayu, the wind god. Hosts of others of both divine and semi-divine descent gathered round the most powerful of them all—Vali and Sugriva. There were bears too—the tribes of the ancient bear, Jambavan. Old almost as creation itself, he had sprung from Brahma's mouth as he yawned.

All these happenings were part of the grand plan of Vishnu, measures to defend the cause of dharma when the inevitable threat arose to its continued existence. The world could only wait and watch, the kings of the earth maintain their vigilance and seize upon the first signs of evil appearing to confront good, might appearing to undermine right. The gods too watched and waited, ready to intervene with blessing, benediction and boon, for on the health and well-being of the world depended their welfare; on its victories rested their triumphs.

The princes of Ayodhya showed great promise of leadership, strength and valour. Studying the Vedas, instructed in archery and the martial arts, imbibing the graces of a cultured court, they soon became the darlings of Ayodhya. Rama and Lakshmana moved in unison like form and shadow, body and soul. Shatrughna followed Bharata with the same devotion and loyalty that Lakshmana showed to his idol, Rama. Their mothers' joy knew no bounds, and the aged Dasharatha could not stop thanking the Gods for

his good, though delayed, fortune.

Maturity dawned on the princes like a gentle morning. Their slender bodies filled out, growing strong and supple, and Dasharatha began to dream of good brides for his sons.

While king and court were planning the future of the young princes, the sage Vishwamitra arrived in Ayodhya, seeking audience with the king. 'Clearly, he has a mission, and a demanding one at that,' concluded Dasharatha, as he welcomed him with royal hospitality.

'I am blessed indeed, Vishwamitra, that you have chosen to grace my court with your presence. I would be honoured to be of service. Whatever be your need, whatever your desire, do not hesitate to name it.'

8

This was just what Vishwamitra was waiting for. 'Indeed, your grace, I come with an urgent request. I am in the midst of a sacrifice—one more step forward in my spiritual journey.'

He paused, hesitating, and Dasharatha felt a faint unease.

'Two powerful and crafty demons, Maricha and Subahu, are tormenting me. They defile my sacrificial altar with chunks of torn and bloody flesh. Each time I have had to start my sacrifice afresh. Finally, I have given up in disgust. These repulsive *rakshasas* have harassed me beyond endurance.'

Dasharatha was now decidedly apprehensive but he waited for the sage to go on.

'As you know, I could easily destroy them. But the rigours of a spiritual exercise are such that I cannot even show anger, let alone curse them. I feel so helpless. . . . '

Dasharatha trembled with a nameless fear as Vishwamitra came to the point of his visit.

'I have come to ask for Rama's help in ridding me of these demoniac pests. He will have to stay with me in my hermitage for ten days till I complete my sacrifice. I hope you will agree to send him.'

Dasharatha panicked at the thought of his young and precious son matching his untried strength with the fierce pair, Maricha and Subahu. There was despair in his voice as he exclaimed: 'Rama fight demons! He is not yet sixteen, a boy, a mere stripling. I beg of you, take me and my army. Rama is inexperienced. He cannot gauge the strengths and weaknesses of the enemy—not yet. Or, at least, if you must take him, take me too—along with my army, all four divisions of it.'

Vishwamitra would not relent. 'You promised me whatever I desire. I desire the services of Rama—no more, no less. I cannot play host to a king and his army. My hermitage is too humble.'

Dasharatha tried one last plea. 'I cannot live without Rama. He is the child of my old age, got with much penance and sacrifice. Do not harden your heart. Free me of this terrible promise.'

Seeing Vishwamitra unmoved, Dasharatha went further. 'I refuse to oblige. This is not a reasonable request.'

Thwarted, the fiery ascetic blazed out at the king: 'You add fuel to my fire of frustration. You, who belong to the dynasty of the Raghus, dare to go back on your word!' As Dasharatha paled at the insult, Vishwamitra fired his parting shot. 'You know how to honour your pledge, indeed,' he taunted, his face distorted with anger and disappointment.

It was a crisis of confidence, and Vasishtha thought fit to intervene. 'Gracious king, you are justice itself, and mercy. Your duty is to protect. Believe me, Rama will be safe. Vishwamitra has weapons and powers that will shield and preserve your son. He will come to no harm, believe me.'

Vasishtha's level tones had a soothing effect on the agitated monarch. Vishwamitra too was appeased, and Rama and Lakshmana, inseparable companions, set out with him. Cool breezes blowing spring fragrances attended their departure. Vayu, the wind god, was blessing their maiden venture into the wide world outside high palace walls. Aware of their sacred mission, eager to shoulder their first manly burden, Rama and Lakshmana stepped out, radiant with hope, radiating confidence.

On the right bank of the Sarayu, a short way out of Ayodhya, Vishwamitra stopped and spoke to Rama and Lakshmana.

'Here I will give you your first weapons, Bala and Atibala. They are daughters of Brahma and mothers of all the skills and sciences. Receive them along with the incantations, the mantras, that lock and unlock them. With these in your armoury, you will feel neither hunger nor thirst, fatigue nor fever. Take the waters of the Sarayu in your hands, purify yourself and with faith in your heart, absorb the strength of these occult powers.'

Rama and Lakshmana felt a flood of energy coursing through their tensed bodies. It was an initiation. They had stepped into manhood, the pranks and pleasures of palace life now truly behind them. Their mission was under way.

Vishwamitra and the princes moved on, passing many legendary sites. The sage launched into story after story, satisfying their growing curiosity. 'This hermitage belongs to Shiva and these ascetics are his devotees. Here, in this very grove, Kama, the god of love, worshipped Shiva. But then, he made the mistake of aiming his arrow at the lord. In a single flash of his dread third eye, Shiva destroyed him. Kama fled, shedding various parts of his body, his *angas*. He managed to survive, but only as a bodiless spirit. Hence, he is known as Ananga, "bodiless"; and this region is called Anga, "limb" or "body".' The princes listened, spellbound. They were wandering through history, myth and legend, acquainting themselves with their beloved land.

They set sail on the river at dawn. Midstream, there was a great roar and rush of waters. Vishwamitra explained to the wide-eyed princes: 'The Sarayu that flows through your city, Ayodhya, comes from the Himalayas, a great distance away. She springs, in fact, from a hoary lake, Manasarovar. Its clean waters in turn were formed by a fleeting thought, the flash of an idea, in the Creator's mind. Here where the waters churn and froth in noisy commotion, the Sarayu crosses the path of the great Ganga. Pay homage to their confluence.' It was a tumultous welcome, indeed, that the Ganga seemed to extend to her fellow river as they met and mingled. It was a beautiful sight, a beautiful sound.

Across the river, they came upon a dark and terrible forest. No chants of ascetics greeted them, no flare of sacred fire, no peaceful settlement. Birds and beasts screeched and growled unchecked, and insects kept up an insistent, threatening hum. It was a place of utter desolation. Rama turned to Vishwamitra with a questioning look to hear the sage saying: 'This was once a thriving settlement, blessed by Indra himself, the site of two beautiful cities. A perverse *yakshini* with the strength of a thousand elephants lives not far from here. She is a forest spirit and the mother of Maricha. Her name is Tataka. Agastya, the great sage, killed her husband with a curse. This threw her into a rage. With her son Maricha in her arms, she rushed at him, wanting to devour him. He turned his wrath on her: "May you turn into a *rakshasi*, a demoness and your son into a demon," he cursed.'

Now, Vishwamitra set the princes their first task: the killing of Tataka. Even as he finished speaking they saw her—a loathsome, misshapen form, running towards them, flailing her arms, raising clouds of dust with her giant footfalls, producing showers of stones and rocks with her black arts.

Rama did not flinch from his first encounter with evil. He raised his bow and plucked from his bowstring a warning note of destruction to come, a twang that echoed in all directions. The quarters heard and trembled, more with hope of deliverance than fear of destruction.

The fight began. Through the pelting rain of rocks and stones he moved swiftly and deftly. Getting close he cut off her hands, her nose, her ears. Finally, as she moved about rapidly, now visible, now invisible, he let loose, under Vishwamitra's instructions, an arrow that could follow the sound of her dreadful cries. With a single shot, he felled Tataka.

'Do not regret the killing of a woman,' said Vishwamitra, clearing Rama's doubts about the propriety of his feat. 'There is divine precedent for such deeds. The occasion dictates the action. Yours is an act of protection and release, not of wanton destruction.'

Nature watched with bated breath, and with Tataka's dying gasp, breathed a sigh of relief. The forest stirred to happy life as the trees tossed their heads, exchanging smiles of full and fragrant bloom as the sap rose once more in their frozen veins. The stillness of death, its gloom, gave way gracefully to the mirth and laughter of life triumphant.

Vishwamitra was pleased with Rama's performance. The prince had gone into his first battle with the skill and expertise of a seasoned warrior. He decided to give Rama the entire range of divine weapons. Smiling with affection and approval, he took the prince aside: 'Tataka is only a taste of things to come,' he said. 'You will need more weapons. Prepare to receive them.

'First, the wheels of Righteousness, Time and Punishment—Dharmachakra, Kalachakra and Dandachakra. They are fierce instruments, each a discus, deadly when hurled. Here is Vishnu's discus, the Sudarshana, and Indra's thunderbolt, Vajra.'

Many others followed—weapons to induce as well as combat drought, floods or intoxication, weapons with bird and horse heads, all powered with divine strengths, fired with the energy generated by goodness, justice and truth. They could change shape and form too, when used by the right people and with the appropriate mantras.

It was a long session of valuable lessons in the art of warfare, both physical and mental. Finally Vishwamitra taught Rama the mantras that would activate this formidable collection of armaments. 'Use them judiciously and with skill,' he advised. Rama began to sense the nature and importance of his mission of destruction.

As the teacher and disciple rose, the weapons materialized, accepting Rama's command over their fates. Some blazed into sight, some rose in columns of swirling smoke, others shone with the softness of moonbeams.

Not long after, the two princes and the sage came to a peaceful grove of trees filled with sunshine and birdsong. Rama guessed it was Siddhashrama, the troubled site of Vishwamitra's sacrifice.

The sage related its traditions. 'Vamana, Vishnu's dwarf incarnation, worshipped here and Vishnu himself sat here in yogic contemplation. It is my turn to stay here and from now on it is yours as much as mine.'

Rama felt quite at home in this world of worship and austerity. He asked

snow and precious metals and minerals, was married to Mena, daughter of Mount Meru, the axis of the world. They had two daughters. Ganga was the elder, Uma the younger. The Gods needed Ganga for their many purification ceremonies, and Himavat obliged by parting with her. Ganga loved her new home and duties. Uma, after many lifetimes of penance, married the bridegroom of her choice, Shiva Mahadeva himself.

'How did Ganga then descend to earth?' asked Rama.

'One of your ancestors, King Sagara, had something to do with that. It is a long story extending over many generations and many mishaps. But first, let us see what happened to Uma and Shiva, for these stories link together at many points.'

Vishwamitra resumed, pleased with the boys' rapt attention.

The love of Shiva for Uma was fierce and all-consuming. He was lost to the world, almost heedless in his passion for her. The gods feared the power of that love, the energy it generated. They began to feel threatened. The offspring of such a union, they feared, could destroy the universe. They had to do something to check this force before it was let loose on an unsuspecting world.

They went to Shiva with folded hands. 'Great god, the welfare of all three worlds is at stake. We beg of you, let Uma become your partner in yogic penance, so that your energies may be contained within you, not flow into her.'

Shiva was very understanding. 'I will keep my energies in check, but should some of my power overflow, in the fullness of my feeling for her, who will receive it?'

'The good earth,' they cried in unison.

And so it happened. The forests of the earth, her mountains, her seas, held the burden of Mahadeva's seed.

When Uma learned of the divine ploy to prevent her bearing Shiva's child, she cursed the gods roundly: 'You shall remain childless—and the earth, too, for her complicity, shall be barren.' And she left with Shiva for the higher northern regions, where they lived for many years, totally absorbed in yogic penance.

Meanwhile, in heaven, Ganga, the elder sister of Uma, served the gods in their sacred routines. But now, the gods were leaderless, after Shiva's departure northwards. From one extreme, his passion for Uma, Shiva had swung to the other, unending austerity. They were in a dilemma, and went to Brahma for help.

'Uma's curse cannot be revoked,' answered Brahma, 'but Agni will salvage the situation. Through him Ganga will bear a son whom Uma will accept and love as her own. This child will lead your armies and be your protection.'

Ganga took the form of a celestial nymph and went to Agni. Her limbs caught fire, her spirit gave out the white heat of sheer energy, as she held within her the power of Agni, god of fire. She found it unbearable, and the growing seed was therefore transferred to the snowbound, forested slopes of the Himalayas.

Much of this shining matter of birth, the stuff of life, veined the

mountainside, lay buried deep as gold, silver and copper, as well as the baser metals. The landscape gave out a blinding radiance, and of that was born Kumara. The gods arranged for the Pleiades, the Krittikas, the constellation of six, to suckle the baby. With his six mouths he sucked simultaneously at all their breasts and grew big and strong. He later became the commander-in-chief of the gods. Men called him variously Skanda, Kartikeya or Kumara.

Rama wondered what his ancestors had to do with the story of Ganga. She seemed to wind through many lives, many worlds.

Sensing the prince's question, Vishwamitra resumed his tale.

Sagara of Ayodhya, Rama's ancestor, performed the Ashwamedha sacrifice. He had two wives—Keshini and Garuda's sister Sumati. By Keshini he had one son; by Sumati, he had sixty thousand. Sagara's grandson Anshuman, an obedient and dutiful boy, was put in charge of the sacrificial horse when it was let loose as the ritual demanded. Indra, wishing to obstruct the sacrifice, stole and hid the horse.

Sagara sent out his sixty thousand sons to look for it. They dug up the earth to a depth of sixty thousand miles, wreaking havoc—destroying crops, disturbing and killing snakes, demons and giants. There was utter pandemonium. The gods ran to Brahma, who advised patience. 'You don't have long to wait. The sage Kapila will be instrumental in controlling these rash youths.'

Sagara's sons returned unsuccessful. They had begun to enjoy their search and the confusion it created. When Sagara ordered them to go out again, they were only too willing to do so. They dug east, south and west, paying homage at each point to the great elephants that guarded the directions and quarters. Finally they struck north, and sighted their quarry. The horse was grazing quietly near the ascetic Kapila, said to be a particle of Vasudeva himself.

The foolish boys thought the sage had stolen the horse, and rushed to attack him before seizing it. But they were courting death in their ignorance. Kapila was speechless with rage. With all the cumulative powers of his prolonged austerities, and the divinity he concealed within him, he let out a blood-curdling, hissing, half-sound—'H'm'. The air crackled with its deadly vibrations, and the sixty thousand sons of Sagara were instantly reduced to ashes.

In Ayodhya, King Sagara began to feel anxious, for his sons had been gone a long while. He sent his grandson Anshuman to look for them. The boy trudged through the tunnels they had dug through the earth, made enquiries of the elephants who stood guarding the quarters and directions. Finally, he came to the huge heap of ashes. Clearly these were his uncles' remains, for the sacrificial horse was still grazing nearby. As he looked round for water to sanctify the remains, he saw the great eagle, Garuda, his great-uncle. Garuda spoke to the young boy: 'Do not sprinkle ordinary water on them. It is only the water of the Ganga that will free them from earthly bondage.'

'And this was where your ancestors entered the life and story of Ganga on earth.' It was a long and complicated tale.

Anshuman returned with the horse and news of his dead uncles, lying damned in the nether regions. Sagara completed the Ashwamedha. But the matter, naturally, did not end there.

Sagara ruled for thirty thousand years, but found no way of bringing the proud Ganga down to earth. She showed no inclination to give up her privileged existence in the heavens. After Sagara, Anshuman, abdicating in favour of his son, Dilipa, wooed Ganga through thirty-two thousand years of penance—to no avail. Dilipa did likewise, for another thirty thousand years. She turned a deaf ear to his entreaties.

Then came Bhagiratha, who set out in a spirit of fresh resolution, determined to vindicate his forefathers and their lives of futile penance. Childless, he entrusted his kingdom to his ministers and practised the severest yet of all their combined penances.

A thousand years he stood, eating only once a month, senses subdued. His arms were raised, his frail body ringed by five blazing fires. Brahma was pleased and pronounced: 'Ganga will descend; she must. Your ancestors will attain salvation. But Shiva has to bear her descent. He must receive her on his head.' Bhagiratha did not flinch at the prospect of praying to Shiva. For a full year, living on air, he stood stock still, on the tip of one toe.

Shiva was gratified at his homage. He would be only too pleased to receive Ganga on his head, he said. The end seemed to be in sight. But they had not allowed for Ganga's arrogance. Now that she was forced to descend, she prepared to come down in a torrential rush. The Ganga in spate, throwing a tantrum! But she had not truly gauged the power of Shiva. Divining her intent, he decided to teach her a lesson. He trapped her in his towering heap of matted locks, and she spent years trying to find a way out of that bewildering maze.

It was very hard on poor Bhagiratha. The fates had dashed his hopes again and back he went on a fresh course of penance. It had become a way of life with him. But this time success was close.

Shiva released the wilful Ganga, somewhat chastened, into the Bindusara lake and from there onwards she divided herself into seven streams. Three flowed left, and three right and one followed the chariot of Bhagiratha as he drove home, older, wiser and well on his way to enlightenment. He had been given the status of *rajarishi* or royal sage, so rigorous and unswerving had his austerities been.

All creation watched the descent of the sacred Ganga. It was a spectacular performance as she ran her blessed course, watering the earth with her riches, scattering largesse on a waiting world. But she had one last prank to play. Bhagiratha looked back to see her pause, then flood the hermitage and sacrificial site of the sage Jahnu. He swallowed her—she had disappeared again. The gods called out: 'She is your daughter, Jahnavi,' and the sage, appeased, released her through his ears.

Bhagiratha heaved a huge sigh of relief. She was with him once more, and

reaching the sea, made her way to the nether regions, where the mortal remains of Sagara's sixty thousand sons awaited their moment of salvation.

And she washed away their sins, and released them from their long wait. Brahma, recognizing Bhagiratha's labour of love and duty, unprecedented in human history, announced: 'On earth, the Ganga is your eldest daughter, Bhagirathi. The world will call her by that name. And because she has flowed through all three worlds she will also be known as Tripathaga, one who moves along three paths.'

Bhagiratha now returned to his kingdom and waiting subjects, who received him with great joy.

2

The Marriage in Mithila

The sage and the princes, now fairly close to Mithila their destination, halted at a deserted hermitage. 'This place has a hoary tradition,' said Vishwamitra. 'The sage Gautama and his lovely wife, Ahalya, a devout and devoted couple lived here. Even the gods envied this blessed retreat.'

But Indra himself was to disturb its peace. One day, when Gautama was away, Indra arrived in the guise of a mendicant, wooing Ahalya with honeyed words and much flattery. She responded with joy and abandon, giving in to his many blandishments.

Just as Indra was about to leave, Gautama returned, surprising the guilty pair. Their expressions gave them away. He raged at Indra: 'You will be childless for your sins.' Turning to his trembling wife, he exclaimed: 'Faithless woman, I abandon you! For a thousand years you will stay here alone, subsisting on air, sleeping on a bed of ashes, invisible to all creatures, turned to living stone. You will have to practise the severest austerities to atone for your treachery.' But he softened the curse by adding: 'When Rama, son of Dasharatha, sets foot in this desolate spot, you will return to me, redeemed.'

Vishwamitra led Rama into the hermitage. Ahalya, till then like a flame veiled in smoke, her splendour dimmed, rose to view, dazzling, wholly purified. She could see the end of her long and lonely vigil of rigours and expiation, as she humbly served the prince and his companions. Her husband Gautama appeared as promised and they resumed their life of penance and worship. The hermitage, too, like its mistress, stirred from the still and stony sleep of centuries.

In a few days the royal travellers were on the outskirts of Mithila. There was frenzied activity—much coming and going, much movement of goods and men. People had begun to gather for King Janaka's twelve-day sacrifice, their goods transported in long lines of loaded carts and carriages.

Vishwamitra and the princes chose a quiet spot to rest and refresh themselves. Hearing of the sage's presence in his kingdom, Janaka himself came to greet them, with his household priest, Shatananda, Gautama and Ahalya's eldest son. The priest had already heard of his mother's redemption. 'Was it you, Vishwamitra, who led Rama to my parents' hermitage? Were you served well? Did my mother wait upon Rama with devotion?' 'They are very well, Shatananda. Your mother is radiant once more, her atonement complete.'

Janaka was more than usually attentive, more than a little curious about

these two handsome princes, and asked many searching questions. Vishwamitra told him who they were, why they were with him, and the story of their heroic exploits—the killing of Tataka and Subahu, the wounding and defeat of Maricha.

The monarch was impressed. He left them to their evening devotions, extending a cordial and respectful invitation to the site of the sacrifice and his morning audience.

The next day they were ushered in with due ceremony into Janaka's presence. Vishwamitra came straight to the point: 'The sons of Dasharatha wish to see the great bow of Shiva.' Janaka was agreeable but wished to first give them the history of the weapon.

It was a bow that belonged to Shiva Mahadeva. At his own father-in-law's sacrifice, he had been overlooked, ignored and insulted. The gods had been a silent party to this humiliation. Shiva drew his bow and aiming at them, teased: 'Your beautiful bodies will shortly meet destruction. Prepare yourselves.' The gods pleaded for their lives. Mahadeva, seeing them humbled, was appeased, and magnanimously handed over the bow to them. They in turn gave it to Janaka's ancestor, Devarata. It was a treasured family heirloom, kept under strong guard and worshipped.

Janaka then told them how it had become the cause of much conflict, even warfare. His daughter had come to him in somewhat strange circumstances.

As he was turning the earth with his ploughshare in ritual preparation of the sacrificial site, he came upon a child, a girl. He named her Sita, 'born of the furrow', and brought her home. She was now his child, brought up in his royal household.

Lines of worry began to show on his noble brow. 'Her marriage is beset with problems, for the bride-price is high—the man who weds her must draw this mighty bow, no less. The bridegroom has to earn her with unchallenged valour. Sita is "Viryashulka", a prize for valour.'

Rama and Lakshmana were listening with dawning interest, Vishwamitra noticed. And so did Janaka.

'Well, prince after prince tried and failed. In their disappointment and

frustration they joined hands and laid seige to Mithila for a whole year. I had to undertake a sacrifice to strengthen my resources, before they retreated.' Janaka unexpectedly announced: 'If Rama is able to draw this bow, Sita will be his bride, I promise.'

There was hope in Janaka's voice—and confidence in Vishwamitra's, as he asked for the bow to be produced. Rama was silent. Sita, princess of Videha, daughter of the earth, had already entered his thoughts.

Janaka sent for the bow. It arrived, enclosed in an iron box, smeared with sandal paste and heaped with flowers. It rested on an eight-wheeled cart drawn by five hundred strong men. Janaka's council of wise men led the way.

'Here is the bow,' said Janaka, a shade doubtfully, his first flush of enthusiasm beginning to fade as he looked at the slender young boys who stood there like twin souls. 'It is a bow worshipped by generations of my ancestors. Even the gods have quailed at the thought of drawing it. Let the princes take a look.'

The counsellors dared not hope. They remembered the many who had failed, their shame, their humiliation. This gentle youth, so quiet and unassuming, would surely recoil, intimidated by its very sight, its lustre, its reputation. Its history of royal defeats would surely overpower him. It seemed a foregone conclusion. Vishwamitra spoke to Rama who stood poised, ready to meet any challenge. 'Come, Rama. Examine the bow.'

Rama strode forward, shoulders squared, long arms swinging gracefully, head held high, eyes wide with dreams of love and conquest. He opened the box, stood with bowed head, silent and prayerful, and then turned to Janaka and Vishwamitra. 'I would like to raise this bow, try to bend it. May I?' he said simply.

Vishwamitra nodded assent. The small gathering watched with growing disbelief as Rama bent down and lifted the formidable weapon with one hand, almost playfully. There was a ripple of interest, a few gasps. Smiling, Rama steadied it with only a slight effort and strung it. The interest had turned to frank surprise. And then, to the utter astonishment of Janaka, he drew the bow. Amazement soon turned to shock as the bow, larger even than its great reputation, snapped in two, as if in final surrender to the hidden strength of the boyish arms that held it.

There was a sound like a thunderclap. The earth quaked. The rumble and roar of it stunned the whole assembly. It was a historic moment for Mithila. For Janaka, personally, it was a moment of unalloyed joy and relief. His daughter, treasured child of the earth, would after all wed a lion among men, Rama, prince and hero of Ayodhya.

Mithila and its king rejoiced. Arrangements were quickly made to inform and invite Dasharatha. On receiving the good news Dasharatha set out for Mithila with his party, led by Vasishtha and his circle of sages, and followed by his armies. Greetings and gifts were exchanged, genealogies too, for the two dynasties prided themselves on their ancestry.

Janaka and Dasharatha, Vasishtha and Vishwamitra also discussed the matter of brides for Rama's three younger brothers. Janaka offered his younger daughter Urmila, to Lakshmana. Janaka's younger brother, Kushadhwaja, had two daughters, Mandavi and Shrutakirti. They seemed ideal for Bharata and Shatrughna. Wise counsel, consultation and negotiation would soon knit the two great dynasties of Ikshvaku and Videha in firm bonds of matrimony.

Vasishtha and Vishwamitra were satisfied with the new links that were being forged between the two great kingdoms of Kosala and Videha and their rulers. The kings exchanged courtesies and expressed wholehearted approval of the four marriage alliances.

The sages too felt greatly honoured, and their status as advisers on matters temporal and spiritual was enhanced. They were put in charge of the nuptial arrangements. Under Vasishtha's direction, Vishwamitra and

Shatananda saw to it that all went smoothly.

Dasharatha performed the rites for his ancestors in the evening and rose at dawn to prepare for the first ceremony of the day, the gifting of cows in charity. Four hundred thousand healthy milch cows, each with a calf, their horns gilded and gleaming, were led away by grateful brahmins. Dasharatha distributed other gifts too, in the name of his sons, as was customary.

The next day, the bridegrooms stood ready, clad in silk and adorned with rich ornaments, each enhancing the other's lustre, and Rama, eldest and best, most radiant of all. Their father sent Vasishtha ahead to say that all was in readiness for the auspicious nuptial hour. Janaka replied that the brides, dressed and fully decorated, were ready and waiting. He requested Vasishtha, as the senior sage, to lead the way and initiate the rites.

Vasishtha, helped by Vishwamitra and Shatananda, set up the altar in the centre of the sacrificial pavilion. Around it were laid out all the ritual articles—coloured pitchers with golden lids, budding branches, conches, incense, flowers and sandal paste. And over everything were strewn clumps of kusha grass, purifying and sanctifying the whole proceedings. Chants and incantations filled the air with sacred vibrations as the ritual fire blazed, ready to stand witness to the princely weddings. For Agni, god of fire, is the supreme witness. With the offerings he consumes, he becomes the carrier of human hopes and desires to the gods in heaven.

Vasishtha then took Sita by the hand and seated her opposite Rama. Janaka, placing her hand in Rama's, gave away the eldest bride. The bond was sealed. So, too, Lakshmana received the hand of Urmila, Bharata of Mandavi and Shatrughna of Shrutakirti. The ceremony concluded with the couples circumambulating the fire, the altar and Janaka. Blessed by the gods, with celestial gongs sounding and conches blowing, the four princes led away their glowing brides as the heavens rained flowers everywhere—on their heads, in their paths, in their nuptial chambers. Boys no more, their senses awakened, they were now young householders with partners to protect and lean on, burdens to shoulder, future fathers, continuers of their line and exemplars for the generations to come.

The time for farewells had come. Vishwamitra left for the Himalayas. Dasharatha and his newly married sons and wives, with their royal entourage, left for Ayodhya. The princesses brought a rich dower with them—gold, silver, pearls, corals, blankets, rich woven cloths and grand attire, thousands of cows, male and female slaves, elephants, horses, chariots and foot soldiers. As they set out, strange birds flew by, screeching. Deer fled in fear, circling in a clockwise direction. Vasishtha explained these portents to Dasharatha: 'The birds point to an unknown event. But the deer indicate that all will, in the end, be well.'

As they stood wondering, a stormy wind tore at the trees and the earth shook. Darkness banished daylight; the directions and quarters were obscured. A thick layer of dust and ashes settled on everything. Fear spread, agitating and unnerving them.

Out of this gloom emerged Parashurama, son of Jamadagni. His matted locks piled high and mountainous, he loomed threateningly over this friendly group warm with good feeling and wedding revelry. On one shoulder rested his famous axe. Slung over the other was a bow and quiver.

Parashurama had circled the earth twenty-one times, killing every warrior and king in sight, because one of their race had killed his father, Jamadagni.

The sages began to whisper to one another: 'Will he swing his deadly axe once more? Will the sight of this royal group inflame him? Has he not shed enough martial blood?'

Controlling their inner turmoil, they welcomed him: 'Have you had a good journey? Do not make us the victims of fresh anger, my lord,' they said, hoping to forestall a possible assault.

Parashurama nodded curtly. With a smouldering glance, he turned to Rama: 'I have heard all about the way you broke the bow. I am here with another famous bow, my father's. It is a family heirloom. Draw it. If you succeed, I will take you on in single combat. Then only can you establish, beyond doubt, your unmatched valour.'

Dasharatha tried to placate him: 'Your enmity towards our class should now end. You are an enlightened brahmin who renounced warfare and weaponry in Indra's presence. You are an ascetic now. If Rama is killed, we are all destroyed.'

It was as if the old king had not spoken, so bent was Parashurama on challenging Rama. 'The world has seen two celestial bows, both worshipped, both designed by Vishwakarma, the divine architect. One was Shiva's which you have just broken. The other is Vishnu's. I have it here with me.' All eyes turned towards the weapon. The bowstring shone like a streak of lightning, eager to let fly in a flash of destruction. 'I happen to know that this is the more powerful of the two, for in a contest, it unstrung the bow of Shiva that you broke. That is why Shiva got rid of it,' he mocked. 'Are you ready?'

Rama, who had been silent till then out of deference to his elders, now spoke up: 'I can understand both your sorrow and your anger against the warrior class. But by underestimating my valour, you have made a grave error of judgement. I will demonstrate my strength and teach you not to treat it lightly.'

And with that the gentle Rama, roused to righteous anger, seized the bow of Vishnu, and drew it, arrow in place and pointing straight at Parashurama. 'I spare your physical body,' he said sternly, 'for you are dear to Vishwamitra, and an ascetic besides. But your spiritual realms are mine to take. With this arrow I destroy your spiritual stature and humble your inordinate pride.' And instantly the towering presence of Parashurama lost its aura and its lustre. His arm unnerved, his eyes lowered before Rama's steady gaze, he pleaded in a tone of abject surrender: 'Leave me only the power to move, to reach the distant Mahendra range where I now live. Even as you seized my bow I recognized the hand of Vishnu. The weapon was pliant, obeying its true master.'

Rama sent the arrow flying at the ascetic's greatest treasure, his spiritual reserves. The dust, the gloom, the confusion, all vanished like morning mist. It was as if Rama had rid the world of the darkness of imminent doom, restoring to it the light of righteousness, dharma.

The party resumed its interrupted journey and reached Ayodhya. They received a tumultous welcome from their adoring subjects and Dasharatha's queens received their daughters-in-law with great affection. Bharata, summoned by his grandfather, Kaikeyi's father, left almost immediately,

with Shatrughna. Rama and Sita made a perfect couple, so lustrous was she, so loving to her brave and heroic husband.

Many years passed. Rama watching his father handle the reigns of government, came to know and love Dasharatha's kingdom and his subjects. He spent his youth, his prime, in observing and absorbing the lessons of life, for these were the years of preparation. Sita, his partner in the pursuit of dharma, his *dharmapatni,* was a tower of strength, a beacon of light to him.

3

The Royal Exiles

Dasharatha loved his eldest son, Rama, and was proud of him. It was not just the blind love of a fond and doting parent. Dasharatha loved him for what he was, for the sum of his great virtues.

Wisdom and restraint marked Rama's actions; courage and valour were never ends in themselves, used merely for personal glory. They were instruments of defence and correction. He was soft-spoken and modest; calm, confident, tolerant and good-tempered; perceptive, compassionate and protective. His causes were just and therefore never lost. He fought as a last resort, but then he fought to win. He was unassuming, yet had a magnetic personality. He drew people to him with his winning smile and ways. He was joy incarnate, hence was known as Rama, 'one who gives pleasure'. He was, indeed, a pleasure to those around him, the pleasure of goodness savoured.

Dharma, or righteousness, was the *chhatri,* the umbrella of power, under which the descendants of Raghu of the Ikshvakus had always taken and given shelter. It shaded a magic circle, defining the limits of righteousness. It was their particular glory and one which they jealously guarded. Dasharatha knew that Rama would dispense justice with truth ever in mind, and mercy following close.

It was spring, the world was in flower, and in the aged king's heart the bud of many a hope dared to blossom; the branch of many a dream, to green.

The stars seemed to favour succession and a coronation. Dasharatha seeking a popular mandate and approval, summoned ministers, courtiers, feudatory kings, overlords and leaders from town and country and announced his plans for succession: 'I have ruled for sixty thousand years and am old and weary. My son, Rama, whom you all know and love will, in my opinion, be an able successor. What are your views in this matter?'

The gathering greeted his announcement with the spontaneous abandon of peacocks dancing at the sight of a rain-cloud. Dasharatha had proved once more that he had his hand on the pulse of his subjects.

'There is no time to waste,' he said to Sumantra, minister and royal charioteer, who went to fetch Rama, driving his horses with the speed of enthusiasm.

Dasharatha watched with a rush of paternal pride as Rama approached the throne. The prince walked with measured, stately steps, swaying with the weight of his own majesty like a processional elephant. Ascending the

steps leading to the throne, Rama, with bent head, greeted his father. Dasharatha seated his son on a jewelled seat beside him, and with an unerring sense of occasion, announced the succession and the coronation to follow. It was a polished performance. The shift of power was made with no stumbles and no awkward manoeuvres.

Alone with Rama, Dasharatha voiced his misgivings. Bad dreams had kept him awake—dreams of tossing tempests and crashing meteors. The stars of his birth were fettered by constricting planets. A strangulation of his fates seemed indicated. . . illness, perhaps death.

'I wish to see you crowned—and soon. I might waver, who can tell? The mind's a funny thing. And Bharata. . . loving as he is, and wholly devoted to

you, might still obstruct the proceedings. Nameless fears clutch at my heart. Let us not delay. Tomorrow you must be crowned.'

Outside the palace gates, the news spread like wild and joyous fire. Vasishtha had already signalled the start of the coronation festivities. Gate and archway, temple, altar and mansion wore a festive look. Festoons and fluttering pennants set the mood; sandal and incense and flowers spread the sweet and heady smell of success and celebration. People collected at street corners, discussing the event to come, the coronation of Rama, the crowning of their hopes for Ayodhya and Kosala.

Rama drove through, acknowledging their greetings. When he arrived at Kausalya's apartments to give his mother the good news, she was waiting with a prayer in her heart and a blessing on her lips. Her pride and joy had flowered into this moment of triumph for her son. Sita was there, too, and Lakshmana with his wife.

For Rama, it had been the first taste of success, of popular approbation too. It was a chastening experience, and he reacted with his habitual wisdom. He needed to share this precious burden, to make a compact with a friend. Who could be better than Lakshmana, the companion of his childhood, his shadow, his image?

'Stand close, Lakshmana, in my hour of triumph, in my hour of need. If I rule, I rule for you. If I live, I live for you. You are my image, my other self.'

It was a private and personal oath of lifelong allegiance, a bond of

brotherhood between princes who found themselves in the thorny realms of kingship to come.

All seemed well set for the great day. Vasishtha was in charge of the festivities, as well as all rites and rituals. The exacting demands of time, place, custom and religious sanction had to be met. No detail could be overlooked, no deviation permitted.

Rama and Sita had their own ceremonies to perform on the eve of the coronation. They spent the day fasting and praying, the night on a bed of kusha grass. It was a ritual gesture of austerity, abstinence and sanctity, calculated to induce in them a sombre and devout frame of mind, suited to the solemnity of the occasion.

28

Long before daylight, the royal householder, soon to be installed as crown prince and heir apparent, rose to supervise the decoration of his apartments. His calm gaze, directed inwards, seemed to settle on invisible goals, his impressive frame ready to receive the rich and heavy mantle of kingship.

Rama's palace, high and white, seemed to sail the clear skies of Ayodhya. The expansive grounds, full of people blooming with hope, looked like a lake of lotuses opening to the touch of a rising sun, and their chatter was the birdsong of a beautiful morning.

Outside, the multitudes gathered, riding a crest of tempestuous joy, a tidal wave of happiness that the city could barely contain. Rama, giver of pleasure, had filled their hearts to the very brim.

On the balcony of Kaikeyi's mansion, a storm was slowly brewing. Manthara, the hunchback, Kaikeyi's personal maid stood idly scanning the landscape.

The jostling, the excitement, the abandon of a city in the grip of a festive mood drew her attention. 'What is the merriment about?' she called out to Rama's maid. 'Tomorrow our Rama will be crowned Regent and heir apparent,' said the maid, all smiles, on her way to one more errand in the delirious round of coronation chores.

Manthara's face twisted with fury. She came down in a rush and shook her mistress rudely awake: 'How can you rest? Your fortunes are being swept away— the tide of events is threatening to swallow us! You must do something to stop it!'

Kaikeyi responded in a daze: 'Are you all right? You seem perturbed. . . agitated. . . ?'

'I am indeed. Deeply so. I fear for you, beloved mistress. Rama is to be named Regent. Your husband is a crafty old man, clever and devious too. He fawns over you, but his true love is Kausalya. You are too trusting and naive.'

Kaikeyi listened to this tirade in utter astonishment.

'I haven't finished. It is much more serious than that. You are clasping a serpent to your bosom. Is he your husband or your mortal enemy? Now I know why he sent Bharata away. How very convenient! Rama Regent!' and she spluttered to a stop.

Kaikeyi's face lit up at the mention of Kausalya's son. He was as much her delight as his mother's. She had never thought of him as other than hers or separate from her world. 'Rama Regent!' she said, ignoring Manthara's angry outburst. 'What could give me more joy? You bring me good news, the best possible. Here, take this ornament,' she said, offering her a precious trinket. 'Take something more. Choose anything. We have cause to celebrate. I make no distinctions between Rama and Bharata.'

Manthara flung the ornament aside in disgust. Things were not going the way she had expected. Kaikeyi would have to be manipulated, or else her ambitions for her mistress and for herself would be so much dust and ashes.

'You are a simpleton. You actually rejoice on the eve of your downfall, your rival's triumph! Kausalya's household will prosper. You and your daughter-in-law will be her slaves, and we her household drudges. We have bad days ahead indeed. You, your son—all of us—will count for nothing!' exclaimed Manthara.

Kaikeyi, disbelieving, brushed her fears aside. 'Rama is high-minded and fair. He protects my son like a father. Bharata is sure to succeed him, I know.'

Manthara laughed. 'You are ignorant of the ways of this world. The eldest son always succeeds. Bharata will be pushed aside. The line of succession will be through Rama. You sit here toying with dreams while your son's fate hangs in the balance—and he is not even here to protect his rights!' She had finally touched a nerve, cast a doubt in the clear waters of Kaikeyi's mind. Kaikeyi looked thoughtful.

Manthara pushed her advantage, playing on a mother's fears and ambitions for her child: 'Move fast, faster than the events which are hurtling past you with the speed of fate.'

There was a trace of menace in the next picture she conjured up: 'Rama will banish Bharata, perhaps even kill him. He holds the reigns of power. Pre-empt him!' As Kaikeyi hesitated, she pressed: 'We are running out of time, dear mistress. It might be too late even now, but there's some hope. Rama must be banished and Bharata crowned Regent. Nothing else will do.'

The poison worked. Kaikeyi's radiant face, no longer wreathed in smiles, set into hard lines of determination. It was a grasping, greedy woman who spoke: 'Rama must go and Bharata take his place. I can see that, Manthara. But how? Can you think of a way to change the course of events?' The evil and corrupting influence of the deformed, conniving domestic was at work.

Manthara almost crowed with delight; she had thought of everything. 'Long ago,' she reminded Kaikeyi, 'when your husband lay wounded in a battle between the gods and the demons, you saved his life at the risk of your own. He offered you two boons then. You did not take them, saying that at some future date you would, and then expect instant satisfaction.'

Kaikeyi recalled clearly both the occasion and the promise. What a jewel her loyal servant was!

'Well,' said Manthara, 'that future date is today and the time, now. Your two boons are clearly indicated—the banishment of Rama and the coronation of your son, Bharata.'

Kaikeyi sighed with relief, and Manthara grew bolder. 'You know the king will go through fire for you. Follow my instructions carefully. Throw a tantrum. Act angry and displeased. Deny him your favours. Play on his emotions. He will come crawling to you. And then you have him in your power. That's the only way. And, as I said, there is no time to waver.'

Kaikeyi was now completely under her spell. 'Manthara, you are no hunchback. Your body bends like a lotus stalk in the breeze, your face is a flower, your waist draws in, shy and slender. And your hump, high and round as a chariot wheel, is a mound of sorcery. When Bharata is crowned, I shall smear it with sandal and worship it with incense. You shall wear a crown of gold and quite eclipse the other maids, I vow.'

Manthara responded to Kaikeyi's lavish praise with a fresh reminder: 'It is no use building a dam after the waters have drained. Act now!'

Like a flame fed with faith, Kaikeyi glowed bright and steady with her purpose. She removed her ornaments, saying: 'I will give up my life if Rama is not banished and Bharata crowned. The king must hear of my resolve.' She was like a coiled serpent, waiting to strike.

In the meantime, the king, weary with the day's activities, was on his way to Kaikeyi, wanting to give her the good news himself. He freshened at the very thought of his favourite wife, so skilled in the art of love and blandishments. Her gardens and courtyards were spacious and well appointed, and soft music soothed his jangled nerves. His bad dreams and his fears were beginning to recede.

His heart missed a beat when he found her couch empty. She never disappointed him. He feared grave displeasure, even a tantrum, but was not prepared for what he saw. Kaikeyi was lying on the floor in soiled clothes, her hair loose and streaming, her face distorted with anger and frustration. The king could not bear to see her unhappy. He bent over her, cajoling: 'The palace physicians will be here immediately. Are you possessed by an evil spirit? Whatever it is, my dear one, speak to me! I am at your service. You have only to ask. I hold sway over a kingdom whose limit is the solar sphere. Nothing is beyond your reach!'

Kaikeyi's voice was harsh and grating. 'I have a wish or two. Say you will fulfil them.'

Dasharatha was hopeful. 'Only Rama is as dear to me as you are. I swear by him to satisfy you.'

The king had walked into her trap. Kaikeyi's next words were ominous. 'May the planets, the directions, night and day, all space and all creation bear witness. . . .'

The king heard her in a daze, unbelieving, as she continued in tones that seemed to turn to a deafening roar in his ears. 'I am about to ask,' she said, 'and you are bound by your promise.' Her tone was threatening.

Dasharatha was numb with apprehension. Why was she invoking the planets? 'I remind you of that day, long ago, when I saved your life. You offered me two boons. I ask for those today.' She spoke quickly and clearly. 'These coronation festivities—let them be for Bharata. That is my first wish. My second, that you should banish Rama to the forest for fourteen years.'

Dasharatha froze like a snake charmed into stillness by a spell. And then blind anger flooded his veins.

'What harm has Rama done you? Or I for that matter? Only the other day you said he was your eldest son. He has served you even better than Bharata. Rama, beloved prince of Ayodhya, its future king, out in the wilds like a common mendicant! Banish Rama! Never!'

Kaikeyi stood her ground. 'A vow is a vow, justified or unjustified. You cannot break it.'

Dasharatha began to lament. 'I can see the blood drain from his face when I tell him, his radiance turn lacklustre. How can I bear it? What of his mother? And what of Sumitra and Sita? There is poison in your heady sweetness. You are a noose fast tightening round my old neck. Spare me, my queen, I beg of you.'

Kaikeyi drew away, spurning Dasharatha as he lay grovelling at her feet. She had turned cold and remote. It was as if Death had sent a warning chill up his spine. And then the king swooned.

Dasharatha recovered consciousness to find Kaikeyi taunting him: 'You are an ocean of truth. Yet the ocean, true to its pledge, never crosses the

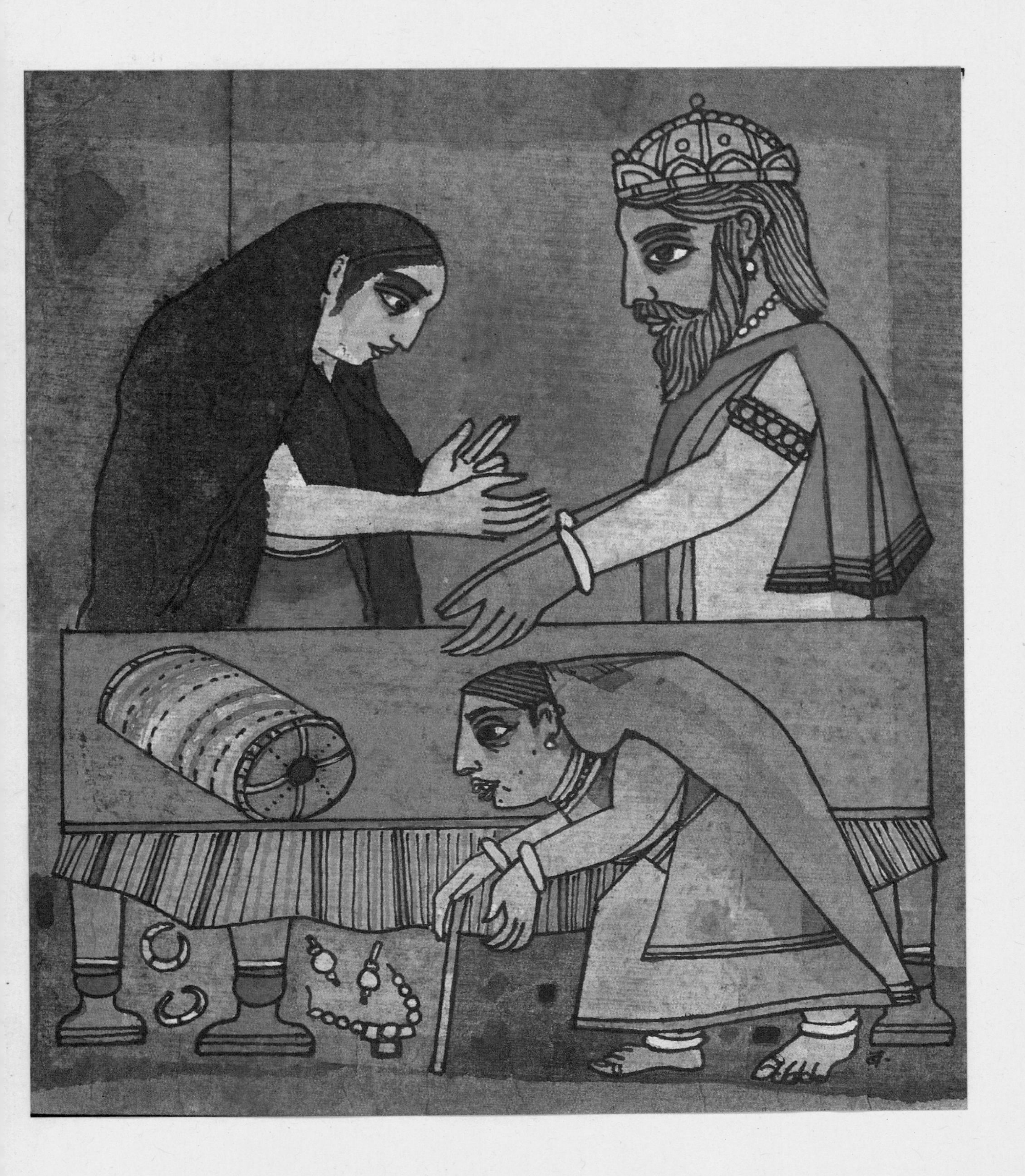

shore, no matter how low-lying it is. How will you face the seers and sages if you go back on your word? Have you thought of that? As for me, I am prepared to die, if you do not grant me my wish.'

Dasharatha said tonelessly: 'I hereby reject this hand of yours that I held in the bonds of holy matrimony, and the son, too, born of that union.' But Kaikeyi did not weaken. 'Send for Rama. It is morning now.'

Sumantra entered just then to announce that Vasishtha had collected everything for the coronation ceremonies. He saw Dasharatha, eyes red with weeping, sagging with the weight of his grief, tottering like an old bullock at the yoke. It was Kaikeyi who said to him: 'Bring Rama here.' Sumantra hesitated, and the king, still in a daze, repeated the order.

Rama started out on his elephant with his retinue of bards, ministers and warriors. His ears were ringing with their praises. The populace cheered him as the cavalcade wound its way through the festive streets. Rama arrived, looking flushed and happy.

Entering Kaikeyi's chambers he could see at once that something was seriously wrong. His father's tear-stained face was a shock to him. Rama drew back like a snake startled by the touch of a passing foot.

'Why is my father agitated? What troubles him? Have you been harsh to him?'

Kaikeyi answered him in level tones: 'Nothing is wrong. He has a wish he hesitates to express. It involves you. Therefore, let me tell you.'

Rama looked up eagerly: 'You have only to let me know. I will do exactly as he says.'

Kaikeyi was gloating as she told Rama: 'Bharata must be king and you must go to the forest for fourteen years. This is what the king finds difficult to tell you to your face. But he is bound by his promise to me, and you, too, have agreed already to do whatever he desires. He desires this in the name of truth, and an old promise made on the battlefield.'

Rama was as good as his word: 'I am pained that the king, my father, didn't tell me himself. Send for Bharata immediately. Let there be no delay. The coronation should proceed unhindered.'

He left Kaikeyi's mansion on foot, no royal canopy over him, no yak-tail fans on either side. These were royal insignia, and he was no longer heir apparent and crown prince. It was his gesture of acquiescence.

Rama set out on his rounds of leave-taking. His mother was the first to be told. 'I wish I had remained barren,' she moaned. 'My heart is crumbling like the banks of a river in spate. I will follow you to the forest like a cow following her calf.'

Lakshmana's reaction was violent. 'The king is a slave to his passions! He is senile,' he exclaimed. And then he threatened: 'I shall rid this city of Bharata's supporters. Let the king be imprisoned or, if necessary, killed.'

Rama consoled and calmed them both. 'Your place is by your husband's side,' he said to his mother. 'I cannot be untruthful for a mere kingdom. Lakshmana, soothe my father and my mothers. These jars of holy water, which were to sanctify my coronation, can now bless my journey to the forest. Dharma, righteousness, is established through truth. And the truth, at this moment, is my father's vow. The fates will it so, otherwise would Kaikeyi have behaved like a common woman?'

Lakshmana would not accept Rama's instant surrender to the workings of destiny. 'You are a man whose merits give you divine strength. Heroes do not bow to fate! They fashion their own destinies with the power of their manhood. Your manhood, your power, can and should overpower fate; lay it low. Let me use my weapons! I will make the whole world lie grovelling at your feet!'

He was shedding tears of anger, helpless, his hands tied and his strength held back by his elder brother. Rama wiped away the tears from Lakshmana's streaming eyes and stemmed the flow of his grief and anger with his gentle persistence: 'There is no other way. I mean to obey my father. This is the right way, the path of dharma.'

Kausalya, seeing that her son would not stay back, showered blessings on him. She invoked his good deeds and her own, the power of the sacrifice, the spirits of the forest and the heavens to guard her son. She invoked time, space and the elements with prayer and rite, sending him on his way, blessed and blessing.

It was Sita's turn next. This would be the most difficult part, reflected Rama. As he entered alone and unattended, Sita ran to him, suspecting something. She noticed his pallor.

'Where is your royal canopy? And those yak fans, white as swansdown? The minstrels, the bands, the ceremonial chariot? And why is your face so pale and troubled? It should be flushed and glowing, the hour of your coronation is so near.'

Rama met her flood of questions calmly and with great fortitude: 'I am banished to the Dandaka forest and Bharata will be king. Those are my father's orders and I intend to obey them. You must stay here and serve my mothers, my brothers and especially Bharata, your king and protector. Kings must not be antagonized. They can be vicious and turn away from their own children, when provoked. Such are the ways of power.'

Sita heard him out and then retorted: 'What you say is unworthy of a prince and a warrior. I have decided to ignore it. A wife and husband are linked inseparably. All other relationships have an independent course. A father, a mother, a son, or a daughter live by the fruit of their own actions. Their destinies are guided by their own hands. A wife lives through her husband and his life. Her salvation is intertwined with his.'

Sita was clear in her mind about the role of a loving wife. 'Wives are supposed to follow their husbands, placing their feet in the shadow of their partners' footsteps. But I will do more. If your path lies through the forest, I will lead the way, clearing that path. Of such stuff am I made. I will learn to love the forest. Take me with you. I will not live away from you.' And Sita painted an idyllic picture of life in the Dandaka forest.

Rama tried to dissuade her. 'The forest is a frightening place. Wild beasts roam about looking for human prey. Crocodiles infest the pools and lakes you so ecstatically describe. Fasting, exhaustion and fear—that will be our lot. Storms howl in those impenetrable woods. Thick undergrowth obstructs your every step. It will be suffering all the way. Stay back in the comfort and security of our palace.'

Sita wept: 'How can I convince you that troubles vanish when you are with me? I fear nothing, because nothing will touch me while you give me

protection. You protect the whole world. Why not me? Besides, I have been expecting this. Astrologers had predicted some years in the forest for me. And I am familiar with its dangers. An old woman in my father's house used to describe them to me in great detail. You must take me, I will not stay back.'

When she saw him hesitate even after such pleading, she resorted to taunts: 'My father judged you wrong. You are timid, a woman in man's form. Where is your famous valour and glory? Will you leave me here to serve others? To be with you is heaven. Where you are not is hell.' She finished with a threat: 'I will kill myself if I am separated from you.'

Rama began to see her strength of character and the strength, too, of her love for him. 'You may come with me, Sita. My happiness, too, is linked to yours. I have no joys, away from you.'

This crisis in their lives had bonded their relationship. Unchallenged until then, their love had now gone through the fire of adversity and come out unscathed and stronger than ever. Rama felt the burden of leaving Ayodhya and his family lightening. Soon the city would cease to be part of their lives, at least for many years.

He asked Sita to give away their possessions—their ornaments, rich clothes, chariots. They belonged henceforth to the dispossessed of the world.

There was still Lakshmana to handle. He had stood by, weeping silently, as husband and wife argued over their future life. He was determined to be part of it too, for, even as a boy, he had thrown in his lot with Rama. 'Take me,' he said, touching their feet. 'I shall walk before you, bow in hand. Life in your absence is insupportable.'

Rama tried to make him stay back. 'If you come, who will guard my mother and Sumitra? Our father is led by his passion for Kaikeyi. And Kaikeyi will not care for them; nor will Bharata, for his mother will influence him.'

But Lakshmana cleverly parried Rama's argument. 'Bharata is dutiful—and if he is not, I shall destroy him and his supporters. Besides, Kausalya is a woman of some substance. She owns many villages and does not lack defenders if the need should ever arise.'

Rama gave in to Lakshmana's insistence. He, too, could not picture life without this brave and impetuous younger brother, so ready with word and action, so wholly committed to his elder brother's welfare.

'Get our weapons together, Lakshmana. Janaka's bows, the two suits of armour, the inexhaustible quivers, the two gold-worked swords. They are with Vasishtha. And after that, bring Vasishtha's son Suyajna here. I wish to shower him with gifts.'

Suyajna came and received ornaments and money and jewelled furniture and Rama's personal elephant, Shatrunjaya. Kaushika and Agastya, the great sages, were also given gifts of cows and gems. To Vasishtha, he gave a chariot; his charioteer received cows and sacrificial beasts and jewels. Much wealth was distributed to other brahmins and officials and servants, according to their status and their service.

The last and most difficult farewell still remained. Rama, with Lakshmana and Sita, started walking towards Dasharatha's palace. The people of

Ayodhya peered through windows, crowded into balconies and stared in surprise and sorrow as the three walked down the streets with no retinue or royal paraphernalia.

'Rama who had a whole army to follow him, now has only Lakshmana and Sita by his side.' 'Sita walks the public highway, exposed to the common gaze, like any ordinary woman.' 'Rama is the root of the tree of humanity. He has been felled, and we fall with him.' Many were the voices of regret in the streets of Ayodhya that morning.

There was a mounting tide of resentment, too, and the citizens openly gave vent to their feelings. 'Let us leave our houses and gardens and fields and follow Rama. May Ayodhya be a desolate place with deserted homesteads. May the snakes and beasts and birds leave their forest homes and come here. Then Ayodhya will be the wilderness that Kaikeyi deserves, and the forest turn safe for Rama, another Ayodhya for us. Where Rama is, Ayodhya is.'

Rama could hear the rumblings of revolt and dissatisfaction, but continued on his way, unmoved. He reached his father's palace and seeing Sumantra, asked him to announce their presence.

Dasharatha sat like a demented creature, his senses numb, his wits wandering. Sumantra announced the arrival of Rama. 'He has come to bid farewell, my lord.'

Dasharatha asked for all the women in the palace to gather for this last meeting with Rama. They came, following Kausalya. It was a silent, grieving group, their eyes red and swollen with weeping.

Rama arrived. Seeing him, the women assembled there set up a loud lament. Rama looked straight at his father and said: 'Permit me to leave—and Sita and Lakshmana too. They wish to come with me.' Dasharatha cried out: 'I have lost my senses, but you are in full control of yours. Put me in prison and occupy the throne! That would be just and fair.'

Rama's heart overflowed with love and compassion. He blessed the aged monarch. 'May you rule for a thousand years. I will return after fourteen years to touch your feet and seek your blessings.'

Dasharatha pleaded: 'Pass this one night with us, just one more night, a few more hours to satisfy whatever unfulfilled desires you may have.' But Rama had already turned his back on what was no longer his—the kingdom of Kosala, Ayodhya, its riches and its subjects.

'I have no desires left, except the desire to honour your word given to Kaikeyi. All this belongs to Bharata. I go willingly, confident that he will dutifully shoulder his responsibilities. And you should not grieve, for a king protects and comforts. It is not proper that you should give in to sorrow.'

At this point, Sumantra, the wise charioteer, broke down and burst into tears. All save Kaikeyi mourned the banishment of Rama.

Sumantra attacked Kaikeyi with the fierceness of a warrior out to kill his mortal enemy. 'The earth should open up to swallow you and your outrageous behaviour! Can sweet fruit grow on bitter trees? You come from bitter stock. Your mother, too, cared little for her husband. She was headstrong, capricious and self-centred. Daughters take after their mothers, it is said. I now know that is true.'

Sumantra paused, then renewed his attack, hoping by his righteous

indignation to make her relent and retract. 'You have led Dasharatha into the path of unrighteousness, *adharma,* you, his *dharmapatni,* partner in dharma! There is time, even now, to correct this grievous injury to the best of men, our rightful Regent.'

Kaikeyi's face was impassive. All the world was against her and she did not seem to mind.

Dasharatha recovered some of his composure and busied himself with preparations for Rama's exile. 'Let him have an army, hunters too and bodyguards and riches from my treasury. Let his royal way of life continue in the forest, though Bharata rules in Ayodhya.'

Kaikeyi was furious. 'You offer my son a kingdom deprived of wealth and strength, a cup of tasteless wine, my lord. I object!'

Rama intervened. 'When an elephant has been given away, why keep the trappings? Give me my robe of bark.' Kaikeyi was well prepared. 'Here are the robes of bark. I have them ready,' she said, cruel in her haste. Rama and Lakshmana both accepted the dress. Kaikeyi held out a robe for Sita too. Sita, whose skin had felt only the softness of silk, drew back, not knowing how to handle the strange, rough material. Rama came forward and with great tenderness helped her with it. The women wept afresh.

Vasishtha, who had been quiet all this while, lashed out at Kaikeyi: 'You go too far. Sita should stay and rule in Rama's place. It would be the right thing to do. She doesn't have to go.' He threatened: 'If Sita goes with Rama, we all leave with him—Bharata and Shatrughna too. And you, perverse woman, can reign over a wilderness. A kingdom without Rama is no kingdom, and wherever he is, even if it is a forest, is the true kingdom. You think you have done Bharata a favour. He will not accept this hollow gift.'

Dasharatha now ordered Sumantra to drive them to the edge of the forest. It was a poignant moment. 'These fourteen years will pass as swiftly as a dream,' said Rama. Sumitra blessed her son Lakshmana. 'From today, Rama is your father, Sita your mother and the forest, Ayodhya.'

The chariot moved, raising a cloud of dust that the people of Ayodhya laid with their tears. Dasharatha, Kausalya and the citizens followed it until, gathering speed, it vanished from sight. They stood still but let their thoughts race with Rama's chariot.

Crossing many rivers, the three exiles and their charioteer reached the river Ganga. Waterfalls lay like braids on the mountainside and ended in whirlpools that seemed to roar with laughter. Fields of lilies and lotuses swept the landscape in patches of red and white. They halted for the night and were welcomed by Guha, king of the Nishadas. He offered Rama his territories, so honoured was he by his visit.

Sumantra knew that the time had come for him to return to Ayodhya. Guha had already made arrangements for Rama to be rowed across the Ganga and a sturdy boat was ready and waiting. Sumantra pleaded: 'I have driven you faithfully and well on your way out of Ayodhya. Let me stay with you so that I can also drive you back at the end of your exile. You are my driving force; I am your charioteer.'

Sumantra was Rama's last link with Ayodhya, the city of his boyhood and youth. Crossing the Ganga, he would also go over the bridge that spanned two worlds—Ayodhya and the forest. But for Rama there was no looking back with regret.

At the confluence of the two rivers, the Ganga and the Yamuna, they came to the hermitage of Bharadwaja. The sage suggested that they stay with him. But Rama hesitated. It was too close to Ayodhya and memories, too easily accessible to its people. They had to move on, deeper into the forest. Only then could they sever the strong bonds that held and drew them. Bharadwaja saw the wisdom of Rama's decision and told him about the Chitrakuta mountain, across the Yamuna. 'Follow the river, keeping west, till you come to a well-trodden path. Cross the river at that point.'

Chitrakuta appeared to be the ideal choice. Winter had given way to spring with its riot of blossom and birdsong. Valmiki too had his hermitage in Chitrakuta. Not far from there, they discovered a clearing, a sheltered and friendly glade.

Here, Lakshmana soon built a hut, thatched thick and cool with leaves. When it was ready, Rama directed the house-warming rites. Lakshmana lit the sacrificial fire, tracked down and killed a black antelope, dressed and cooked it. Rama then recited the appropriate prayers and set up sacrificial platforms in all four directions, thereby inviting the gods to enter and bless their modest dwelling, the cottage of their dreams and hopes, their island of peace.

4

The Throne of Ayodhya

Sumantra returned to Ayodhya. There were fresh outbursts of grief and recrimination. Kausalya found it hard to forgive her husband. The king whipped himself up into a frenzy of grief and self-pity. 'I am paying for my past misdeeds,' he told Kausalya. 'When I was young, I was out hunting one day. I heard what I thought was the sound of an animal drinking water. I was eager to test my newly acquired skill in archery; so I aimed, fixing my target by the sound alone. It was not an animal I struck but a young ascetic, Shravana. He had come to fetch water for his blind parents. He was their sole support and I had killed him.'

Dasharatha carried out the boy's dying wish. He took the water to the parents and revealing his identity, gave them the news of their son's tragic death. They cursed him, saying 'You will one day grieve over a son, grieve to the point of death,' and setting alight their own funeral pyre, they died.

'That curse is taking effect now. The flame of life has no more oil to feed on and is flickering to a stop. I can sense the nightfall of death, its darkness covers the land of my being. My senses fail. I can see but dimly, hear but faintly.'

When the end came it was swift and unseen. Kausalya and Sumitra woke up to a morning of death and widowhood. The whole of Ayodhya mourned, pointing accusing fingers at Kaikeyi for the calamities she had brought down upon them.

The ministers conferred and decided that Bharata should perform the funeral rites. Dasharatha's body was placed in a stone vat filled with oil, for Bharata was away and it would be some days before he arrived. Vasishtha sent off messengers to him at Rajagriha. 'Give him my best wishes and ask him to start back at once with Shatrughna. Display no grief. Give away nothing.'

At Rajagriha, Bharata had spent a night troubled by bad dreams, dreams he feared to disclose. His companions tried to divert him, but the uneasiness persisted. One of his close friends asked him the reason. Bharata confided: 'I have had disturbing dreams throughout the night. My father, hair dishevelled, in faded clothes, fell from the top of a mountain into a dungheap below. He wallowed in that filth, bursting into fits of maniacal laughter. I saw the ocean dry up, the moon come plummeting down, the earth split open. Again, the king dressed all in black, wearing red garlands, sat in a chariot drawn by asses. Finally, a monstrous female demon lured him

playfully on and away. I think the ass-drawn carriage points to a funeral pyre. My throat is dry at the thought. I see no reason for fear, yet I am tense. I have given in to this dread that is nameless. It seems to loom over my activities, my pleasure, my whole day.'

Even as Bharata was talking about his nightmare, the messengers from Ayodhya rode in saluting him: 'We bring presents and greetings to your uncle and grandfather. You must hasten back. An urgent matter awaits your return.'

Bharata asked immediately: 'Is the king my father well?' And then followed a shower of questions: 'Are Rama and Lakshmana all right? And Sita and Sumitra? And my ambitious, aggressive mother, Kaikeyi—what message do you bring from her?'

The envoys answered evasively: 'They are all well. Great prosperity awaits you. Prepare to return immediately.'

His grandfather and uncle bade him a fond farewell, loading him with rare and costly gifts—precious elephants, dogs bred for hunting, with great fangs and lashing tails, antelope skins, horses, mules and much gold.

But Bharata's heart was leaden with fear and the memory of his dream. The envoys' sudden arrival and their insistence on an immediate return only increased his fears. He made his way anxiously back to Ayodhya with Shatrughna.

On the seventh day they were outside Ayodhya. Even from a distance Bharata sensed that all was not well. The bustling city seemed to have come to a standstill. The amusement parks were deserted, the highways held no traffic.

They entered the city and Bharata turned to the charioteer: 'The streets are unswept. There are no flowers and garlands, sounds of music or signs of joy. No temple bells sound, no sacrificial fires burn. The city seems to be mourning. . . .' They were now in the precincts of the royal palace. Bharata entered, looking for his father.

Not finding Dasharatha, he sought out his mother Kaikeyi. She rose to greet him and then made fond enquiries, keeping up a stream of chatter: 'When did you leave Rajagriha? Is my father well? And my brother? Tell me everything.'

'I left seven days ago,' said Bharata, with a slightly distracted air. 'I left behind the gifts they gave me because it would have slowed down our progress. The messengers said something needed my urgent attention. Do you know anything about it? Where is Father? He's usually with you. Is he with Mother Kausalya? I must find him and pay my respects. I've been away for some time now.'

Kaikeyi had to break the news. She tried to sound casual and down to earth. 'He has gone the way of all human beings. He has met the fate that awaits each one of us. What did you expect?'

Bharata threw himself on the floor, covering his face, and wailed like a child. Kaikeyi rebuked him: 'Men of royal blood do not behave like this. Control yourself, my son.'

But Bharata was deaf to her entreaties. 'I miss my father. How he would have caressed me! How lovingly he would have wiped the dust of travel off my limbs! Take me to Rama—my brother, my friend. He is my father now.'

Then, suddenly, he demanded: 'What were my father's dying words?' Kaikeyi answered: 'He called out "O Rama, O Sita, O Lakshmana" and then cried out "Those who will see them return are the fortunate ones." That was the last thing he said.' Bharata looked at her with unblinking eyes and said, slowly and heavily, dragging out the words as if by force: 'And where are they, that they should return?'

'They are in the forest, exiled...' and Kaikeyi told him everything. 'Give up grieving,' she said, 'and take possession of your kingdom. Move as fast as I moved. You must establish your claims to the throne of Ayodhya before any awkward questions are raised.'

Bharata could not stop the flood of accusations that came thundering down on Kaikeyi like a deadly avalanche. 'You rub salt into my wounds. My father is dead, my brother banished. What will I do with a kingdom? You are like the dark night of doom. When my father took your hand in marriage, he grasped a handful of fire!' Bharata was outraged. 'I, King! I am not reared for kingship. How did you even think of such a thing? Who put the idea into your head? Have you no integrity, no character? I am amazed at your ambition. King of Kosala, I? You are not only evil, you are ignorant. Don't you know that eldest sons always inherit the throne?' He was shouting with helpless rage.

He had more to say, much more. He spared her no blame, no censure, attacking her mercilessly. 'Do not mourn your husband whom you have killed with your cruelty. Weep for me, your son. For I am dead to you, and you to me. I will bring back Rama and work as his slave. That is my rightful place. And you—you should take your own life, before you find yourself in the blazing hell of your own evil designs!'

Bharata howled and moaned and roared like a lion in pain, trapped in a high mountain cave. When he regained some control over himself, he called the council of ministers and formally repudiated Kaikeyi. 'I do not wish to rule. I have no part in this. As you know, I was far away in the kingdom of Kekeya with Shatrughna when all this happened.'

Meanwhile, Kausalya asked to see him. In a voice full of reproach, taunting him, she said: 'The throne you have always coveted is now yours. Your scheming mother has managed it.'

Bharata was deeply hurt. 'You blame an innocent man. I curse the wretch who advised my mother, for she was ill-advised, that is for certain. May that wretch, whoever he is, wander the earth an outcaste, stained with the guilt of a royal murder. May all the sins in our scriptures be his to expiate.'

Kausalya was moved. Drawing him to her, she blessed him, and wept tears of love for her banished son and for this noble prince, mourning like one orphaned and alone.

Vasishtha thought it was the right moment to raise the question of Dasharatha's funeral rites. He tactfully reminded Bharata of his duties as a son. Bharata lifted his father's body out of the vat of oil and laid it down on a rich couch set with precious stones. The cortege began to move. People walked before, scattering gold and gifts. Some collected various kinds of wood and rare aromatic essences for the funeral pyre.

Offerings were first made with silent Vedic prayers and then followed the sombre sweet songs of the Sama Veda. The bodily fires were ritually

extinguished with oblations of water. Dasharatha had returned, through the five elements, to his cosmic self.

The funeral was over. Shatrughna and Bharata sat brooding over the tragic events of the past few weeks.

'Lakshmana should have put up a fight,' said Shatrughna to Bharata, whose thoughts were far away in the forest with Rama. He was working out ways and means of making him return. 'Rama will have to come back. I will make sure of that,' said Bharata, his face haggard and drawn with the strain of events that seemed to overturn all his plans. Suddenly they heard raised voices followed by a scuffle at the door. The brothers looked up to see a group of frightened women looking on as the guards entered, dragging in Manthara after them.

'Here is the monster who was behind this whole plot. She is solely responsible for your father's death and your brother's banishment.'

They could see that Manthara was already beginning to benefit greatly from the new order of things. She was decked out in fine jewellery, dressed in richly embroidered silks fit for a princess and smeared liberally with sandal paste. She was shamelessly flaunting her wealth. Her companions stood around her deferentially, in awe of her newly acquired status. They knew she was the power behind the throne.

Shatrughna sprang at her like a tiger. He caught hold of her and shook her till her bones rattled and her ornaments scattered like so much grain all over the floor. And then he beat her to within an inch of her life. She fell, screaming and shrieking, calling out to her mistress for help. Kaikeyi came running and pleaded with Bharata to save Manthara before Shatrughna killed her in his anger.

'Let her go,' said Bharata sternly to Shatrughna. 'One should not kill a woman. Rama will have nothing to do with us if he gets to know of this. That is the only reason why I spared Kaikeyi,' he said, turning on his mother a look full of hatred and scorn. 'Otherwise she would have met with death at my hands.' Shatrughna released Manthara, still scowling furiously. Her friends fled in fear and confusion. Slowly, Manthara's cries and groans subsided as Kaikeyi stroked her, murmuring soft words of comfort and consolation.

The twelve-day period of mourning was now over. The ministers and counsellors met and formally announced the successor to Dasharatha. They unanimously chose Bharata.

But Bharata refused to accept the throne of Ayodhya. Grim and determined, he said, 'You are well aware of the family tradition. Amongst the Ikshvakus, the eldest son has the unquestioned right to the throne. You cannot proclaim me king—that is Rama's right. I will bring him back here immediately. I am leaving for the forest to seek out my brother and install him as regent. I will then escort him here in a fitting manner. He shall enter his beloved Ayodhya as king. Get everything ready, Sumantra, everything necessary for a coronation. Preparations are almost complete in any case, you have only to shift them to Rama's forest camp.

'Repair the roads and level them,' he commanded, 'so that they will be free of all obstructions. The path to Rama's throne must be a smooth and royal highway to glory. We need to cleanse ourselves of the disgrace of his exile.' The ministers blessed him as they shed tears of happiness. All who heard him wished him joy and prosperity, for Bharata had spoken with the true voice of the people of Ayodhya. Rama had been their spontaneous and heartfelt choice.

The royal party got ready to leave. Ministers and priests led the party. Nine thousand richly caparisoned elephants, sixty thousand chariots, a hundred thousand cavalry and countless archers followed in formation. Next came the three queens, Kausalya, Kaikeyi and Sumitra, and prominent citizens from all walks of life along with their wives. Artisans and workmen brought up the rear.

They halted on the banks of the Ganga to rest and refresh themselves, to feed and water their animals. Bharata also took the opportunity to offer libations to his dead father on the banks of this holy river.

Guha, king of the Nishadas, saw them from a distance and suspected foul play. Bharata might have come, he surmised in his anxiety, to attack Rama. Otherwise why would he bring such a large army with him? Not satisfied with his banishment, he wanted to kill him. . . .

He asked his men to be on the defensive and alert, manned his fleet of sailing vessels with fighter squads and instructed them to be prepared for any eventuality. Then, taking gifts of fish, flesh and honey, he crossed the river to meet Bharata and take stock of the situation,

Sumantra, seeing him, introduced him to Bharata as Rama's devoted friend and ally. Bharata greeted him warmly. 'I am impatient to meet my brother and these forests are totally unknown territory to us. You must guide us,' he said, hoping for immediate help.

Bharata seemed genuinely eager to meet Rama. But with what motive? Could he be certain. . .? Yet this prince seemed friendly. 'Tomorrow I will provide you with a guide who will lead you to Rama, but. . .' and he faltered to a stop. Bharata, sensing his reluctance, asked: 'Why do you hesitate? Is there something on your mind?'

Guha decided to come out in the open, and Bharata's response, full of loyalty, love and sheer devotion, allayed his fears. 'Rama is a father to me. I have come to take him back. His family and his subjects are waiting to welcome him. Ayodhya can have no other king.'

Guha was relieved. This brother of Rama's was free of all taint, like the high dome of heaven on a clear day.

The party retired to rest. But for Bharata the night seemed long and endless. His heart was a dark forest of despair where wild beasts of fear ranged, howling in the tangled undergrowth of nagging anxieties. A hidden fire raged, ready to break out and spread in the hollow spaces of his heart, dry with sorrow and regret. There would be no peace for his troubled soul till he met Rama and persuaded him to go back to Ayodhya.

He sat up with Guha, unable to sleep. 'Tell me about Rama, Sita and Lakshmana. Are they well and in good spirits?' Guha gave him all the news and his eyes seemed to swim with images of their life here.

'This is the very spot where they slept the night before crossing over.' And Bharata's sadness sharpened into intense and overwhelming grief. He stared at the spot and wept.

'This grass bed, pressed by his hallowed body, these specks of silk from Sita's garments, they go through me like daggers.'

For deep down in his heart, there was a knot of fear and hopelessness that seemed to tighten with every passing moment. It would be difficult, perhaps impossible, to make Rama retrace his steps to Ayodhya and the life he had left behind so instantly and without regret. A throne had weighed so lightly against his father's word, given in a moment of weakness to a wilful queen. Bharata was ready to leave with the first light. Anticipating that, Guha had already made provision for their onward journey. 'The sage Bharadwaja who has his hermitage at Prayaga will direct you to Rama. But first, you must cross the Ganga.'

Guha called for a huge fleet of river craft, in all five hundred rafts, boats and barges, to ferry them across. Bharata was impressed by the speed and efficiency with which everything was done.

The two princes and the queens sailed in a splendid barge royally decorated and appointed and navigated by Guha himself. With a canopy of pure white fabric, it rested on the waters like a swan, full of grace and majesty. Guha's kinsmen and servants helped the rest on to their craft, and with all their animals and goods safely aboard various vessels, they set sail for Prayaga. Rowed by skilful boatmen, they were soon safely across, and disembarked in good time. It had been a swift, smooth operation, expertly handled. No mishaps marred the journey and Bharata was grateful to Guha for all the help he had so readily extended to them.

The party prepared for a morning's halt while Bharata and his counsellors set off almost immediately for Bharadwaja's hermitage. The prince had changed into simple clothes. He wore no armour or royal ornaments and carried no weapons. When they got to the hermitage, Bharata ordered the others to stop and went ahead with Vasishtha to meet Bharadwaja.

Seeing Vasishtha, Bharadwaja came forward eagerly, with many warm words of welcome. But it turned out that he too had doubts about Bharata. 'Why have you come with such a large army? I question your intentions. Rama has suffered enough and given up enough. We will do all in our power to shield him from further harassment.'

Bharata wept as he declared: 'If you too doubt me, I am lost, indeed. I would not harm my brother even in thought, let alone by word or deed. I have come here with the sole purpose of taking him back. The army is here to escort him so that he enters Ayodhya with the appropriate royal fanfare. He is born to rule and I intend to see that he does. Please direct us to wherever he may be.'

Vasishtha looked at him with the pride and affection of a father, and Bharadwaja too was satisfied. There was no mistaking the utter sincerity of his words. 'Your brother lives on the Chitrakuta mountain, not far from here. You can start off for his place in the morning. I would be happy if you stayed the night. Tell me,' he said, smiling affectionately at Bharata, 'why did you leave your army behind when you came to my hermitage?'

Bharata was apologetic. 'My army is large and they, especially the animals, can be difficult and unruly. They would have trampled on your grass, uprooted trees and generally disturbed the peace and quiet of your hermitage. That is why I ordered them to stay some distance away from here.'

'Send for them, my son. I would like to entertain you royally. It is within my power to do so, and I would consider it a privilege.'

The ascetic then stood close to the sacrificial fire and with eyes closed, sent up prayers and requests to Vishwakarma, the divine architect, and to other gods. 'May the rivers flow with wine and the sweet juice of sugarcane. May Kubera, shower his wealth of gold and Soma produce pleasures for the palate, undreamt of before. . . .' His thoughts ran on, summoning up scenes of hospitality fit for a king and his retinue, tired with travel and aching to rest.

It worked wonders. An expanse of green grass, soft and pliant, stretched as far as the eye could see. Music filled the air and perfumes wafted by on gentle, cooling breezes. There was a cloudburst of flowers that fell, settling in soft heaps of colour. Trees laden with fruits and flowers sprang up everywhere. Parks and pleasure gardens transformed the austere hermitage into a city of joy.

A river flowed past and on its banks were houses and mansions and a grand palace that towered over them all, furnished with the best that money could buy. Kubera, god of wealth, seemed to have emptied his pot of plenty on its lavish appointments. Bharadwaja conducted Bharata, Shatrughna and the queens into this luxurious building. A golden throne seemed to wait for its king, and seizing a yak-tail fan, Bharata took a low seat as if in readiness for the arrival of Rama. It was a touching gesture.

The army settled down to rest, refresh and enjoy themselves. There were baths provided for all, with scented oils and waters, and piles of food flavoured with heavenly condiments and sauces. Troupes of divine nymphs from the courts of heaven, dazzling in their finery, danced and sang far into the night. They also kept filling and refilling pitchers of wine and jars of food. It was a night-long scene of revelry by starlight under a cloudless, moonlit sky. It was, too, a celebration, a blessing and a gesture of tacit approval on the part of Bharadwaja. Bharata's mission was a praiseworthy one, a battle-cry for dharma in the face of his mother's greed and ambition.

The next morning, Bharata said his farewells and prepared to leave. Bharadwaja gave him detailed instructions. 'A few miles from here, in the midst of thick forests, is the Chitrakuta mountain. The river Mandakini lies north of it. Follow its course. Between its wooded shores and Chitrakuta, a little way up the slope, you will spot Rama's cottage. The landmarks are clear and easy to follow.'

Bharadwaja then asked Bharata to introduce the three queens. 'That lady, slender with fasting and ravaged by grief, is Kausalya, Rama's mother. By her side, like a tree with fading blossom, drooping sadly, is Sumitra, mother of Lakshmana and Shatrughna. And there, apart, standing tall, shameless and unrepentant, is my mother, Kaikeyi whom I am ashamed to own.'

Bharadwaja considered the three in silence and consoled Bharata: 'Do not reproach your mother too much. Rama's exile is a blessing in disguise. Gods, demons and sages will benefit greatly from his banishment,' he finished mysteriously, in the tone of one who knew much more than he

could, or would, reveal.

Bharata, who was like an angry serpent with hood raised and ready to strike, calmed down. There was so much to do. A whole army had to go through unfamiliar territory, and he himself had to face Rama and present the case for Ayodhya and justice as he understood it. It was not going to be easy.

Just before Bharata's arrival, Rama and Sita had been exploring the forests around Chitrakuta. The riches of nature lay spread out before them—flowering trees, soft grass, birdsong and the hum of bees. The dark mountain face spurted white ribbons of foaming water, like elephants in rut, frothing at the temples. Veins of precious minerals, blue, yellow, white and red, streaked the hillsides, and at dusk, the light played tricks with the skyline, changing plain rocks into mansions and parks and looming monoliths. At night, herbs with magic healing powers glowed in their hundreds, fire-tipped, ghostly in the moonlight.

The Mandakini too flowed through their lives. Devout ascetics stood waist-deep in its clear waters, raising their arms to the rising sun in daily salutations. Nature here seemed to aid man as he reached out to God, and all creation was drawn into one undivided whole, the sum and substance of existence. Rama and Sita were getting to know the forest and its moods, getting to know each other too, in a private world of growing love. They were young enough to forget, to let their feelings expand and enfold them in a golden haze of mutual admiration and passion.

Rama was totally wrapped up in the radiant beauty of his wife. She glowed, earthy and fresh, like her mother, the earth, in the springtime of early love. He responded with the ardour and gallantry of a prince. He would pick flowers and put them carefully in the dark, shining coils of her hair and laugh with joy when she threw fragrant garlands round his beautiful neck. They were weaving, through these simple pleasures, a mesh of love that brought them closer and closer together.

He watched over her with obsessive care. One day, while drying their scant reserves of meat for preservation, Sita tried in vain to ward off a persistent crow. He pecked at her, clawed her necklace and flying close, flapped his wings, right in her face. Rama lost his temper. Picking up a blade of grass, he uttered an incantation, and it became a deadly weapon, charged with destruction. It hovered over the crow threateningly till the frightened bird was forced into submission. 'Save me,' he cried. 'I have no one to protect me.' Rama relented, but having once taken aim, he had to destroy. 'Give up some part of your body and then you will be released,' he said. And the crow chose to give up one eye. Which is why, it is commonly believed, the crow turns and twists his head, always on guard, for he can see only out of one eye.

Sitting with Sita, Rama heard the din and clamour of an approaching army, and asked Lakshmana to investigate. Lakshmana climbed a tall tree and scanning the horizon, said: 'It is a huge and well-equipped army. I can see more clearly now. It is Bharata's chariot and his banner. I have no doubt he comes with intent to kill.' His voice was high-pitched with excitement. As

usual, he had jumped to the worst conclusions, and was ready to fight. 'We must defend ourselves and fight back. Kaikeyi will see her son fall like a tree snapped by an elephant. I will go through them and finish them like fire through dry wood. Chitrakuta will see rivers of blood today, I declare,' he finished, as he stared at the approaching army.

Rama met this frenzy of fury and pent-up feelings with his usual calm. He admonished him gently: 'You speak in anger and haste. With Bharata killed, why would I want a kingdom? All that I ever desire, I desire only for my brothers. And nothing will I acquire, not even a kingdom, except through fair means, just means, true means. There is only one way for me, the way of right, the rule of dharma. Killing Bharata will not be the way of right and truth, it will be the way of might and arms. It is not my way.'

Chastened by Rama's rebuke, Lakshmana said, partly to pacify him: 'I could be wrong. It might be our father come to see us.' The army was in full view now, but there was no royal canopy in that vast cavalcade. That was unusual and a cause for some anxiety.

Ordering the army to pitch camp, Bharata set out on foot with Guha and Shatrughna, towards a cluster of huts. One of them particularly, drew his attention. It was beautifully built with leafy branches of many kinds, well thatched and spacious. Through the open door he could see the floor laid thick with kusha grass. On the walls were weapons of great beauty and power—bows, quivers of arrows, swords and daggers sheathed in scabbards

of silver and gold. They were designed for a prince. Bharata came closer and looked in. And there, sitting cross-legged on the floor, his once immaculately groomed hair matted and spread out over his massive shoulders, was Rama himself, and with him were Sita and Lakshmana. As their eyes met, the exhaustion, the anxiety, the sorrow and the despair of the past few weeks burst their bounds, and Bharata fell at Rama's feet, sobbing like a lost child. 'You should live in a city palace, enthroned and crowned, and hold court over an assembly full of luminaries. Instead, you sit here, surrounded by wild beasts! Your hair should be elegantly groomed, not hang limp and straggly, in tangled clusters like a common mendicant's! Your body should be smeared with sandal and wrapped in soft silks, not clad in rough bark and antelope skin. I am responsible for this, I alone!' he said, as his tears bathed Rama's feet in floods of penitence.

Shatrughna, too, wept, overwhelmed by the sight of their elder brother, reduced to living in a forest hut. Rama embraced them both and drawing Bharata on to his lap, in a voice full of concern, began to question him closely about Ayodhya.

'Is the king well? Do you rule by good counsel, taken in good time? Do you perform your sacrificial rites? Are you alert to danger? Have you chosen your advisers with care? It is better to have one wise counsellor than to have a hundred fools who will confuse every issue. I hope your subjects do your bidding out of love, not fear. Has your army got a good leader, and are your men well fed and paid? Disgruntled soldiers can eat into your strengths. Have you appointed a good messenger, an excellent ambassador? Do learned men flourish in your kingdom? Do you protect your women? Do you make frequent public appearances to reassure your subjects? Do you balance duty, profit and enjoyment? Are you fair, are you just, are you true, dear Bharata? Good governance is made up of many things. A king cannot afford to be slack or neglectful. A good king rules the earth and exercises absolute power, but not for his own profit or glory. He fills his coffers, strengthens and enlarges his boundaries and performs sacrifices, only for the sake of his children, his subjects. He lives for and through them, ever mindful of their welfare, ever heedless of his own. Such a ruler is a true monarch of the earth. Such are we, the Ikshvakus, and such you must be, Bharata.'

Bharata listened to Rama, drinking in his words. How could he ever attain such heights of perfection? Rama fell silent and then asked: 'Why have you come?'

'O, Rama, our father is dead, killed by the woman he loved, my mother, in her greed for power. He could not survive your banishment. I returned from Rajagriha to find him gone. It is an unbearable situation. I feel my hands are stained with the blood of my father's death. What is worse, they ask me to sit on a throne, to accept a kingdom which is yours by right. I will not commit this crime, for crime it is. You must come back to Ayodhya. This vast army is here to escort you. Everybody wants you back.' And Bharata bent low to touch his feet once more in a gesture of renewed subjection.

Rama parried his appeal. 'A father has the right to banish and a mother the right to command, equally. We must respect their wishes. You must rule, and I must wander the forest, clad in bark robes. That is the order of things.' Bharata tried again. 'This is neither fair not just. The elder son always inherits the throne. You know it.'

Rama was no longer with him. He had been trying to control his grief at the news of Dasharatha's sudden and untimely death. He broke down and lay on the floor grieving, face to the wall. To Bharata he said: 'My father died, sorrowing for me, and I was not even there to perform his last rites.' Bharata, Shatrughna and Lakshmana raised him, saying that he should perform the ritual even now, for he was not only the eldest but the favourite son. And Rama did.

On the banks of the Mandakini he filled his cupped palms with water and offered it to his dead father. Then, placing the ritual ball of food on a heap of kusha grass, he laid his dead father's spirit to rest. The rites of water and food both performed, they walked back, grave and thoughtful.

The people in the camp, meanwhile, had come to their own conclusions, for they could hear sounds of loud lamentations. 'They have met, the princes have met!' they said, and there was a stampede in the direction of the sounds. They could not wait to see their beloved Rama.

Kausalya and the two other queens walked ahead with Vasishtha. It was a scene of many regrets and accusations. They parted for the night, wondering how Bharata would set about persuading Rama, what arguments he would use.

It was an uneasy night for everybody. The brothers met in the morning and Bharata appealed once more to Rama. 'The kingdom of Kosala was given to me. But I give it back to you. The flood of events has caused a breach in our dynasty—only you can mend it. A donkey cannot keep pace with a horse, nor can I follow in your footsteps.'

Rama was firm. 'All that comes together, parts. That which rises, falls, union leads to separation, ripeness to decay, life to death. Death is our constant companion. It sits, stands, walks with us. Death moves, shadowing life. Even as the sun rises, it has begun to set. Each season is a source of joy, but spells death; death of the season preceding it and its own approaching death. You mourn our father too much, my banishment far too much. Accept the fact that I mean to honour my father's word, and accept the kingdom which is your destiny.'

It was a losing battle and Bharata was beginning to lose heart. He was pitting his meagre strength against the moral might of a giant among men. He tried a last, desperate measure. Spreading a heap of grass, he lay down on it, saying: 'I refuse to move till you return .

But the others by then had begun to see Rama's point of view. 'Rama is right. You should accept responsibility for Ayodhya.'

Bharata could still not think of ruling in Rama's place, yet he was the only one who could be king of Kosala. There seemed no way out. He felt cornered and helpless.

'Give me your sandals,' he begged of Rama. 'Step on them so that your powers and energies may flow into them. I shall rule guided by their lustre, far from Ayodhya, for Ayodhya is your capital. It will wait for you. And remember,' he threatened, 'not a single day more than fourteen years will I rule—or live if you delay.'

Rama slipped his feet into his sandals and Bharata touched them

reverently to his head. 'I shall wear bark robes and rule under the shadow of your feet. I hold the kingdom in trust, waiting for your return. I rule, under protest.' They returned to Ayodhya. Bharata's mission had failed, but not for want of trying.

Ayodhya seemed a city of the dead, desolate and joyless, a waveless sea, a fallen meteor, a dry river bed. Its roaring success as a capital city was a faint and fading whisper. There were hardly any signs of life.

Bharata saw the queens settled into the palace and himself moved to Nandigrama, a village outside Ayodhya. Rama's sandals were taken there in a royal procession and enthroned. The royal canopy of power and authority shaded them, not Bharata. He never allowed himself to forget even for a moment that the kingdom was being held in trust for Rama, its rightful occupant. Every problem was referred to the hallowed sandals through prayer and meditation. Bharata ruled, as it were, sitting at Rama's feet.

Kaikeyi had wanted Bharata to step into Rama's shoes. But he chose, instead to enshrine and worship them, to humbly conduct the affairs of state from under their royal shadow. Her dreams of power and glory had, after all, come to nothing. It was hard to tell who had won and who had lost in this battle of wits, wills, ambitions and crossed purposes.

The arrival of Bharata and his army had disturbed the ascetics of Chitrakuta. They feared, too, the repeated depredations of the *rakshasas,* demons who defiled and destroyed their homes and their sacrificial fires. They decided to leave. An old ascetic advised Rama to move too. The demon Khara, brother of Ravana the ten-headed demon-king of Lanka, was terrorizing the area, he said. But Rama decided to stay on. Seeing him unperturbed and fully prepared to fight Khara, some of them stayed back and the peaceful hermitage limped slowly back to normal.

But there were too many memories that churned Rama's heart. Father, mother, brothers, his beloved Ayodhya and those harrowing scenes with Bharata—these were bonds he had to loosen. And the only way was to move on, farther into the forest, where family, Ayodhya and his subjects would be truly things of the past.

Rama, Sita and Lakshmana started for the deep, dark woods of the Dandakaranya. Stopping briefly at the hermitage of Atri and Anasuya, they spent the evening recalling the past. It was now firmly behind them. The future had to be planned. And the future loomed ahead, dark with the roving forms of demons going unchecked about their work of senseless destruction.

5

The Rout of the Demons

The friendly warmth of Chitrakuta gave way to forbidding jungle terrain. They began to get used to the sounds and silences of the forest. The rustle of leaves as an animal brushed past, hidden and swift, no longer made them start.

They came to a hermitage. From a distance, the circle of huts seemed set in a heap of pulsating light. Rama recognized it as the radiance of spiritual fire, the aura of the true ascetic.

It was a pleasant clearing, cool and welcoming. But there was more than a hint of menace in the air. The hermits had hair-raising tales to tell of demons who swooped down on them, defiling, destroying, killing. 'As our prince, we expect you to protect us. We cannot fight these man-eating monsters,' they said. Rama's response was ready, reassuring. He would do all in his power to help them.

At dawn the next day, they met a fearsome creature of giant proportions. Clad in a tiger skin dripping with blood, he came towards them, roaring, mouth open and ready to swallow his prey.

He grabbed Sita and shouted: 'This lovely woman shall be my wife. But, first I must drink your blood, you trespassers!'

Rama grew pale with fury. 'How dare he touch Sita,' he said hoarsely, turning to Lakshmana who was equally outraged.

The demon challenged them. 'Who are you? Speak up!'

'We are warriors of the Ikshvaku dynasty. Who are you?'

'I am Viradha. No weapon can harm me, I would have you know. Go away and leave this woman behind and you may escape with your lives.'

Rama was speechless with rage. Two arrows struck Viradha and seven more, feathered and gold-tipped, sped as one missile. Viradha fell, letting go of Sita as his hold on her slackened. Almost immediately he rose again to attack them. The fight was long and indecisive, for Viradha was impervious to weapons. Ultimately, his arms were broken off and he lay prone, gasping for breath.

'I am a celestial cursed by Kubera, and you are my deliverer. That was foretold.' He was sinking fast. 'You are new to these parts. I can only give you advice. Go to the hermitage of the sage Sharabhanga. He will guide you. He lives just a short distance away. And now put me out of my misery. Bury me alive, for no weapon can kill me. Start digging, young men. What are you waiting for?' he gasped.

Sita stood there, trembling like a leaf. 'The forest has dangers I never dreamt of,' she thought, 'but then, my protector is no ordinary man. He has the power and strength of an army of gods!'

At Sharabhanga's hermitage, they were treated to a divine vision. Indra himself, golden and luminous, hovered over the hermitage in his aerial chariot. Around him, like attendant planets, stood the heavenly hosts. Rama was excited. 'That is Indra himself, I think. And do you realize, Lakshmana, how young they all are. They are twenty-five years old, and will stay so, for they are blessed with eternal youth. I am going closer to make absolutely sure.'

Indra, seeing Rama approach, said to Sharabhanga: 'I had come to take you to Brahma's heaven, but now you will have to follow on your own. I do not want Rama to see me now. There is a task he has to accomplish,' he said, looking secretive and a little complacent. 'After that, I will reveal myself to him,' said the chief of the gods to whom all the world offered sacrifices. And he vanished.

'Who was that?' asked Rama.

'That was Indra. I was to go with him, but that can wait. I am blessed that I was able to see you. I would have missed you. But now I must hurry. I suggest you go on to meet Sutikshna. He will help you plan your next course of action. Follow the Mandakini and it will lead you straight to him. Now I am ready to go. I would like you to stay here while I shed this troublesome body of mine. It hampers my progress.'

He lit a fire, sanctified it with offerings and, chanting certain mantras, consigned himself to the sacred blaze. And as they watched, he soared into the heavens, young, revived and resplendent, on his way to Brahma's world of bliss everlasting.

The three royal bystanders grew thoughtful. The forest had its own share of lessons to teach them. The mystery and the power of spiritual growth and its rewards were slowly unfolding in their young and impressionable minds. Their own individual destinies too were beginning to take firmer shape.

The ascetics in Sharabhanga's hermitage gathered round Rama as if by common consent. They knew they had struck a deep chord of sympathy in this young and dynamic prince.

Rama studied them keenly, his curiosity and interest awakened by this seemingly motley crowd of professional penitents. There were those who lived on the moon's rays, or did penance standing in water. Some slept on the bare ground or lived out in the open all the year round. Yet others sought the scorching heat of the sun or subsisted on water and wind alone. Then there were those who fasted or prayed endlessly or sat perched on high mountain peaks.

Abstinence of one kind or another, in varying degrees of severity, seemed to be a whole new way of life; giving up, more giving up and yet more giving up.

Rama knew what was in their minds even before they began their clamour for protection. 'Blessed is the king who defends his weak and helpless subjects. You have only to see the havoc caused by these demons, the trail of human carnage they leave wherever they go.'

Rama pacified them. 'I am here to save you from these marauders. I am

your refuge. Understand that. My brother and I will both prove our mettle, do not fear!' And with this reassurance they left.

After a night's halt at Sutikshna's hermitage, they prepared to move on. Rama wanted to visit all the hermitages in the Dandaka forest. He seemed to have taken his mission of protection very seriously indeed.

In the meantime, Sita too had given the matter a good deal of thought. She decided to confront Rama with her conclusions. 'There are three major wrongs that arise from worldly pursuits,' she began very tactfully, 'falsehood, taking another's wife and violence without provocation or enmity. You have shown no signs of the first two, ever, and will not, either. But I notice that you have begun to betray some signs of the third—a readiness to harm or destroy those who are not your enemies.' She paused, surprised at her own boldness, and hesitated.

'Yes. . .?' said Rama, encouragingly. She spoke on, gathering courage.

'You are in the forest to honour a pledge, to live the life of an ascetic, entertaining no thoughts of violence or killing. You are not here as a king or a warrior. Yet you have sworn to seek out and kill these demons, with whom you personally have no quarrel. Their quarrel is with the sages, not with you. This can only lead to trouble, as it happened once in a similar situation. Let me tell you.'

And Sita told him the story of a great ascetic whom the wily Indra had managed to divert through a simple ruse, so simple that the sage did not see through it. All Indra did was to hand him a sword, asking him to guard it with his life. The sage carried it around with him wherever he went. Gradually, by sheer association and proximity, the sword put thoughts of violence into his head and he began to strike warlike postures. It was only a matter of time before thought was translated into deed.

'To cut a long story short,' said Sita, 'he went to hell for his misdeeds. Weapons breed violence. The process is insidious. A warrior's duties are linked to the sword, it is his strength. It is the fuel that feeds his valour. You are not here as a warrior whose duty it is to fight. You are here as an ascetic. In my humble opinion, my lord, your weapons are beginning to colour your thoughts. I disapprove of this journey through the Dandaka forest in search of demons. I speak out of concern for you. My words are a reminder, not a rebuke. Who is there in this world that can correct you in matters of right and wrong?' she finished, in some agitation.

'What you say is true, Sita,' said Rama, who had given her his undivided attention. 'But you forget my role as protector. Although I am exiled, my responsibility remains. These sages have no other refuge. They themselves cannot fight, although through penance, they have acquired powers more deadly than any weapon could ever unleash. Any act, or even thought of violence will wipe out their spiritual reserves.

'Warrior princes carry weapons in order to anticipate, pre-empt harassment. Here, in Dandaka, the limits of forbearance have long been crossed. These sages have had to seek the protection they should have got, unasked. Besides, I have given my word. I cannot go back on it. You should know, that to me, the honouring of a promise given takes precedence over all else—even you and Lakshmana.

'I appreciate your concern and your great love for me and your preoccupations with matters of truth. But I too am bound. I have my compulsions. You must continue to have faith in me.'

It was another landmark in their life together as man and wife. It was not a blind following of a pre-set goal by an unquestioning wife. It was a relationship where dialogue and debate cleared the path to a common goal—right conduct and right living in the pursuit of truth.

Rama, Sita and Lakshmana roamed the forest of Dandaka for ten years, visiting almost every hermitage, living with the ascetics, sometimes for months at a stretch. Then Rama decided it was time to return to Sutikshna. After a few days with him he said: 'I would like to pay my respects to Agastya. I know he lives in this forest but I have not come across him in all my travels. I will need your guidance to get to him.'

Sutikshna thought it was a good idea for them to visit the great sage. 'I was going to suggest it myself. You should start off immediately. South of my hermitage, not too far from here, lives his brother. He will tell you how to reach Agastya.'

They had no difficulty in finding Agastya's hermitage. It was a jewel of a glade. The leaves of the trees shone and sparkled with the special care lavished on them, the deer were fearless and tame, and did not shun human company. In true ascetic tradition, plants and animals were treated as sentient beings, handled with love and care and constant attention. Over the whole area clung a rare fragrance that revived the travellers' tired spirits.

'Here there are no demons,' explained Rama. 'Agastya's powers have banished them. He swallowed Vatapi, the fiercest of them, and consumed Vatapi's brother, Ilvala, with a single glance. And when the proud Vindhya mountain raised his head, wanting to block the sun, Agastya bore down on him with his spiritual powers, keeping him firmly in check. I would like to spend the remaining part of our exile with him.'

Lakshmana announced Rama's arrival and a disciple showed Rama into the renowned ascetic's presence.

Agastya radiated an aura born of penance and austerities. Rama felt flattered by his attentions. 'I have been waiting for you, Rama, waiting with special weapons. You will leave here armed with the might of the gods.

'This is a bow of Vishnu's, studded with diamonds and inlaid with gold. And here are two inexhaustible quivers, filled with arrows that blaze like torches, a silver scabbard and a gold-worked sword. And the Brahmadatta missile. I hand over all these to you. May they strengthen your hand and bring you glory.' There was a prophetic ring to Agastya's voice as he blessed Rama. His destiny as a warrior in the cause of right seemed now clearer than ever before.

As Rama accepted the treasury of divine weapons, Agastya praised Sita. 'Most women are fickle, ruled by their changing moods. Your wife is steadfast and loyal, a true partner to her husband in prosperity and adversity alike.'

Agastya then extended the traditional ascetic's welcome. Water was brought to wash and cool tired feet, and then offerings of forest produce—fruits and roots. 'You have offered to stay with me but I know you long for a home, however humble.' Rama nodded assent. 'Could you suggest a place,

somewhere quiet and secluded, full of trees and flowing streams?' he asked.

'I have just the right place in mind. It lies south of this region, on the banks of the Godavari, and is known as Panchavati. The surroundings will delight Sita with their flowering woods and abundant birdlife. It is just beyond that mountain—not too stiff a climb.'

Rama, Sita and Lakshmana began the journey to Panchavati. It was time to strike roots. A home was in sight after years of wandering, a place to spend the remaining four years of their exile.

On the way to Panchavati, they encountered a giant vulture. The brothers suspected he might be a demon in bird form. Demons had the power, they knew, to change their form at will. Their tone was rough as they asked him

aggressively: 'Who are you?'

The bird answered in a voice that seemed to stroke them like a fond and loving parent. 'I am Jatayu, son of Aruna, brother of Garuda, monarch of the eagles. I knew your father. Sampati is my elder brother. We are descendants of the Prajapatis, superhuman beings of another age, and Kashyapa was my ancestor. It is from the same race of beings that the whole animal and bird kingdom came into existence. Our closest kin and deadliest enemies are the serpents.

'We tread pathways in the skies trodden by none. We see sights beyond the range of normal human vision, for the eye of an eagle or a vulture travels far. It pinpoints the invisible with superhuman clarity. I will watch over Sita and take care of her when you are away,' offered Jatayu. 'Let me be part of your group.'

Rama willingly consented and the four started off for Panchavati. At Panchavati, they chose a sheltered spot with the river Godavari flowing close by. Lakshmana started to clear and level the ground and built a spacious hut that would house the three of them comfortably. Mud walls and a bamboo frame supported a roof thatched with leaves and branches, thickly interwoven with reeds and grass of all kinds. It was a modest but sturdy dwelling, made to withstand the rigours of forest life. Rama was touched anew by his brother's unswerving loyalty, love and devotion.

Winter had now set in. Mist lay over hill, river and tree. The wind blew, its

breath icy with the touch of mountain snows. The sun veered south, leaving the north pale and desolate like the forehead of a woman bare of the auspicious vermilion. Elephants put out their trunks to drink water and withdrew hastily, shying away from the cold. Waterfowl stood rooted to the river bank, shunning the water like cowards who shrink from the thought of battle. The trees slept, their sap withdrawn, and the lotus, beloved of the sun, no longer bloomed, red and fiery.

Rama, Sita and Lakshmana watched the season settle into its cycle of short, chill days warmed by a weak sun and long, cold nights lit by a dim and frosty moon. They thought of Bharata and Ayodhya with sharp and intense longing. Lakshmana still raged at Kaikeyi. Rama would chide him gently.

'Kaikeyi is our mother and second among the three queens of Ayodhya. You must not harbour a grudge against her. But I miss Bharata's love and affection, and when I think of him, I weaken.'

Life was a lake of rippling memories that peaked now and then into a wave of sorrow and regret.

One day, while Rama sat chanting the scriptures, a female demon happened to see him. She was ravished at the sight of this handsome man in the prime of youth, radiant and near-divine. His dark and splendid body, wide, shining eyes and heap of matted hair drew her like the god of love himself.

They were a study in contrasts. He was spare and slender, she heavy and squat. His eyes were large, his gaze steady—she had a pronounced squint. Rama's voice rang out like a clear bell, while hers tore at the air, brazen and harsh. Sullen, haggard and altogether repellent, she had fallen in love with this utterly captivating and youthful ascetic.

Coming close to Rama she asked: 'Who are you, clad in bark, armed with bow and arrow, wandering this forest which is the preserve of demons? Why are you here?'

Rama was quick to reply. 'I am Rama, son of Dasharatha who was a powerful king. I am here with Lakshmana, my younger brother and my wife, Sita, princess of Videha, to fulfil a vow. And who are you?'

'I am Shurpanakha, sister of Ravana, demon-king of Lanka. Kumbhakarna, Vibhishana and two others, Khara and Dushana, warlike and terrible, are also my brothers. I want to be your wife,' she declared, looking at him with eyes full of love and longing. 'I can change my form at will,' she ventured. And then, more hopefully, 'Abandon Sita—she is a miserable sickly creature. I mean to devour both her and Lakshmana, before the day is out.'

Rama was in a mischievous mood. He decided to have a little fun at her expense. She cut such a sorry figure, ridiculous in her abject surrender to him. 'I am married,' he said, 'and rivalry between you and Sita would be bothersome. Lakshmana is young and single and waiting for someone like you, large-eyed and lovely.'

Shurpanakha was easily swayed—after all, both brothers were equally desirable. Either would do.

She went running to Lakshmana, who met her frenzied proposals with a clever ploy. Rama had started a game and he went along with it, carried away somewhat with the cruel humour of the situation. 'Do you want to be the wife of a slave?' he asked. 'For that is what I am, my brother's slave. You deserve better. And let me tell you, Rama will give up his peevish old wife with a little persuasion.'

Shurpanakha sensed no sarcasm or trickery. She went running back to Rama. 'This hag is standing in our way. I will eat her up and your brother too,' she exclaimed and rushed at Sita. Rama stopped her and said angrily to Lakshmana: 'Stop taunting this demon. Sita is in danger, don't you see?'

Lakshmana was ready to attack, drawn sword in hand. Rama ordered: 'Don't kill her. Just disfigure her and let her go.' Lakshmana, quick to obey his brother's slightest command, cut off Shurpanakha's nose and ears. Injured and bleeding, she ran to her brother Khara in Janasthana and threw herself at his feet.

Khara flared up at the sight of his sister, mutilated and streaming blood. 'Who has dared to stir the sleeping serpent of my wrath,' he thundered. 'Who is this man who goes about his day's work unaware that the noose of death is about to tighten round his neck? The earth will drink his blood today and the vultures tear at his flesh!'

Shurpanakha, choking with sobs, said: 'Rama and Lakshmana, sons of Dasharatha, are responsible for this violence done to me. And all for the sake of Rama's wife, a young and beautiful woman. I must drink their blood. I demand it.'

Khara called for fourteen of his bravest demons. 'Go after those two young men. My sister's thirst must be quenched.'

The demons attacked Rama and Lakshmana with spears. But Rama broke the spears mid-air with his arrows. It was an unequal battle. They fell like trees before the woodcutter's axe.

Shurpanakha set up a loud wail as she ran to Khara and told him of Rama's triumph. Khara reprimanded her: 'Fourteen of my best men gone, and you still complain! Why are you thrashing about like an angry serpent? You shall drink their blood, fresh and warm as it is spilt, I promise!'

Khara himself set out in his golden chariot, yoked with excellent horses. Fourteen thousand demons went with him. Janasthana resounded to their blood-curdling war cries.

The heavens sent warning signals through bad omens and portents, but Khara, blind with anger, chose to ignore them. Comets came tumbling down silently, dark clouds rained showers of blood, stars clustered thick as fireflies though it was still day, parrots screeched and a vulture perched ominously on his golden standard.

'I can conquer even death,' Khara boasted, defiant and foolhardy. And the vast demon army hurled themselves at Rama and Lakshmana, starting a battle such as Janasthana had never hoped to see. The gods rejoiced, and so did the sages. A blow for right against might would finally be struck, they felt, as the two princes braced themselves for the attack.

Rama waited, fired with energy, intent on destruction. He spoke words of encouragement to Lakshmana as the enemy advanced like vast clouds rolling towards them, their golden chariots and armour like a blaze of morning sky.

'Smoke rises from my arrows ready to fly, and my bow moves of itself, eager to attack. My arm throbs in anticipation of victory. I can see the enemy vanquished, Lakshmana.'

The enemy hordes converged on Rama in all their fury and strength, showering weapons and missiles. Rama took them like a vast ocean receiving the rivers flowing into its endless waters. The attack continued in a storm of arrows. Rama stood his ground like a bull who blinks away drops of rain, unperturbed.

His arrows began to fly, flaming like lit torches, drawing enemy blood. The demons were like dry wood to flame, like trees falling in a storm raised by the rush and rustle of the giant eagle Garuda's wings.

Only Khara and Trishiras, leader of the army, survived. Trishiras undertook to fight Rama. 'Let me go first, Khara. I will avenge the death of my demon warriors.' Three-headed and terrible as he was, he played havoc

with his weapons. His arrows hit Rama's forehead and Rama cried out: 'I wear your arrows like a garland on my brow. Now get ready for mine.' And Trishiras fell, all three heads severed by Rama's flaming arrows, his chariot shattered, his horses killed.

Khara felt a sudden twinge of fear. His army was in a shambles, his leader slain. He rushed to the attack, like a moth to the flame, courting death. A battle of words began as the two met in single combat.

'Oppressor of the ascetics of Dandaka, your end is near,' cried Rama. 'Evil deeds bear bitter fruit. My arrows will pierce your flesh like snakes boring through an anthill.'

Khara called out, his anger mounting: 'Warriors do not boast, especially when they are on the brink of death, as you are now. Fourteen thousand demons have died in battle. I mean to dry the tears of their dear ones by killing you.'

Khara hurled his magic mace that came hurtling through the air, reducing to ashes every tree that stood in its way. But Rama struck it, and it fell like a serpent, charmed and powerless. Khara then snatched a tree and swinging it in a great arc, hurled it at Rama. But Rama hit the tree, snapping it as it fell, away from him. And then he let loose a powerful arrow that struck Khara, burning him to death.

Fourteen thousand demons had been slain in the holocaust at Janasthana. It signalled the end of a reign of terror and oppression. Dandaka was once again a haven of peace for those who embraced the ascetic path. The gods and sages rejoiced and Sita, in a rush of love and joy and wonder, tended to her brave husband's wounds.

6

The Abduction of Sita

Akampana, Ravana's messenger, had managed to escape the carnage and return to Lanka. He reported to his king, eyes wide with horror: 'Janasthana has been devastated. The demons have all been killed, and Khara too. It's a wonder I am alive to tell the tale.'

Ravana's fiery red eyes seemed to smoke with anger and his voice was like a clap of thunder. 'Who has dared to massacre my people and ruin Janasthana? No one can save him from my wrath. I order the march of time; the very winds blow at my command. I burn fire and kill death. Tell me, Akampana, who is he?'

'He is Rama, son of Dasharatha, a lion among men, with powerful shoulders and long arms,' said Akampana as he recalled Rama in action at Janasthana. 'His voice is deep and resonant like a drumbeat, his face full and glowing like the moon.'

'Was he helped by the gods?' asked Ravana, in utter disbelief.

'Lakshmana, his younger brother, was the wind to Rama's fire, fanning his energies into the blaze that destroyed Janasthana. It was not the work of the gods, but the power of his serpent-headed arrows that consumed the demons like a forest fire swallowing trees.'

'I shall kill them both,' threatened Ravana, half rising from his seat.

'First hear me out, gauge Rama's full strength,' advised Akampana. 'With his arrows he can check a river in spate, shift the ocean, make it flood the earth, then raise the submerged earth from the flood waters once again. He can destroy whole worlds, create new ones. Such is the power he wields, such is his reputation. You cannot defeat him in a straight battle.'

Ravana was listening, trying to get the measure of Rama. Akampana said, in a conspiratorial tone of voice: 'There is a way out, the only way I can think of. Rama has a wife, a dusky, golden beauty, exquisitely proportioned, in the full bloom of youth. You must separate them for a while, somehow, then carry her off. He will not live without her.'

Ravana liked the idea and decided to act on it without delay. He called for his chariot and went to the demon Maricha, Tataka's son, an ascetic. Ravana did not waste words or time. 'Rama, you know, has destroyed Janasthana. I want you to help me take Sita away from him.'

Maricha was stunned. He had escaped with his life once, long ago, when Rama, then a mere boy had attacked him and his brother Subahu. And again, more recently.

'Whoever has put this idea into your head? He is an enemy, not a friend.

He expects you to extract the fangs of a deadly serpent with your bare hands, no less. Carry away Sita!'

Maricha could not believe his ears; he went on in a daze, frozen with fear. 'You are rousing a sleeping lion to whom we demons are as deer, easy quarry. You hurl yourself into an ocean of dangers, seeking certain death. Return, Ravana, to your palace and your women. Stop dreaming of Sita; she is Rama's and Rama's alone.'

Maricha had been so vehement that Ravana had second thoughts about abducting Sita. It was sheer madness to think of her, he was now convinced.

Shurpanakha had by then heard of the demons' humiliating defeat. She started off for Lanka, her sense of grievance and insult heightened at this

fresh setback. She arrived in the city and went straight to her brother's palace.

Ravana was holding court, dazzling the assembly with his ten heads and twenty arms. There were marks of former victories on his great body. Indra's elephant Airavata had scarred it, and the Vajra, Indra's thunderbolt, had also left its mark. Ravana was a law unto himself, going on the rampage when he felt like it, breaking every moral law, carrying off other men's wives, defiling sacrificial altars, trampling heavenly gardens. Because of a boon given to him by Brahma, he was impervious to the attack of gods, demons, aerial or subterranean spirits. Shurpanakha became acutely aware of his strengths, powers, reputation and renown as she looked at him, seated on his golden throne. She was going to demand revenge and get it.

She held her ravaged face up to him, raving and ranting. 'You take your defeat lightly. Rama has wiped out a whole tribe, fourteen thousand of them, and killed your brother Khara too. You should feel threatened. Instead, you sit here wallowing in pleasure, indulging your senses, lulled into a feeling of false security. You will be swept off your throne like a stray wisp of straw.'

Ravana was forced into taking notice of what his sister said. She had pointed out grave flaws in his character, revealed the chinks in his armour. Was he, after all, being too complacent? Rama's show of strength had been a challenge; his treatment of Shurpanakha, a blatant insult. He could not

afford to ignore either. His reputation was at stake. And he was intrigued too.

'Who is this Rama?' he asked his sister. 'Why is he here? What does he look like? Tell me.'

Shurpanakha, pushing her advantage, waxed eloquent. 'He is love and beauty embodied. He exudes strength and power and energy. His brother worships him and follows him like a shadow, a second self. As for his wife, Sita, she walks the earth like a second moon, her skin the colour of molten gold, her body swaying with the weight of its own loveliness, rounded and soft and full of sweet promise.'

Ravana's interest was now definitely aroused, his dormant desire

awakened by Shurpanakha's ecstatic description. She finished deceitfully. 'In fact, it was to get her for you that I went near them. She would make you a fitting consort.'

There was no stopping Ravana now, Shurpanakha knew. Her ploy had worked.

Ravana went again to Maricha, this time with a firm plan. 'Assume the form of a golden deer. Attract Sita. She will want to have you and will make Rama and Lakshmana go after you. She will then be alone and unguarded and I will carry her off. And Rama will die of grief. I will be rid of him,' he gloated.

Maricha dissuaded him. 'I have become an ascetic just to escape Rama's arrows. He is my nightmare. Sometimes I see a thousand Ramas lurking in these woods.'

Ravana was too intent on his scheme to listen. He barely heard him.

'Give up the idea, Ravana. It is not a simple matter. Rama is virtuous and loved by the whole world. Sita is devoted to him and her virtue shades him like a halo of spiritual protection. Besides, compare your strength with his. Sita will be your downfall and the downfall of all of us. Consult Vibhishana and your other ministers before you venture on this rash mission.'

Ravana was furious. He was set on his course of action and would brook no resistance. 'Your gloomy talk and despondent mood exasperate me. I have not come here to consult you, but to ask you for help. You are foolish to deny that to a king as powerful as I am. All you have to do is to play the part of a golden deer and captivate Sita. Having done that, you may return. In any case, you have no choice. If you refuse, I will kill you. By going near Rama, you only risk death. By refusing me, you make certain of it!'

Maricha had to agree, but warned Ravana: 'You will drag us all with you to certain destruction. But those who are doomed to die turn away from good counsel. That is the way of the world.'

Ravana was all sweetness when he and Maricha reached Panchavati. 'Here is Rama's hermitage. Put our plan to work!'

Maricha transformed himself into a golden deer, speckled with silver. His antlers, tipped with jewels, branched majestically in wide curves over his head, glinting and gleaming in the morning sun. His mouth was rose-red, his ears and rounded belly the blue of a clear sky. He stepped proudly on emerald hooves, his neck held tall and straight, and his haunches rippled rainbow hues as he moved in and out of the trees, a shifting mass of light and colour. He leapt and ran, flashing through the tracery of leaves, dazzling the senses.

Sita was in the hermitage garden gathering flowers when she saw this radiant, jewelled vision. She watched him gambol and frolic, come up tantalizingly close or move away almost out of sight. She was ravished by his beauty and could hardly take her eyes off the deer as she called out to Rama and Lakshmana: 'Please come at once. I've seen something wonderful and strange—a golden deer, washed in all the colours of the rainbow.'

They watched the animal for some time. Lakshmana was suspicious. 'That is Maricha, I am sure, trying to lure unwary kings on their royal hunts. It is no ordinary deer. It is an illusion, a result of black magic.'

But Sita had set her heart on having the deer. 'I have seen many beautiful creatures around our hermitage, some of them semi-divine, but this deer enthrals me. What a feast for the eyes! You must catch it alive. How beautiful it will look in the palace gardens of Ayodhya when we return,' she said dreamily. And then stubbornly—'I must have it. I have never wanted anything so much in my life. And if you can't capture it alive, the skin will make a lovely spread. Is that a cruel thought for a young woman to have? I can't help it,' she said looking at Rama, flushed with excitement, carried away on waves of wild anticipation. 'Oh, how I long to sit on it, and feel its shining softness, and watch the precious gems flash back at me. It's a treasure fit for a queen.'

Rama looked indulgently at her and said to Lakshmana: 'Who would not be charmed? See how the creature yawns, shooting its tongue out like a flame licking the air. How its radiance lights up the forest! Even if it is Maricha,' he declared, anticipating Lakshmana's objections, 'I must kill him and rid the forst of his evil presence. He's been spared by me twice already!'

Rama instructed Lakshmana before he left: 'Watch over Sita. Don't leave her alone till I return with the animal, dead or alive. Jatayu is also here. Guard her with your life, Lakshmana.' And Rama went, following the elusive creature who led him deeper and deeper into the jungle, away from their hermitage.

It was a merry chase. The deer dived into thickets and emerged, quick and nimble, weaving its way in and out like lightning streaks in a mass of cloud. It was becoming difficult for Rama to keep track of its flashing form. Just when he thought he was catching up, the creature would leap high and away, and then stand quite still, waiting.

Rama was getting impatient. The hunt was beginning to tire him and he decided to end it by killing the deer. Taking out one of his deadlier arrows he aimed straight for the heart.

The arrow drew blood and the animal lay on its side, gasping with pain. Rama saw the golden form vanish into thin air and in its place was the huge figure of Maricha. So Lakshmana was right! What trickery was this?

Just then Maricha, assuming Rama's voice and tone, cried out in agony: 'O Sita, O Lakshmana!' It was his final act of treachery.

Rama was frantic. What would Sita do when she heard that voice? And Lakshmana? He would be in a mighty quandary. 'I dare not think of what must be happening there at this very moment. I'd better get back as fast as I can,' he thought, as he quickly shot another deer, slung it over his shoulder and hurried back.

It was worse than Rama had imagined. Sita was urging Lakshmana to go. 'Lakshmana, he is being overpowered. Go quickly! He must be in great danger to call out like that.'

Lakshmana, however, was reluctant to go. His brother had ordered him not to leave her alone. Seeing him hesitate, Sita grew desperate. She accused him of disloyalty, and worse. 'You desire me. You want him to die so that you can have me!'

Lakshmana tried to reason with her. 'Nothing and no one can defeat him, of that I am sure, neither god nor demon nor man. I can't leave you alone, I mustn't. That voice is not his. It is a demon simulating Rama's voice.'

Sita lashed out: 'You are evil and full of deceit—always have been. You came with us, hiding your wickedness under a mask of love and affection for Rama. You lust after me. Do you think I can love an ordinary man like you after consorting with a man like Rama? Or are you Bharata's agent?' She went on, losing all sense of balance and proportion. 'Have you been sent to kill us so that nothing will stand in the way of your ambitions?'

Lakshmana could not bear to hear any more. 'You are a goddess to me, you know that. Your words pierce my ears like hot arrows. I am not surprised at this angry and unreasonable outburst. Women don't think before they speak. They are heedless and fickle and cause dissension. You are wicked to accuse me so. May this forest bear witness to my innocence and your harshness, and may its deities protect you! Will I see Rama with you when I return? I wonder.'

Sita was hysterical. 'If anything happens to Rama, I will kill myself,' she cried. Lakshmana tore himself away, and as he went, he turned to look, again and again, as if to fix her in his memory forever.

Ravana lay in wait, under cover of dusk, disguised as a mendicant. As soon as Lakshmana left, he appeared, clad in saffron, staff and waterpot in hand. His whole bearing spoke of goodness, abstinence and humility.

He could see Sita clearly now. She sat in the gathering shadows of dusk, her face bathed in tears, golden and glowing and utterly desirable, her yellow silk garment falling about her in soft folds. He stood for a moment, eyes riveted to the slender form weighed down with grief. Then he began to walk up to her.

The trees, sensing the presence of evil, grew still as the winds stopped in their tracks. The river Godavari slowed down almost to a stop, barely rippling. Nature held her breath in fear.

Ravana spoke to Sita in soft and pleasing accents. 'Are you a divine nymph or are you the goddess Lakshmi herself? You feast my eyes. With garlands of flowers round your beautiful neck, you seem to me a lotus pool of joys in full bloom. What are you doing here alone?'

There was no reason to suspect this gentle ascetic. Sita went in to get food and water for the weary traveller and begged him to make himself at home.

And all the while, anxious and uneasy, she searched the growing darkness with her large, lustrous eyes for some sign of the returning brothers.

Ravana dropped all pretence of being a mendicant, declared his true identity, and showed himself in his true colours. He painted glowing pictures of Lanka, offering Sita a life of ease and pleasure and luxury, the riches of both earth and heaven. 'Five thousand maids will wait upon you in my capital city, Lanka, jewel of the southern seas.'

Sita recoiled in horror, her heart pounding in her ears. 'You are a clumsy bear who craves a lioness. You will burn, cut or drown, for you wish to grasp the lustre of the sun, lick a razor's edge, cross an ocean with a stone tied round your neck. You want Rama's beloved, no less! You are doomed to failure and disaster.'

Sita was burning with shame and indignation. She looked at him with disdain. 'Rama is an elephant and you are a common cat. He is a stately swan, you are an ugly bird of prey; he is the fragrance of sandal, you are a lump of

clay.' She could not stem the flow of her hatred and scorn. 'You walk on spears, trying to reach me. You gather a burning fire in your garment, trying to hold me. You swallow a diamond, you little fly, by wanting to possess me. Remember, and be warned, I am Sita, beloved of Rama.'

All she could do as she stood trembling with rage was to heap insult upon insult, and by doing so, wipe out the indignity of Ravana's advances.

Ravana's pride was wounded. He bragged: 'I am the brother of Kubera, god of wealth; I can destroy Death himself. You had better come with me.' And Sita replied: 'Even if you have sipped the waters of immortality, you will die.'

'You have taken leave of your senses, woman. This is my true form. Take a good look.' He stood there, dressed in blood-red robes, all his ten heads glowering down at her, his twenty arms outspread. Catching her by the hair, he bodily lifted her into his chariot and began to rise into the skies. Sita desperately invoked the trees, the river, the sylvan deities, asking them to tell Rama of her plight. She saw Jatayu, perched on a tree, drowsing. She called out: 'I know you cannot fight this evil demon, but tell Rama I have been carried away by force.'

Jatayu snapped awake. He had to think and act very fast. He tried persuasion.

'A king is the repository of good and evil, an example to his subjects. How can you take another's wife?'

Ravana did not even slow down.

Jatayu then threatened: 'I am sixty thousand years old. You are young. But you cannot take her past me, just as you cannot demolish the wisdom of the Vedas with logic. You will fall from your chariot like ripe fruit from its stalk.' When Ravana continued to move, ignoring him, Jatayu rose, and throwing all caution to the winds, blocked the demon's path.

They clashed like storm-driven clouds or winged mountains. Air currents set up by Jatayu's flapping wings rocked Ravana's chariot and warded off his arrows, now flying thick and fast. Jatayu broke first one bow, then another, snapping them in two with his vice-like claws. Then he hurled his huge bird-form at the chariot till it broke and fell apart.

Ravana sprang to the ground, still clasping Sita, and brandished his sword. Short of breath, gasping with pain, Jatayu managed to say: 'You are a poor fish. . .who has swallowed the hook. . . of Rama's wrath along with the bait. It will stick in your throat and kill you. You cannot escape.'

Seeing the aged Jatayu exhausted, his strength slowly but surely ebbing, Ravana flew up again. Jatayu pulled himself together, wounded and bleeding, and rose with him, plucking out his hair, tearing the flesh off his back and arms. Ravana, descending once more, released Sita, and in a fit of fury chopped off Jatayu's wings and feet.

The brave bird fell and lay on the earth, bathed in his own blood. Sita ran to his side and gathered him to her breast in a rush of love and gratitude.

Ravana turned to find Sita no longer where he had left her. He gave chase. As he stooped to pick her up she slipped away and ran from tree to tree crying out for help, trying in vain to evade his grasp.

It was no use. He grabbed her and they were soon high up in the sky, on their way to Lanka. Her hair loose, her yellow garment streaming, her jewels scattered, Rama's young wife travelled the skies like a flashing meteor.

The forest animals fled in confusion, following Sita's shadow, away from the scene of her abduction. The evil they had sensed had come to pass. Strangely enough, the gods were pleased, for with this great wrong, the wheel of righteous destruction had been finally set in motion. There was no stopping it now. Brahma announced to the assembly of gods: 'My work is done, my mission accomplished.'

Ravana moved like a blazing volcano in the sky, supporting Sita's golden form; around it, billowed waves of yellow silk.

Sita spoke harsh words but they fell on deaf ears. 'You shall see the gold-branched trees of hell, with emerald leaves that cut sharp and deep even as you pluck them; and its dread river, flowing blood. Such will be your fate, Ravana.'

Sita looked down at the earth again and again, as if to draw strength from her mother. And she saw, on a high mountain, five huge monkeys looking up, as if they could hear her cries for help. On an impulse she threw down her mantle and jewels. Ravana, crowing with satisfaction, noticed nothing. It was death and destruction that he cradled in his arms; indeed, she was the golden tree that grew in the hell of his own wickedness, bound to bear bitter fruit. But for now, he was in a heaven of delight.

He reached Lanka in a mood of great triumph. Taking Sita straight to the inner quarters, he instructed his women: 'No one is to meet her, man or woman, without my permission. Give her whatever clothes and ornaments she wants. Serve her well. A single harsh word to her and you incur my displeasure, remember that!'

Ravana then ordered eight strong and valiant demons to go immediately to Janasthana and somehow kill Rama. 'I cannot sleep in peace till he is destroyed. Keep me informed of your movements—and his progress,' he said.

His mind already filled with dreams of Sita and her beauty, he gave himself up to thoughts of wooing and winning her. First, he decided to show Sita the splendours of his palace. Golden stairways led to rooms with marble floors and ivory doors and windows inlaid with precious stones. And looking out, one could see the sprawling palace gardens with flowering trees and lotus pools and shady arbours of rare creepers. They walked past fountains and flowing streams and stopped under a tree.

'This is not all,' he tempted. 'Not counting the aged and the infants, many millions of demons inhabit Lanka. I personally command ten thousand powerful demons, each of them in turn offering me a thousand slaves. You will be their queen, the queen of all my consorts, indeed, queen of all Lanka and of my own heart, full of love and desire for you.'

He added contemptuously: 'Your Rama is a man with no kingdom, no resources, an exile, a forest dweller with no prospects. What can he offer you? Leave him and be mine. Lanka is invincible. Rama cannot dream of getting here. He will not even consider it, believe me.'

All through this Sita stood, her face covered, silently weeping. Ravana was sure he would have her before long. He humbled himself before her. 'I touch your lovely feet with my ten proud heads that have never before bowed to a woman. Accept my offering of love, O Princess.'

Sita wiped away her tears and, holding her head high, placed a tiny blade of grass between them. It was a gesture full of meaning, her way of indicating the impassable barrier between them. It was also her valuation of all the temptations, he had offered her. They weighed lightly, or not at all, to a woman who loved and had lived with Rama, proud princess of Videha and daughter of Janaka.

'If Rama had been there when you came, you would not have lived to talk such nonsense. He can bring the sun and moon down to earth, dry up vast oceans with his powers. You might think Lanka is invincible. Rama will soon prove that it is not. Lanka will be razed to the ground and desolate because of you and your folly. Can the royal swan accept the common fowl for mate?'

Ravana was enraged. 'I give you twelve months to yield. If at the end of it you still persist in your foolish dreams of returning to Rama, the palace cooks will chop you up for my breakfast.' Sita replied calmly: 'That will be perfectly acceptable to me. This body of mine is a lump of insensate flesh, empty of my spirit, my soul. That is with Rama and no one else. I am indifferent to the fate that awaits my body.'

Ravana stamped his feet, making the earth tremble and the female demons guarding Sita, quake. He ordered them: 'Break her will, as a trainer breaks in a wild elephant. Use sweet words, threats, anything but she must come to me suitably tamed.'

And he stamped out, fuming with anger and frustration. He was not used to being thwarted. His wealth and power had always got him whatever he wanted, and he wanted much.

In Panchavati, Rama had come to know of Sita's disappearance and possible abduction. As he was hurrying back after the killing of Maricha, he met Lakshmana halfway. Lakshmana was alone, slouched in an uncharacteristic posture of dejection, his face grave and troubled.

Rama poured out all his doubts and anxieties. 'Why are you alone? Where is Sita? Why did you leave her alone? I had ordered you not to. What on earth could have made you disobey my strict instructions? You should not have left her unguarded. I fear the worst!'

Lakshmana listened to his tirade and explained unhappily: 'I did not want to move—would not have moved. But when that voice rang out saying "O Sita, O Lakshmana", she was as one demented. I tried to reason with her but she was adamant. I stood my ground, I was equally adamant till she accused me of unspeakable things. She said I wanted you out of the way so that I could have her, that I was conspiring with Bharata to kill you. How could I stand there and listen to such cruel words? I was sure it was a trick, but what could I do?'

'It was a trick,' said Rama, heavily. 'That was Maricha. You should not have given in to her and your sense of hurt pride.' As they had feared, the hermitage was empty. There were no signs of Sita anywhere. Just for a moment, he thought she might be hiding to tease him. He went round like a mad man asking the trees, the birds, the river, for news of Sita.

The first warning came when he looked at the deer who had been following him. Their eyes were filled with tears. 'Lakshmana, all is not well. See how the deer are shedding tears. They weep for Sita.' He began to hope again. She might have gone to the river to gather lotuses. But she was not there either.

Rama stared at the herd of wild deer who sat mutely near him, huddled together. 'They are trying to say something, Lakshmana,' and in a pathetic tone of voice choking with sobs, Rama asked them, 'Where is Sita?' The herd rose and turned in unison, their heads pointing south, their necks craning as if to stress a point. Rama and Lakshmana started walking southwards and the deer walked before them leading the way, turning round every now and then to see if they were following.

The clues started appearing. First, her flowers. Rama recognized them immediately. 'I gave them to her,' he said, picking them up. They saw her footprints next, tracing a crazy path, up and down, round and about, followed by larger ones and then, fragments of her broken ornaments. The evidence was mounting. A magnificent bow lay shattered, bits and pieces of a golden suit of armour were strewn about. A royal canopy had been knocked down, a chariot overturned, and mules grinned up at them with monster heads, all dead. Next to the wreckage stood the dead charioteer, whiplash and reins still in his outstretched hands.

'It must have been a mighty demon who carried away Sita,' said Rama. And then the anger welled up in him like a tidal wave of destruction. 'Today, Lakshmana, you will see the terrors that lie hidden in me rise up to take the world by storm, a storm of destruction. If the gods do not restore Sita to me today, all three worlds are as good as wiped out. Nothing will survive my anger. Hand me my bow, Lakshmana, and all my weapons. Watch every arrow loosed, every weapon hurled, every missile launched. My quivers shall be emptied, my armoury expended.'

Rama drew his bow and placed an arrow on it. Lakshmana, pale with terror, spoke out: 'Why destroy the world for one man's sins? This does not seem to be the work of an army. There are signs here of a desperate struggle, but it was almost certainly between two individuals. We must find out who it is, identify the enemy, before destroying mindlessly.

'You are the soul of justice and compassion. It is not proper that you lose control and hit out like this. Let us search, and search till we trace her, humbly, patiently, prudently. If we fail then you may, in all fairness, let loose your anger on an unjust world ruled by heedless gods.'

Rama calmed down, but he grieved deeply and refused to be comforted. Lakshmana soothed him with words of wisdom and solace. 'All beings are subject to adversity. You too have come face to face with grief. You must bear it and resolve to find your enemy and destroy him. Wisdom must prevail and life must go on.'

In this manner Lakshmana finally persuaded Rama into making a systematic search of Janasthana.

It was Rama who saw Jatayu lying in a pool of blood. 'This is the villain, the demon who took a vulture's form to devour Sita,' he said rushing to kill him.

Jatayu was spitting blood; he said: 'I did not kill Sita. I was left here to die by the demon, Ravana. I fought him with all my strength, even broke his chariot and killed his charioteer. But I proved too old and feeble for him. My strength failed and he took Sita by force, flying up with her into the air. She

is alive.'

Rama knelt down and embraced him. Jatayu's voice was hardly audible and his eyes were veiled with approaching death. 'What did Sita say? How did she look? Describe Ravana to me,' said Rama, bending close. 'He is the son of Vishravas, and brother of Kubera,' whispered Jatayu, with a faint gasp. 'Speak up, tell me more,' pleaded Rama.

Jatayu's beak moved silently, once or twice, his eyes closed in the sleep of death and he lay still. 'Lakshmana, our father's friend Jatayu is dead. Do my misfortunes have no end? If I jumped into a vast ocean now, my grief would dry it up.'

Rama performed Jatayu's funeral rites. He killed a few deer and offered up the ritual balls of flesh, reciting the scriptures, and on the banks of the river Godavari he made the ritual water offerings. Jatayu's spirit, they hoped, would soon soar into regions reserved for the brave and the selfless, for he had died shedding blood for his friends in a losing battle.

The princes crossed Janasthana and went farther afield looking for Sita. Near the hoary hermitage of Matanga they met a demon. His single eye, set in his chest, glared hatefully at them, and his mouth, cut into his belly, gaped open, ready to devour. He had long arms that extended from one part of the forest to another. Lakshmana trembled at the sight of this terrible monster, and even Rama felt some fear. 'I am Kabandha,' roared the demon, 'and you two are my first morsels for the day.'

Guessing that his arms were both his strength and his only means of support, for he lived by grabbing most of his victims before they even saw him, the brothers, moving to right and left, quickly chopped them off. As Kabandha fell, he learnt who they were and why they were there. He told them that Rama was meant to deliver him from a long-standing curse. 'Light my pyre. When the flames consume me and I take on my original form, I will show you the way to someone who will lead you to Sita. But the fire must first consecrate me.'

Kabandha, no longer misshapen and monstrous, rose from the flames in a chariot drawn by swans. He spoke to them: 'Go west, till you reach Lake Pampa. On its banks rises the great mountain Rishyamooka, specially created by Brahma. There, in a cave hewn out of the surrounding rockface, lives Sugriva, son of Surya, king of the monkeys, with his four companions. Look for Sugriva, for he will help you in your search for Sita. My good wishes go with you.'

The brothers left. The evil darkness of Dandakaranya seemed to lift as they reached the Matanga woods, sacred to the great sage. There all animals lived at peace with one another and flowers of every season bloomed all at once, all the year round. 'Those flowers are watered by the sweat of Matanga's disciples, the sweat of their brows fevered with the heat of spiritual fires,' Kabandha had said.

They reached the hermitage of Shabari, the aged female ascetic who had served there for many years. She seemed to be expecting them. Rama made the usual enquiries as Shabari touched his feet. 'Have you subdued the two fires of anger and hunger? Has austerity become a part of your life?'

'I have been blessed indeed, in my pursuit of austerities, thanks to my gurus, the disciples of Matanga. As soon as you set foot in Chitrakuta, they

left for their heavenly home, their minds at rest; for you, Rama, are destined to deliver me from earthly bondage.'

Shabari spoke with bowed head: 'I sensed your approach, and have been waiting here with these wild fruits gathered from the banks of the Pampa. Accept my humble offerings, lord, and bless me.' Rama put out his hand in the act of blessing and ate the fruit.

As he was in the hallowed precincts of Matanga's hermitage, Rama wished to experience something of its sacred spirit. 'I have heard of your great teachers. Could I be shown their haunts?'

Shabari took them through the woods. 'This is no ordinary forest. The mantras of my gurus still echo for those who listen, the sacred fire still lights up the four quarters, blazing in all directions, and the seas of the world flow by because those ascetics were weak with austerities and unable to move. Their bark robes still hang, moist with sacred life, and the blue lotuses offered by them never fade.'

Shabari stopped, and leaping into the fire she had already set blazing, rose into the air, a flame of pure light.

Rama and Lakshmana felt wrapped in the aura of spiritual effort and salvation. It felt like a protective armour. They felt cleansed of the violence and wrong which had become part of their lives. They dared to hope once again as they set out, renewing their search for Sita.

In the distance, they could see Rishyamooka. They walked till they reached Pampa, its waters clear as crystal or the polished minds of sages. Rama and Lakshmana bathed in its cool, pure waters, shedding for a while their burdens of sorrow and longing.

Spring danced in, breeze in hand, rampant, through flowering trees and blossom-fall, stirring the birds and bees into a buzz of chatter and song. It stirred the garden of Rama's heart too, quickened it with the bud and blossom of pain and the bee-hum of yearning for Sita. He mourned her absence, summoning up her presence with past scenes of joy—Sita's delight in birdsong and cuckoo-call, leaping gazelle and dancing peacock or mango blossom with its maddening scent. Each simple event of growth had been a celebration of life with her. Spring magic was in the air once more, turning all heads with dizzy joy. But for Rama it was a spring without Sita, without love, without life.

7

The Kishkindha Alliance

The two brothers were now almost at the foot of Rishyamooka. Sugriva saw them arrive. Their gait, their regal manner and the fact that they were armed, filled him with fear and suspicion. Could they be spies of his brother Vali come to do him secret harm? He hid himself and watched with growing dread. He had to consult his advisers.

He summoned his ministers and expressed his doubts, now turned to certainty, about them. The counsellors were quick to act. They moved swiftly and surely and cordoned off Sugriva in a ring of close protection. Then, for the benefit of the strangers, they put up a show of their destructive powers. They jumped from crag to crag, shaking the hillside with their leaps. They tore down trees and put all the animals to flight.

After that, one amongst them spoke sternly to Sugriva. It was clear that his voice carried some authority. 'There is no cause for fear, none at all. It is your monkey nature that makes you restless and jittery, fearing shadows. You are distracted and agitated and that is not a good state to be in. You are our leader.'

Sugriva was defensive. 'Seeing those two, who would not be unsettled? Vali is crafty. And kings have many friends. We should not be complacent and off guard.' He suggested an exploratory mission. 'I think you, Hanuman, should approach them disguised as a mendicant and engage them in conversation. Their manners, their gestures and their speech will reveal much to an observant eye. Go at once. You are just the person to tackle them.'

In a single bound Hanuman stood directly in the path of Rama and Lakshmana. He had, of course, discarded his simian form and was a mendicant, gentle and softspoken. But his manner was forthright, calculated to inspire respect and confidence.

'Who are you, and why have you come, disturbing the peace of this forest? You wear matted locks, yet stride like warriors, fully armed with bow and quiver and sword. Sugriva, king of the monkeys, banished by his brother and without a kingdom to his name, extends his hand in friendship. I am his minister, a monkey, born of the wind, sent to bring you his message of goodwill, disguised as a mendicant at his command.'

Hanuman waited for them to respond, and Rama said softly to Lakshmana: 'Speak to him courteously. He is impressive. Only one learned in the Vedas and fully conversant with the rules of language could speak so

well and flawlessly, and to the point.'

Rama was enthusiastic and excited. 'He has an excellent personality, a perfect physique, a cultivated voice that handles sounds and words with skill and consummate ease. Each syllable is clear. There is harmony in his well-modulated voice. He attracts with the dignity of learning and mastery of self. A king who has such a messenger is bound to meet with success in any venture. He charms me with his eloquence.'

Lakshmana was as direct in his approach. 'We are, in fact, looking for Sugriva and now wait for your guidance.' Hanuman was happy for Sugriva. He decided on an immediate alliance with the two ascetics. It had definitely been a meeting of true and like minds, auguring good for both.

Hanuman, assuming his monkey form, lifted Rama and Lakshmana on to his powerful shoulders and leaped across the waters to Sugriva. They exchanged news and information on the way and when they arrived, Hanuman introduced them to Sugriva, telling him how Sita had been abducted.

Sugriva extended his hand in a formal gesture of friendship and love, and then followed a simple ceremony. Rubbing two sticks together, Hanuman lit a fire and made an offering of flowers. Sugriva and Rama circled it. They had sealed their friendship, and Agni, lord of fire, had witnessed the pact.

Sugriva broke off a flowering, leafy branch and spreading it, he and Rama sat down. Hanuman spread a flowering branch of fragrant sandalwood for Lakshmana, and they settled down to talk. Sugriva began: 'You are my friend and ours is a common sorrow. Vali has banished me and taken away my wife, Ruma, by force.'

Rama replied: 'I will kill your brother and restore your wife to you.' And Sugriva solemnly declared: 'I will bring back Sita to you be she in heaven above or hell below. And I think I have a small clue. . . .'

He told Rama how, one day, seated on a high mountain peak, he and his friends had looked up to see a woman being carried away, struggling to break free, and crying out 'Rama, Lakshmana!' 'That must have been Sita. She dropped her mantle and jewels, as if on purpose. I have them with me.' Rama was impatient. 'Bring them to me, quickly, please. I can't wait.' When the jewels came, Rama identified them and held them out to Lakshmana. 'These are Sita's jewels, beyond doubt, aren't they, Lakshmana?'

Lakshmana glanced at them briefly and said: 'These are earrings and an armband. I only know Sita's anklets, through daily worship of her feet. I have never wished or dared to look higher than that.' He was thinking of their last meeting and her wild accusations.

Rama shed hot tears of sorrow, holding the jewels close, remembering Sita. And then, shaking off all signs of weakness, he exclaimed: 'That villain stands at the gates of death, unlatching them. I will send him speeding up the pathway to Death's open door!'

Sugriva began to tell Rama about his banishment.

'Vali is my elder brother and I loved him. He inherited the throne when our father died, and ruled from our capital city, Kishkindha. I was his subject and served him loyally.'

afraid for your life?'

That was enough to provoke Dundubhi, who was only waiting for an excuse to start a fight.

'Come out and fight, Vali, but first embrace your women and bid them farewell, and give Kishkindha, too, a last glance.'

Vali attacked with his bare hands, catching hold of him by his horns. Then he used rocks and stones. Dundubhi lay still, spreadeagled on the ground. It was a swift and ignoble death.

Vali lifted him and flung him out of the way. The impact shattered his jaw. Blood came pouring out of his mouth in floods and the wind carried droplets of it to Matanga's hermitage, defiling it.

The sage saw the corpse of Dundubhi and guessed it was Vali's work. He cursed him: 'If he who has defiled my hermitage, broken my trees and trampled my plants, ever enters these woods, he will die—and his monkey followers too will suffer if they set foot here. They will be turned to stone for a thousand years.'

'This turned out to be a blessing in disguise for me,' said Sugriva. 'Vali cannot come anywhere near Rishyamooka and so it has become a refuge for me and my ministers. Here at least I am safe from his wrath.' His eyes were full of fear. He was clearly terrified of his brother.

'How can I convince you that Vali is no match for Rama?' said Lakshmana, showing the forbearance of the truly strong.

'These tall trees that you see before you used to shed their leaves in fear when Vali passed by or touched them. You see, he had struck them many times, both individually and collectively, with a single arrow. If Rama can aim at just one of them successfully, I will judge him to be a capable warrior. Secondly, if he can kick Dundubhi's carcass with one foot and send it flying to a distance of two hundred bow-lengths, I will risk a confrontation with Vali.'

Sugriva was apologetic. 'Do not misunderstand me or take offence. I am a coward, afraid to face Vali without adequate proof of your strength.' Rama had been waiting for him to finish. He put out his foot and effortlessly, with a flick of his toe, he flung the carcass well beyond the stipulated distance.

Seeing should have been believing, but Sugriva's confidence had been so badly shaken by Vali that he still had lurking fears. 'There is a great deal of difference between a fresh corpse, heavy with flesh and blood, and this heap of dry, light bones. I still can't make up my mind, Rama; I have to be doubly sure. Your second test will measure your strengths more accurately. Forgive my persisting doubts. They arise from my diffidence and fear. I do not mean to draw comparisons and insult you.'

Rama was patient. He drew his bow and aimed. The arrow went through all seven trees, through the mountain, then piercing the earth, it returned neatly to its quiver.

Now Sugriva knew that, beyond any doubt, Vali would meet his match.

Rama took charge and worked out a strategy for Sugriva to follow. 'Let us go to Kishkindha straightaway. While we stand hidden, ready to attack, you must challenge Vali. From that point on, the battle for your kingdom as well as for your reputation will begin in earnest.'

They reached Kishkindha and halted in a wooded stretch outside the palace. Sugriva had regained some of his old confidence. His challenge to Vali was a roar of newfound courage. Vali rushed out, livid and blustering. His brother had dared to challenge him and in this impudent manner!

They met, fist to adamantine fist, palms clapping thunder. Rama watched, taking careful measure of their progress, waiting for the right moment to intervene.

But an unexpected problem arose. The two monkeys looked alike, grappling, falling and rising, their roars of victory and pain almost identical. Their tawny gold bodies shone with a blinding brilliance as they met, locked and parted in repeated bouts of combat.

Sugriva fought valiantly but was beginning to tire. He was no match for Vali—never was. He wondered why Rama was not coming forward to kill Vali and save him. Was he backing out of their pact, letting him down? Was he getting cold feet?

Sugriva was taking no chances. He ran for his life and Vali, taking pity on him, let him go like an errant child who needed only to be checked, not severely punished. Besides, Rishyamooka was out of bounds for him and he knew Sugriva must have gone straight there.

When Sugriva met Rama and Lakshmana, he was both ashamed and reproachful. 'Defeat seems to be my lot in life, even with a powerful warrior like you on my side. If you did not want to kill Vali, you should have warned me. I would never have put myself in this position. Being a runaway and a homeless wanderer is bad enough, but to be chased back like a whipped animal after that proud challenge you talked me into, is humiliating. I could have spared myself that.'

Rama's voice was placating. 'Sugriva, try to understand my dilemma. Vali and you were like twins. I couldn't distinguish you from him. That is why I did not shoot. How could I risk killing you?'

Rama was persuasive. 'Challenge Vali to another fight. But this time, wear something on your person that will mark you out.'

Rama asked Lakshmana to give Sugriva a flowering creeper to wear as a garland. Sugriva was somewhat mollified and they started off for Kishkindha once again. This time, the monkey ruler was in a better frame of mind, all doubts and suspicions cleared and sensing the end of his long travail. He would, given just a little luck, be living once more in his beloved Kishkindha—he could see its turrets rise in the distance. He said to Rama: 'Look how the golden walls of Kishkindha catch the sun. And the monkey guards—the ramparts are bristling with them, ready for instant attack.'

Rama was not afraid. He told Sugriva so, and promised him victory. 'Take heart. Vali is so full of himself that he will walk into your trap. Let him. Come on, do your best. That should be good enough.'

Sugriva's spirits soared with fresh confidence. He had whipped himself into a state of high courage like an ocean lashed by a tempest. When Vali heard him roaring at the gates again, calling him out to fight, he was furious. It was exasperating to be interrupted when his senses were being fuelled with the choicest pleasures. His wives were round him fussing, pampering. And here was Sugriva again, making a nuisance of himself. He would put an end to this impudence, once and for all.

As he sprang up, shouting, his wife Tara put an arm around him lovingly and held him back. She was a wise woman and reckoned that Sugriva would not have dared to challenge Vali without making sure of support from a formidable ally. She had kept her eyes and ears open too, unlike her husband.

'You are acting too hastily. Go to him tomorrow when you are calmer. There is more to Sugriva's challenge than meets the eye. He would not dare to confront you without some great and hidden strength, and I have an idea what it is.'

She told him what she knew. 'Rama of the Ikshvakus is here these days with his heroic brother, Lakshmana. Our son, Angada, has heard from his more reliable spies of a pact between him and Sugriva. It would be unwise to antagonize Rama. You know his reputation very well. Rama is always on the side of the weak and oppressed, a refuge for those in distress. Sugriva's battle for reinstatement is just the kind of cause he is likely to champion, and what Rama champions meets with instant success.'

Vali showed no signs of relenting. Tara drew closer to him, hoping to win him over with love and affection where persuasion seemed to have failed.'Sugriva is your brother and natural ally. You are like a father to him. Make conciliatory gestures and strengthen your hand. In fact, you have no alternative, Vali. Believe me, you will not be lowering yourself in any way. Sugriva is a worthy kinsman, and friendship with Rama is a highly desirable move.'

Vali, however, was in no mood to listen to commonsense. Life was turning a point of no return for him and destiny beckoned with a misleading hand.

Vali left, reassuring Tara: 'Rama is the soul of righteousness. He will not do anything that is not either fair or just. So don't be afraid. And I will not kill Sugriva, only give him a good thrashing and humble his pride, I assure you.'

And he charged out, calling to Sugriva: 'I will finish you with a single blow of my fist.'

Sugriva was equal to the threat. 'My fist will go through your skull, Vali.' They fought, drawing blood, wrestling like maddened bulls. Sugriva, as expected, was the first to show signs of weakening. Rama's golden arrow flashed past like a tongue of flame and brought down Vali, wounding him fatally. He had been caught off guard. He sank, bloody and bruised, like a tree in scarlet bloom, felled by a sudden storm. Indra's son lay on the ground like his father's mighty banner, brought down and trailing in the dust.

Vali was breathing and still resplendent, for his father's necklace hung gleaming on his massive chest, guarding his lustre. As Rama and Lakshmana approached him softly, thoughtfully, he looked at them with sorrow, disappointment and shock. He argued justly, but harshly.

'The world sings your praises, Rama, and so did I. You are supposed to be just and righteous, brave, learned and enlightened. You come from the Ikshvaku clan, famed for its unblemished glory. Yet you struck me while I was busily engaged in fighting another, struck me without revealing

yourself. You killed slyly, like a snake that strikes a sleeping man and slips away unseen. I would have expected you to come out in the open and challenge me. If you had done that, you would be dying instead of me.

'You have flouted certain codes by which the warrior class lives. I was not your declared enemy; you had no quarrel with me. People fight for land, gold, or women. Why did you fight me? What was there between us?

'I am no fit adversary, no equal. I am a mere monkey. You are a man, and a prince at that. Even my skin is no use to you, not permitted by custom to wear it. And the flesh of a monkey is forbidden food. Why, then, did you kill me, Rama? Was it to ingratiate yourself with Sugriva? I heard of your pact. I would have brought you not only Sita, but that demon Ravana, chained for his sins. Sugriva will ascend a throne unjustly won. If he had waited, he would have had it rightfully.

'I am not afraid of death, but how will you explain your conduct to your elders and betters, the guardians of law and order in your realm? I feel sorry for you.' And with that, Vali fell silent.

Rama countered his arguments briefly and succinctly.

'You speak like a child. My chief, perhaps only role is to protect the laws of justice and good conduct in my brother Bharata's kingdom. You have transgressed these laws and ignored social custom by lusting after Sugriva's wife and living with her while her husband, your younger brother, is still alive. That is a sin punishable by death, you know that.

'Release comes from expiation for both sinner and dispenser of justice. If I do not punish you, your sin is transferred to me. That should answer your question about my killing you needlessly. As for hiding and not declaring my presence, those are the rules of the hunt. You are an animal. Snares and traps are quite in order.'

Vali accepted Rama's explanation graciously. It was an impartial assessment of a moral predicament, difficult to justify in human terms. He began to think of death at Rama's hands as deliverance. 'Look after Angada,' he said. 'He is my only son. And don't let his mother, Tara, suffer for my misdeeds. You must see to that.'

His face shadowed by the darkness of the unknown, he waited. There was little else he could do.

Tara grieved over the dying Vali: 'The earth is your wife, I know, for you are a king, but have you no love left for me that you embrace her so? Your blood covers you like the silken spread on your couch.'

Vali's general, Nila, pulled out the golden arrow of Rama. Fresh blood gushed out, and with it fresh floods of grief from Tara. Angada, their son, was inconsolable as Vali handed him over to Sugriva, saying, 'Look after him; he has no one. And take my divine necklace while I'm still alive and wear it—the glory and the power that it has will vanish with my life-breath. Keep it blazing.'

Sugriva was heartbroken and guilt-ridden. 'My better self takes over, fired by guilt, leaving behind the dross of my sin. I suffer the pangs of sorrow and regret; I grieve for my brother. Is the kingdom worth it?'

Time, the source of life and its course, had run out for Vali, the valiant king of Kishkindha. It now bore him inexorably towards death. For time is also the source of death and its course. It is the human journey.

Vali was cremated and Sugriva crowned with Rama's blessings. Angada was installed as heir-apparent. Bound by the vow of exile in the forest, Rama could not enter the city of Kishkindha. He and Lakshmana retired to Mount Prasravana to wait out the rainy season. Sugriva promised to send his armies out in search of Sita, immediately after the rains, when the skies cleared.

The rains came. The skies were gashed red, wounded by the sun, and at twilight, lay sickening, pale saffron with love. The winds blew moist and heavy enough to drink. Clouds riding high held flapping banners of lightning that whipped the skies and made them roar with pain. Peacocks fanned out their wings and danced. Frogs woke up from the long, dry sleep of summer, croaking with joy; birds sipped raindrops from leaf-folds and bees sucked hungrily at wet lotus-cups.

Rama was pensive. 'The world goes home, Lakshmana. The swans make their way back to the Manasa lake. Cranes fly in glad formation, garlanding the sky like lotuses. Travellers everywhere return to their wives. Sugriva rejoices in his kingdom, drowning in new-found happiness. He will think of me when the time comes to search for Sita, I am sure.'

Lakshmana too was waiting, sharing Rama's thoughts and feelings and hopes. They had four long months to go.

In Kishkindha, Sugriva showed no signs of putting plans into action for Sita's search and recovery. Hanuman reminded him somewhat sternly: 'You should make friends and learn to keep them. That is how your kingdom will grow in glory. Rama, your powerful new ally, is waiting. You must fulfil your obligations to him. He will hesitate to raise the matter on his own. I would advise you not to delay to the point where he has to remind you. Do not make an enemy of him.'

Sugriva responded promptly with a command to Nila, leader of his armies. 'Instruct all monkeys, wherever they may be, to gather here in full strength with their leaders and generals. Anyone who delays and is not here within fifteen days will be executed.'

Hanuman had gauged the situation correctly. Rama's melancholy deepened as he brooded over Sugriva's indifference. The rains were definitely over, he noticed. The world sparkled, newly washed and spread out to dry. The nights came clothed in white moonlight, starry-eyed with autumn. The river receded from its banks like a veil drawn slowly back to reveal hidden charms. It flowed lovely and languid, girdled with silver fish, like women dreamy with love. Autumn stabbed sharp with the call of cranes and wild geese. Rama remembered: 'Sita would call back, imitating their cry.'

He remembered and was angry. Resentment grew with every passing day. 'Kings are already out on their campaigns; the roads are clear and dry. But I see no signs of Sugriva getting an expedition ready for us. These four months have dragged like a hundred slow years. Has Sugriva no thought for me, no pity? Or does he think he can ignore me because I have no ally, no army, no kingdom?' He was furious at the thought. 'Go, Lakshmana,' he said, 'and convey this message to Sugriva: "Even beasts refuse to feed on the flesh of an ungrateful being. Do you wish to see Rama's golden arrow fly,

hear his great bow twang as he goes into battle with you? The path by which Vali travelled is wide enough to take you and your whole family!"

'Tell Sugriva to honour his pledge and begin the search for Sita, or else I will send him in search of Vali!'

Lakshmana, quick to take offence and always ready to settle scores with a fight, set off immediately for Kishkindha.

His progress was devastating. He plucked up trees, crushed rocks to get them out of the way and stormed up to the ramparts of Kishkindha. He could see now how impregnable it was, this citadel high up among the mountains. Huge monkey guards emerged from their hideouts and stood around threateningly with uprooted trees in their hands, ready to strike. This enraged Lakshmana even more.

It was Angada who went out to meet him. Lakshmana asked him to announce his arrival as an emissary of Rama. His tone was forbidding. The monkeys chattered nervously and occasionally roared to keep their courage up.

Sugriva, who had been lying in a state of drunken torpor, woke up with the noise and wanted to know why there was such a commotion. He sent for Hanuman who said pointedly: 'You are so involved in your daily round of pleasure that you have lost track of time. I told you it is high time we set out to look for Sita and honour our pledge to Rama. Now, Lakshmana is at your door, stamping with rage. You had better deal with him. Use soft words and somehow calm him down, otherwise we are all in for a rude shock.'

Angada escorted Lakshmana to Sugriva's palace in the city. Kishkindha was a mountain fastness of huge caverns set amidst flowering forests, deep ravines, steep gorges and labyrinthine pathways cut into the rock-face. Its citizens were semi-divine simians, majestic and impressive, able to change their forms at will. Around it, mixing with the scent of sandal and aloe and lotus, hung the heady fumes of wine brewing from wild honey.

The royal palace stood perched on a high white rock, gleaming with gold and jewels. It had the severe grandeur of a mountain fortress, rich yet restrained and forbidding. Lakshmana entered and went through courtyard after courtyard, seven in all. Inside, all was sheer luxury and soft ease. Couches of gold and silver gleamed through doorways, and lovely women sat weaving garlands of flowers.

He was right inside the women's quarters. The tinkling of anklets irked him. He plucked his bowstring in annoyance, as if to drown out these sights and sounds of feminine frippery, withdrew to a corner and waited unobtrusively for some word from Sugriva.

Sugriva knew that Lakshmana had arrived and was at this very moment in

the women's apartments. But he did not as yet feel confident enough to face him. He sent Tara, saying to her, 'He is angry. Win him over with your usual tact. He will not harm a woman. After that, I shall see him.'

Tara came, swaying slightly, her eyes red with wine and lack of sleep. But she spoke sweetly and well. 'We have watched the wildfire of your anger spreading. What is the cause?' she began, innocently.

Lakshmana was in no mood for polite conversation. 'Sugriva is self-indulgent and seems to be lost in sensual pastimes. He has lost his sense of time, for one thing, in flowing cups of wine, I can see.'

Tara was quick to defend him. 'To the restless monkey, pleasure is a normal activity. Why hold his nature against him? Besides, you do him an injustice. He has already made preparations for the search. The monkey armies are gathering from all directions, in full force. Come with me, Lakshmana. Let me take you to Sugriva. He is waiting, ready to receive you.'

Sugriva shone with the splendour of the Sun, his father. 'Kingship sits well on him,' thought Lakshmana, grudgingly. The monkey king watched Lakshmana as he walked up, still smouldering with suppressed anger, eyes full of fire that might flare up any moment to scorch the beholder.

The two warriors took quiet stock of each other. Then Lakshmana spoke to Sugriva, accusing him of falsehood and gross ingratitude. 'You have been false—for that there is some expiation. To lie about a horse is equal to killing a hundred horses. To lie about a cow is like killing a thousand cows. To lie to a man and let him down is to destroy oneself and one's family. Your falsehood is of the last kind.

'But you have been worse than false; you have been ungrateful. And there is just no expiation for the sin of ingratitude. You are truly damned, unless you act immediately and wipe out the ignominy of your conduct.'

It was Tara who dared to stand up to Lakshmana. 'You speak harshly and judge without mercy. Sugriva has been terrorized and hunted down. He lived in daily dread of Vali for a long time. If he has forgotten himself and his obligations for a while, you should be generous enough to overlook it. And what is his sin, after all? Even great sages have lost track of time indulging their senses. And we are only monkeys.

'Sugriva has no intention of shirking his responsibilities. He is already getting his vast resources together and marshalling his army of monkeys. You will need these hordes of helpers to spread out in search of Sita, for she must be under heavy guard, and hidden. And later, too, they will be needed to tackle Ravana and his demon hordes. It is not a job for a handful of monkeys, however powerful, sitting here in Kishkindha. It calls for concerted effort and much planning. Give up your anger, Lakshmana. You make us monkey women quake with fear.'

Sugriva knew that he had been forgiven but the volatile Lakshmana had to be handled carefully. 'Rama needs no support to fight Ravana or recover Sita. I will only stand by with my forces out of gratitude for what he has done, hoping to be of some small service. And if I have erred in any way or betrayed his faith and trust in me, I humbly beg forgiveness.'

Lakshmana was impressed with his humility. 'Who, at the height of his power, would humble himself thus and acknowledge his fault? You are

indeed a worthy ally. Forgive my reproaches and allegations. They were made in the heat of the moment and out of the great love I bear my brother.'

The tensions and anxieties of the long wait seemed to lift as both sides removed all barriers and prepared to work together towards a common goal— the recovery of Rama's lost wife.

Hanuman now sent off in all directions a second set of messengers, to summon the monkey hordes and expedite matters. No monkey escaped the wide net cast by Sugriva's ablest minister.

The monkeys came pouring into Kishkindha. From the great mountain ranges of the north, south, east and west; from forest and seashore and regions close to the sun they came, bearing rare herbs and fruits and rocks as offerings to Sugriva. They came out of respect and regard, curiosity and a sense of adventure. They came in fear and trembling and great expectation. Some of them came reluctantly, not knowing or questioning or even caring why. But they came, for the word of Sugriva was law to their kind. It was the largest gathering of monkeys ever to collect under a common banner for a common purpose.

Sugriva called for his palanquin and royal canopy. Fanned by yak-tail whisks, he set out with Lakshmana in full and splendid regalia. Armed monkeys guarded his royal person and followed his royal train as they proceeded to Prasravana to present themselves to Rama. They wound their way there in slow and stately procession.

Rama looked at them and his heart filled with hope and courage. Before him, spread out like a great lake of lotus buds, were Sugriva's retinue with his handpicked leaders. Success would blossom wide open and glorious and flood the earth with its sweetness. He could already scent it in the air. And the face of the dark and handsome prince bloomed like the unfolding of a blue lotus bud.

Rama looked up to see the monkey army marching towards him, raising clouds of dust that obscured the noonday sun. They stood to attention with their leaders whose names were a roll call of honour and reputation. Each had come with well-trained troops that ran into hundreds and thousands. There was Shatabali and Sushena, Tara's father, who moved like a hill of beaten gold. Ruma's father shone out like a youthful sun. Then there was Hanuman's father, Kesari, Dhumra with his company of bears and the veteran, Jambavan, a venerable bear, who had also joined them. Completing the list were Nila, young Angada ready for his first campaign and lastly, Hanuman himself, the real power behind the throne of Kishkindha and the entire project.

It was a proud moment for Sugriva, a landmark in his association with Rama. He had the privilege of offering what he knew was valuable service. He was placing at Rama's disposal a deal of monkey power—the strength, the cunning, the agility, the tenacity and the fierceness of the breed. And the divinity that rested in the best of them would rise to the occasion and shine, blessing this venture when the time came to act.

'Here is your army, Rama. Do with them as you please. They await your orders.'

Rama put Sugriva in charge after giving just one direction: 'Find Sita and

take us to where Ravana lives.' And he said to Sugriva: 'You shall instruct them, Sugriva. When it comes to confronting Ravana, then I will take over and you will execute my orders. Till then, you are in complete charge.'

Sugriva began to deploy his forces. He had a clear plan in mind. He proceeded to explain it and hand out clear directives.

'Search the land, search it hard and minutely. Every inch of territory must be covered.

'First the eastern quarter. I would like you, Vinata, to tackle it.' Sugriva then went over in detail the rivers, forests and special spots that Vinata would have to reach and search, the tribes he would have to investigate.

'You will cross the rivers Bhagirathi, Sarayu, Yamuna, the red river Shona and its wild tracts, the red and dreadful sea, Lohita. Passing the mansions of Garuda, the giant eagle and Ananta, the thousand-headed serpent, go on to the Udaya mountain where the sun rises and begins its journey across the skies. This is the gateway of the world, the east. Nearby also is the mountain stepping on which Vishnu measured the earth in three strides. Beyond this the sun does not shine, nor the moon. That is the limit of your search and you must turn back. And the time limit allotted to you, remember, is one month from this day.'

Next came the turn of Angada, who had with him many of the great monkeys, chief among them being Hanuman, along with Nila, Jambavan, Gaja and Gavaksha.

'You will touch Utkala, Kalinga and Vidarbha among other regions, cross the Narmada and Godavari rivers and go over the Vindhyas. You will be in Pandya, Chola and Kerala country, see sandal forests and the golden Mahendra mountain placed in the ocean by Agastya and visited regularly by Indra. You will visit Bhogavati, city of snakes, where Vasuki, the king of serpents, lives. Beyond the Rishabha mountain, shaped like a bull, you will cease to look; for here, in Yama's territory, death holds sway and those who cross that border, cannot return. You too, shall return here in a month.'

Sushena, Tara's father, was sent west. Sugriva mentioned desert tracts that his troops would have to cross and important landmarks on their way.

'You will see the mountain named Chakravan, where Vishnu acquired both his discus and his conch. After that Mount Meru, blessed by the sun with the words "You and your entire range, with all beings who dwell on it, will shine like gold by day as well as by night." The light never fails in this region, this quarter guarded by Varuna, lord of the waters.

'Go on to where the celestials gather at dusk every day to worship the sun as it sets behind the Asthachala range. Beyond this point lies the vast unknown. Do not attempt to explore it. Death is my punishment for those who delay beyond the time limit of one month set by me.'

Shatabali was assigned the northern regions, the domain of Kubera, god of wealth. 'Explore the Himalayas. Go to Mount Kailasa where you will see Kubera's mansion built by Vishwakarma, the divine architect. And on to Mainaka and Krauncha. You will see the splendours and the riches of these mountains and meet gods and celestials, divine and semi-divine beings. Your limit is the Soma mountain. Turn back from there. I expect you here exactly in a month.'

After these general directives to the leaders of the four monkey divisions, Sugriva called Hanuman in for a special session. He praised Hanuman, and the praise was fulsome.

'Your speed, your power, speaks of your origin, for you are the son of Vayu, god of the wind. Nothing can stop you on earth, at sea, or in the skies—you fly and leap over all obstacles. You are blessed with strength and valour and wisdom in equal measure. In you, qualities of body, mind and soul are held in perfect balance. You have an uncanny sense of time, place, occasion. To you therefore I entrust all our plans, all our hopes for success. From you, I expect much, knowing fully well that you will not disappoint.'

As Rama watched these two, king and minister, he sensed the strong bond of trust that linked them, a trust based on past strategies planned and campaigns won. Rama recalled his first meeting with Hanuman. Even then, as early as that, he had impressed with his manner and appearance. Even at that time Rama had felt hope flooding his heart. Now, listening to Sugriva, Rama knew that Hanuman would determine the success or failure of this campaign.

Rama gave him his signet ring. Hanuman would need it to establish his identity if and when he met Sita. The monkey held it to his head in a gesture of reverence as he bowed to touch Rama's feet. Between Rama and Hanuman too a link had been forged of mutual respect and regard.

After the armies had dispersed, Rama asked Sugriva in wonder and admiration. 'How did you become such a treasure-house of facts about this sprawling country? Your descriptions were vivid and detailed. I went on a journey in my mind while you were giving instructions!'

Sugriva smiled. 'Everything has a bright side. I fled from Vali, moving like a hunted animal from place to place, not able to stop anywhere for long. That is when I got to know this country, its vastness and variety, its many rivers and mountains, forests and oceans, its cities and towns and sacred spots. Finally, I came to rest, thanks to Hanuman, who told me about Matanga's curse, and how Vali could not set foot on Rishyamooka and the Matanga woods. Otherwise, I would still have been on the run, or more likely, dead, for Vali would have caught up with me and finished me off.'

The monkeys searched in all directions for Sita—north, south, east and west. One by one the armies returned, for the month had gone faster than they had imagined. Vinata was the first to return. The eastern quarter had yielded no clue, no hint. Then Shatabali trailed in, dragging his steps with fatigue and disappointment. The mountains had been wonderful but their object had not been achieved. There was no sign of either Sita or Ravana. Sushena came next. He knew the western regions like the palm of his own hand, he had left out no corner of that difficult terrain, but he had no news to give of Sita. It had been a futile search, a frustrating month.

But he had not given up hope. Standing before Rama and Sugriva as they sat on a promontory high up on Prasravana, he declared: 'It is Hanuman who will bring us news of Sita. He will not return like us with sad hearts and empty hands.'

Sugriva too hoped, and Rama refused to give in to despair. That magnificent minister, golden and calm and wise, would search not only with

his eyes and mind, but with all his heart and soul. He was a devotee, if ever there was one.

Things were not going too well with Hanuman's group. They had searched the caverns of the Vindhya mountains where water was extremely scarce, and found themselves next on the shores of a vast and roaring ocean. They were tired and hot and beginning to lose hope.

Angada had attacked and killed a demon, mistaking him for Ravana, and had since then given in to a mood of deep dejection bordering on despair. He was afraid of facing Sugriva and Rama. Failure would not go unpunished, he felt. He began to imagine the worst.

'Our time is up and we have found nothing. What will I tell Sugriva? As it is, he resents me. It was Rama who made me heir apparent, not Sugriva. He will make my failure an excuse to get rid of me. Rama too is going to rage at fate and we as instruments of that fate are bound to suffer.'

Angada could only think of desperate remedies: 'Let us starve ourselves to death; it is the best way. If we are to die, let us choose the time and place and manner of death ourselves.'

Hanuman tried to dissuade him. 'Sugriva will not harm you. He will do anything to please your mother!'

But Angada was sceptical. All his suppressed hostility towards Sugriva surfaced. 'Sugriva is a man without any moral scruples. He lives with his elder brother's wife who is like a mother to him. He had forgotten his pledge to Rama and if he started the search for Sita, it was not out of a sense of obligation but for fear of Lakshmana. He will throw me into prison when I get back. No, it is better that I die here.'

The other monkeys rallied round him and they all sat down sipping water, facing east, on heaps of kusha grass whose tips pointed south, signifying death.

Hanuman realized he had a minor rebellion on his hands. He stood nonplussed, contemplating his next move. He looked at those monkeys sitting like a group of hillocks, loudly lamenting their fate, and almost gave in to a feeling of defeat and failure.

While they sat there, talking of their approaching death, a giant vulture emerged slowly from its cavern in the rocks and looked down at them. The bird had overheard everything and was overjoyed. 'I will eat them up, one by one, as they die. What luck! My prey has literally walked into my mouth.'

Angada paled. He said: 'Because we have failed in our mission, death stalks this place, claiming us. The world bends to Rama's will, Hanuman. Jatayu gave up his life for Sita at Janasthana. . . .'

The great bird stopped moving and said in a voice choking with sorrow: 'Who speaks of my brother Jatayu? Do I have to hear his name spoken after such a long time, only to hear that he is dead? Tell me how he met Rama and how he died. I am Sampati, his elder brother.'

He walked to the edge of the cliff and said: 'You will have to help me down, for my wings have been burnt by the sun and I cannot fly. I am helpless and old.' Though the vulture seemed feeble and tremulous and genuinely grief-stricken, the monkeys hesitated.

However, common sense prevailed. They had made up their minds to die anyway. 'He will make quick work of us. It might be better than a slow death by starvation.' Angada helped him down and told him about Sita's abduction, Jatayu's valiant effort to save her, his fatal battle with Ravana and subsequent death.

Sampati wept. 'I cannot even avenge his death. When we were young and foolish and full of pride in our strength, Jatayu and I flew up to the sun to test our stamina and to find out who was the superior of the two. . . .

'The sun was at its zenith. Jatayu began to swoon with the heat. I could see his wings grow still and his head begin to droop. I quickly spread my wings to shield him and that is how they were scorched. I fell on this mountain and have been here ever since. A whole century has passed. I never found out what happened to Jatayu.'

Angada asked him: 'You have been here a long time. You sit perched on this high mountain, scanning the skies with your sharp eyes. Do you have some clue to the demon Ravana's whereabouts?'

'I think I can help you,' said Sampati. 'Sitting here, I see much, as you very rightly guessed. The other day, I saw a lovely woman struggling to break free, in the arms of a huge demon. She called out "Rama, Rama" as they flew overhead. That must have been Sita. I can tell you more than that, for we are descended from Garuda and are blessed with a sixth sense. We see far and away and beyond. Ravana is in Lanka, a golden city situated on an island eight hundred miles south of here. Sita is there, too, under heavy guard. You must cross the ocean and go to her.'

The monkeys sprang up joyfully. 'We will live, after all, for we have news of Sita!' Sampati's tale was not yet over. They listened eagerly.

'My son brings me my food because I cannot fly. You know how voracious we eagles are. Hunger tears at our vitals like anger raising the hoods of serpents. We are never satisfied.'

Sampati's son had stationed himself on the Mahendra mountain waiting for prey. A huge demon passed by with a woman in his arms. He pounced but the demon pleaded humbly to be let off and he relented. The woman's name was Sita.

And that is how Sampati came to know that Sita was alive and with Ravana.

Old Sampati took his own time telling the story. There was still more to come. 'When I fell, I fell near the hermitage of a sage whom Jatayu and I used to visit as children. He saw my wings and predicted: "You have been brought here to give news of Sita to the monkeys. You will regain your lost wings, your powers, even your lost youth when the monkey army arrives. You must wait here for them".'

As Sampati spoke, he felt his shoulders tingle with new life. Fresh blood raced through his aged veins, his eyes grew bright with youth, and great new wings fanned out. He could fly.

The vulture moved his wings as if testing them, drew back his giant beak, lifting his head. The monkeys felt a rush of feathers and power and good fortune. Life seemed all the more precious and worth living after their brush with death. They were bound to succeed.

Jumping and shouting with delight, the monkeys made their way to the

southern ocean. They stood there, looking at that vast sheet of water that at times seemed asleep and at times playing with its own shores. At times it seemed to threaten with a wave that rose bearing sea creatures with it.

Angada said: 'Who will cross over? Who can? Let each one declare his capacity!' 'I can leap a hundred miles. . . I can do three hundred. . . I, five hundred. . . six hundred. . . seven hundred.' As the clamour died down, Angada declared: 'The distance is within my capacity but I am not sure I can do it twice—I may not be able to return.'

The wise Jambavan said: 'I don't think you should try. You are the leader, the root of this expedition. We can't risk cutting it. You can't stake your life,

you must preserve it.'

Angada who was quick to despair, said: 'We are back to where we were—death by starvation seems to face us all over again. Therefore, Jambavan, with all the wisdom of your great age, give the matter serious thought.'

Jambavan did have a solution: 'There is one amongst us who can do it, and do it with ease. Only, he sits apart and silent.'

Jambavan looked meaningly at Hanuman and asked: 'Why are you quiet? You equal even Rama and Lakshmana in strength. You were born of the wind, of his love for your mother, Anjana. You are driven by his force.'

Jambavan felt it was time to tell the rest the story of Hanuman's birth because clearly, from now on, he would play a major role. Hanuman's mother was an *apsara*, a divine nymph. She was born as Anjana, a monkey, because of a curse, but she could change into a woman whenever she felt like it. She loved the mountains. One day, she went walking through cloud and rain and silver mist. Her silken garments clung to her, her jewels and garlands glowed about her person and her face shone with happiness. The wind blowing about her, playing with her hair, her flowers, her clothes, was thoroughly charmed and fell in love with her unearthly beauty. He caressed her with loving gestures, fondling her till she sensed his presence and cried

out, alarmed: 'Who is this who embraces me? I am the chaste and faithful wife of Kesari, the great monkey. What will happen to me?'

The wind god, Vayu, reassured her. 'This is a meeting of two enamoured minds and from our union will be born a son of surpassing glory, as golden as our experience, endowed with my speed, my power, my intelligence.'

Jambavan said to Hanuman, 'You were blessed, too, specially, and will die only when you wish to. Recognize your strength and put it to use in this good cause. Save the monkey tribes, Hanuman.'

Hanuman responded by stretching out and yawning like a lion coming awake. It had dawned on him, his great strength. He flexed his arms, taking

delight in his waxing powers, which settled on him like a magic mantle. Suddenly, it was a superhuman being who spoke: 'I am the son of Vayu, whose element is space. He leaps, circles, dives, lives, moves and has his being in space. I can circle the great mountain Meru a thousand times without pause and churn whole seas. Like my father, I devour space.'

8

Hanuman in Lanka

Hanuman had now assumed his full, gigantic form. He seemed to fill the sky, dwarfing even the ocean. He had come into his own, recognizing, at a critical moment his destiny as a saviour.

He looked around for a suitable site to launch himself, a mountain plateau that could take the impact of his great leap forward into space — to Lanka. He strode about searching for the right spot, stopped, swished his great tail and then, coiling it, laid it against his back like a resting serpent. He stiffened his arms, drew in his neck and crouched, ready to take off. 'I will fly, fleet as Rama's arrow, and if I don't find Sita, I will bring back Ravana, or Lanka itself, plucked out from the ocean. But something tells me I shall find Sita.'

He leapt, dragging whole flowering trees with birds nesting in them, knocking down mountains. He rose into the sky in a shower of petals like a blessing of the gods, a fragrant benediction.

The monkeys called after him: 'We shall wait here, standing on one foot, till you return. That will be our penance.'

Hanuman, son of the wind, adviser and minister of Sugriva, king of the monkeys, was airborne and finally on his way to Ravana and Lanka.

The great monkey moved in space, his eyes glowing like fires lit on a mountain side. He shone red and coppery like the sun and his tail waved like the victorious banner of Indra. As he flew, the sea rose in great waves, carrying fish to greet him.

The ocean heaved with yearning to help, for he owed his very existence to King Sagara of the Ikshvakus. He asked the winged Mainaka mountain, submerged in the ocean as a bulwark against the evil spirits of the netherworld, to rise so that Hanuman could rest his limbs, weary with flying. Mainaka was glad to oblige for he, too, had a debt of gratitude to pay. As Hanuman passed overhead, Mainaka emerged, an impressive, wooded peak capped with blossoming trees and streaming with waterfalls, a veritable garden in the sea.

Hanuman, however, mistook him for an obstacle, and bore down on him with his powerful chest to crush him and push him back. Mainaka only cried out with joy and said: 'I was only offering myself as a resting place, Hanuman. Your father helped to hide me when Indra cut off the wings of all the mountains.'

Hanuman released him saying: 'I am pressed for time. I cannot wait.'

Then touching him gently in greeting and blessing, he went on.

A little later, he encountered a real obstacle. Surasa, mother of serpents, took a female demon's form, blocked his path and opened her mouth, ready to swallow him.

'You are the food reserved for me. So please enter,' she said.

'I shall certainly do so on my way back, after I have seen Sita,' replied Hanuman. Surasa insisted: 'I have been granted a boon that nobody should cross my mouth, once it is opened.'

'Well, then, open your mouth wider; I won't fit,' he said, and began to grow bigger and bigger as she opened her mouth wider and wider to accommodate him. And then, before she realized it,he shrank to a miniscule size, ran quickly in, and out again.

'I have fulfilled my obligation and your boon has not been in vain. I entered your mouth. So, now, let me go.'

There was one more obstacle that the gods had designed to test him. Singhika was a female demon who could capture people by catching hold of their shadows. She grabbed at Hanuman's vast shadow. The monkey suddenly felt he could not move and wondered what was sapping his energy. When he looked around he realized what it was. Gauging the size of her mouth, he contracted to the right dimensions and dived right into her. His body, hard as a diamond, tormented her as he forced his way through, and his nails tore at her entrails. He emerged and she sank, destroyed.

The gods were happy, for Hanuman had proved that he was a perfect combination of the four qualities that make for success—determination, foresight, wisdom and skill. Rama would be ably assisted in his campaign against Ravana.

Hanuman sighted Lanka and began to descend. He let himself down gently on the Trikuta mountain. It would be unwise to attract undue attention.

The journey had not tired him in the least and the freshness of spring revived him. He walked through green fields and honey-scented woods full of spring blossom and new beginnings. All round him was birth and growth and burgeoning. Life, which had been undercover and dormant, was forcing its way through into the open, flaunting its triumph over the death of winter.

From a safe and hidden vantage point, he got a giant's-eye view of Lanka, perched right on the summit of the mountain. For he was still striding tall and broad, though unobtrusive.

It was his first real view of the city built by Vishwakarma, architect of the gods, for Kubera, god of wealth, and later acquired by Ravana, Kubera's demon brother, who was now king of Lanka.

It was an ethereal city, all white and gold and laced with the green of lush foliage. Even the ramparts that circled it were gold. Fierce demons, armed to the hilt, stood at the main gates as well as at all strategic entry points. Hanuman was observing, recording every impression, every little fact. After all, he was on enemy territory as a messenger and spy.

One thing was amply clear. Lanka was so closely and heavily guarded that not even a puff of wind would go undetected. What would Rama have done, thought Hanuman, even if he had been here now? You just could not take this enemy by surprise or catch him with his defences down. Only four among even the wily monkeys could hope to slip past these sentries—Angada, Sugriva, Nila and Hanuman. The security arrangements were near-perfect.

'We can worry about that later,' thought Hanuman, concentrating on the job in hand, brushing away these nagging anxieties. 'I have undertaken a task that needs all my attention. A messenger can make or mar a mission. In this case, I can't risk a single wrong move!'

Hanuman had planned his first step. He would become a small monkey, no bigger than a cat, and attempt to enter the city under cover of night.

At sunset he approached the city and managed to enter it soon after dark. Just as he expected, he was spotted almost immediately. A fearsome woman stopped him and rudely demanded: 'Who are you and what is your business, you little monkey?'

Hanuman answered meekly and mildly: 'I will tell you all you want to know. But first, tell me who you are and why you are so angry.'

The woman replied even more harshly: 'I am Lanka, the spirit of the city, in person. I guard it with my life, under Ravana's command.'

Hanuman refused to be intimidated. He explained calmly: 'I have come to see Lanka—its palaces, parks, gardens and groves. I have heard so much about this beautiful city.'

She lost her patience. 'You don't seem to understand. You cannot go wandering through this city. I refuse to give you permission.'

Hanuman stood his ground. He repeated: 'I shall go away after seeing the city. I have come all the way just for this.' Lanka lost her temper and attacked him with her hands. Hanuman, forgetting himself for a moment, struck back with clenched fist. She looked at him in surprise as she fell. Such strength in this little monkey! He is no bigger than a cat, she thought.

Hanuman regretted his hasty action. He had struck a woman. That was an ignoble thing to do. She surprised him. Instead of raising an alarm, she looked at him submissively, all her bravado gone. 'The hour has come,' she said mysteriously, lowering her voice. 'The creator had prophesied that the day a monkey overpowered the spirit and presiding deity of Lanka, Ravana and his demons would cease to be invincible and Lanka would become vulnerable. Spare me, for the strong can, and sometimes do, show compassion!'

Her voice was subdued. 'You may go where you like, see what you like. The hour has come,' she repeated, in a daze, as she watched him leap over the wall and into the city.

Cool, smooth and white, the moon sailed swan-like down a star-bright sky. Hanuman walked the streets, past houses where women laughed and drank and sang to men whose sole business seemed to be pleasure. They lived and loved as they pleased, beautiful, dissolute, abandoned.

People drank and revelled or drank and brawled. Voices rose and arms waved in drunken argument or pointless debate. Groups of demons went about singing Ravana's praises. Music mingled with Vedic chants.

Hanuman walked the streets of Lanka, city of demons, and saw it for what it was—opulent, decadent, heedless of the morrow and what it would bring.

And he searched for Sita, searched in likely and unlikely places. In the distance was Ravana's palace, at a greater height, shining white and aerial. Hanuman got back to it after doing the rounds of the city and its sights, the breeze roaring in his ears and beating against his face like the sea itself. Lanka was a windswept island, blustery and tempestuous at times.

He had searched the whole palace complex including the mansions of Ravana's brothers, Kumbhakarna and Vibhishana, and the palace of Indrajita, his son, keeping his eyes and ears open all the time. Sita was nowhere in sight.

He entered Ravana's palace. The atmosphere was tense. At times a silence prevailed, the silence of dread; at others, waves of sound rose and fell. It was all a matter of mood—Ravana's moods. He could smile or laugh one moment, scowl, growl or roar with anger and demoniac laughter the next.

Everything to delight the senses was here in abundance. There was a garden within a garden. Clay and wooden mountains mocked nature with forest ranges, lotus pools and blossoming trees, the products of fine art and artifice. No thought had been spared, no effort, no expense, to create a heaven on earth of pastimes and delights. In an enclosure, set apart and well guarded, was the famous Pushpaka, Ravana's aerial chariot. It stood carved, gilded, and gem-set, with many chambers, pavilions and balconies, like a lofty mansion that soared into the skies, poised for flight. Fuelled by thought and driven by the mind, it was Ravana's most prized possession, acquired through penance and valour, hard-won and fiercely protected. Hanuman gazed at this golden vision, flowering like spring. It had jewelled birds with moving wings, flowers and fragrant breezes, and was the handiwork of Vishwakarma's heavenly artisans. Ascending it, he surveyed Ravana's spacious living quarters.

As he stood scanning and observing minutely, all his senses alert, he picked up a faint scent, the inviting smell of food and wine, the subtle aroma of a royal banquet. He followed it and soon came to what was undoubtedly Ravana's apartments, the scene of his nightly revels.

He entered and began to explore. Spread out before him, in room after room, were hundreds of women dressed in fine clothes and jewels, lying exhausted, dishevelled, spent with the effort of pleasing Ravana. They were fast asleep, soft smiles still playing on their beautiful faces, dreaming in maudlin confusion of an evening passed in sensual delights, reliving it.

Some of them embraced each other as if Ravana were still by their side. They lay hand in hand, limbs flung about in attitudes of drunken abandon, wine-scented breaths gently moving their diaphanous veils about their faces and forms. They filled the vast halls like garlands of bright flowers, carelessly flung aside, bruised and lovely.

'These are the best of women,' thought Hanuman, 'wives of sages and celestials, brought here by force, now enslaved and enthralled by Ravana's great wealth and charms.' Could Sita be amongst them, he wondered, having yielded too? He dismissed the thought as quickly as it arose.

At the very end, in a chamber lit by four golden lamps, Ravana slept like a heaving mountain, his breath an ominous hiss that filled the room with its dread sound. Near him, in a pool of soft lamplight, lay a woman, slight of build, flower-like, exquisite, apart. 'That must be Sita,' he thought and thrashed his tail and hands about in a monkey-dance of sheer delight.

His joy was short-lived. Sita would not sleep or dress and adorn herself without her lord, he reminded himself. 'This must be Mandodari, Ravana's chaste and beautiful wife.'

He continued to search, walking through more rooms. He saw great bowls of choice meats, pitchers of rare wines and more women, drunken and dissolute. Hanuman felt chastened and contrite. He had looked upon the sleeping wives of other men, a reprehensible act. But how else could he search? He had to look in the women's apartments and in Ravana's bedchamber. He had searched high and low, in loft and attic and basement, secret chambers and recesses. He had searched till not an inch of space was left to go through, so thorough had he been. Sampati had directed him to Lanka and Ravana's palace, but his search for Sita seemed to be in vain and fruitless.

Where was she? Where was Sita, beloved of Rama, the sole object of this mission? Fear gripped him as his agile mind ran over the dread possibilities. Had she fallen in flight and drowned, struggling with the demon? Had she been crushed to death in his powerful arms? Or, looking down at the tossing ocean, died of sheer shock? Had he or his wives eaten her up, or was she in some corner of this vast palace caged like a talking bird for their demoniac amusement?

His thoughts raced, tearing through his mind. 'I can't face Rama with the fact of failure. He will kill himself. Lakshmana will follow, then Bharata, Shatrughna and all their mothers. Sugriva, too, will destroy himself and Tara is sure to follow him with Angada. The Ikshvakus and our tribes will both face annihilation. I dare not go back and declare failure. I would rather renounce the world, starve to death or kill myself, kill Ravana and fling him to the other shore where the monkeys wait, praying. . . .'

As he emerged from the oppressive atmosphere of Ravana's palace into the garden, hope born of courage from some hidden, inner source filled him once more, banishing despair. There was just one spot he had not searched in that whole massive complex and it lay now directly in front of him—Ravana's grove of ashoka trees in rampant bloom. Hope seemed to well up and wash over him like a springtide of fresh life, promising success.

He prayed. He summoned up in thought Rama and Lakshmana, all his gods, all his strengths and all his reserves of concentration. He summoned them all and focused them on the ashoka grove, till Sita and Rama filled his thoughts to the exclusion of all else.

It was a grove of sheer delight, full of fruit and flowers. Hanuman stepped on ground strewn thick with fallen petals, fragrant and yielding, followed paths that wound through arbour and bower designed to shade, past streams, waterfalls and lotus pools and a golden, thousand-pillared pavilion. All was silent and still except for birdsong or the drip and splash of water. There were no other signs of life, no sign of Sita.

And then, through the ripple and murmur of a stream, his sharp ears picked up the sound of anklet bells. He quickly stepped aside and climbed a tree, looking out for women, for Sita. Surely she would come here to this private garden, pining for Rama, thinking of him with longing and desire....

He peeped through the leaves and saw a lady in soiled garments, weak and sighing, quite overcome by sorrow. Her long hair, braided and snaky, fell to her knees and below. Surrounding her were a circle of fierce, female demons. What a picture of dismay she was! 'This must be Sita,' he thought, as image chased image in his mind, recalling his visions of her.

She was a single, slender digit of a new moon once rounded and glowing and full, the lean spirit of prosperity on the wane, the echo of a prayer without any meaning. 'She is faith shaken by doubt, a clear intellect clouded, fame stained with censure. She is like fair speech turned thick with blurred edges of sense,' he thought, as her misery flooded his imagination and churned his heart. She was beside herself with grief, perhaps not herself at all, maddened with despair. There was no doubt now, as he scrutinized her. She was Sita. The clothes she wore matched the ones dropped by Sita on Rishyamooka, and the jewels too. Hanuman praised Rama and enshrined Sita in his thoughts. Even as he looked upon the ugliness, deformity and misshapen terror of the demons and felt Sita's burning sorrow, he shed tears of joy. He thought again of Rama, and yet again, with gratitude. He needed to pray, to bless and be blessed. Prayer and benediction would work where all else had failed, pave his way to Sita and success. The end seemed finally in sight. He sat still and thought hard.

It was late night, passing into dawn. Ravana woke to Vedic chants, sounds of music and thoughts of Sita. Desiring her, he set out immediately for his pleasure grove, determined to woo and win her with all the resources at his command.

He went with an impressive entourage. The grove was bright with golden lamps, golden pots of water and wine and golden staffs. A hundred women, their eyes heavy with sleep, swaying languorously, went with him. They were carelessly dressed, their girdles slipping, their garments and jewels out of place.

Hanuman hid himself behind a leafy branch, and waited expectantly. He recognized Ravana whom he had left sleeping only a short while ago. The king shone with a lustre that dazzled even Hanuman. Pride, desire and wine had reddened and widened his eyes, glowing fierce and coppery in the lamplight.

He stood before Sita who tried to hide her beautiful breasts, bending low in fear and modesty, trembling at this public display of unashamed passion. She threw her mind back, clinging to thoughts of Rama, her lord, her protector. She seemed a bruised lotus stalk, wilting in the sun, a river run dry in the sweltering heat of summer. She could not bear the hot blast of his desire, his brazen, though ardent, wooing. She shrank into herself and he, courting destruction, approached her with words and gestures of frank seduction.

'Why do you shrink from me? I love you to distraction. When my eyes stray over your lovely body, they feast on its unending delights. I yearn to unite with you. We demons take our pleasure where we please, when we please, but I do you the honour of waiting till you accept me. Do not delay. Youth passes like a flowing current, never to return.

'Accept my love; be chief among the loveliest women in the world. Range the skies and walk the sea-washed shores of Lanka in my company.'

Sita was quiet, her mind fixed on Rama. Then placing a blade of grass between them, a barrier of contempt and distaste, she said with all the courage and dignity she could muster: 'Dissuade yourself. Keep to your own women.' And she turned her back on him, and on his lavish praise. 'Just as your wives need and seek protection, so do other men's wives. You took me by force when Rama and Lakshmana were away. I know you for a cur who would flee in terror at the mere hint of their presence—those two tigers among men. You will be destroyed. I shall see you cowering yet when the arrows fly thick and fast, bringing death and destruction to Lanka. Rama will drain your vital breath as quickly as the sun dries up a puddle.

'Restore me to Rama, make friends with him before it is too late, before you hear the twang of his bowstring.'

Ravana stormed: 'Only my love for you holds back my anger, like a charioteer drawing in his restless horses. My desire for you saves you from instant death. But my patience and your time are both running out. Two months is all you have, Sita! Either you share my bed or I have you chopped up and cooked for breakfast—I repeat my threat, just to remind you.'

Sita's reply was even more cutting: 'Is there no adviser in Lanka who could dissuade you? Who dares to even think of me as his mate and escapes destruction? How is it that your eyes, looking at me, daughter of Janaka, don't fall out? How can your tongue, uttering such calumny, not tear to shreds? It is Fate's mysterious way of destroying you, Ravana. Your end is near.'

Ravana glared, towering above her like a mountain, his strength and power barely contained. She stood trembling and frail but prepared to take him on. It was a headlong confrontation.

Ravana left, instructing his demon guards: 'Bring her round. Use any means. Try persuasion first, and if that fails, use threats. Frighten her; force her!'

The demon women wasted no time. One of them cited his lineage: 'He is the grandson of Pulastya, born of Brahma's mind. You could not ask for higher credentials.' Another appealed to her vanity: 'He is giving up his other wives for you. Accept him.' A third tried to frighten her: 'When he

passes by the wind blows softly, the sun pales, trees shed flowers in fear, mountains cry out for help. Aren't you afraid?'

Sita walked away as they followed her about, teasing, pestering, threatening, till she stood under the very tree on which Hanuman sat, his head buzzing with plans to meet and talk to her.

There was menace in their tones now. They began to see her as a choice morsel of human flesh, a rare delicacy. They began to relish the thought of feeding on her.

'I will pluck your juicy heart out and eat it. Ever since I set eyes on you, I've wanted to chew on your head, to bite your soft limbs.' 'Let's squeeze her slender neck. Why are we wasting time? I'm sure Ravana will let us eat her once she is dead. He is a generous man.' 'We must make a fair division,' said another as she saw signs of a coming scuffle. 'Let's chop her up fine, make equal balls of flesh and distribute them. There will be no quarrel then. Arrange for a banquet. Bring out the wine and decorate the place with flowers.'

'I agree,' said Shurpanakha, Ravana's sister, sanctioning the feast, happy at the thought of avenging her humiliation. 'Let's eat her, wash her down with wine and then dance before our patron goddess, Nikumbhila, in joyous celebration.'

Sita was terror-stricken, but put up a brave front and said proudly, defiantly: 'I won't touch him even with my left foot, come what may. Why talk to me of Ravana? Talk of Rama and his valour, instead. Who wiped out fourteen thousand demons in Janasthana?'

Why was he not here already, she thought wildly. Was he dead? 'Lanka should by now have been a burning ground of dead demons, a cemetery,' she cried out loudly, suddenly breaking down, lamenting her fate, beginning to lose faith. 'Has he forgotten me, or ceased to care for me? Love weakens with distance and lack of contact. . . . No, that can never be!' And she threw herself on the ground, tossing, turning and rolling about, her face bathed with tears, her lovely body caked with the dust of her mother Prithvi, the Earth.

The demons stepped up their threats, screaming and roaring. But one among them, Trijata, restrained them.

'Listen and be warned,' she said. 'I have had dreams. Rama in an aerial chariot, made of ivory, drawn by a thousand horses . . . Lakshmana in white, with garlands . . . Sita in white, on a white throne surrounded by the sea . . . Sita with Rama, radiant . . . Rama rode the Pushpaka, going north and Ravana, shaven, oiled and bloodied, fell from the Pushpaka, dragged down by a woman . . . Ravana in a chariot drawn by donkeys, clad in red, drinking oil, signifying death . . . Ravana, headless . . . dancing and garlanding him, Kali herself, it seemed, destruction personified. And then she dragged him southwards, in the direction of Yama, god of death. Death and destruction all round . . . except for Vibhishana, over whom was held the royal white canopy of power. And everywhere, in hundreds, demons tumbling into the ocean, raving, eating dung. I fear for Ravana, for Lanka, for us. Don't touch her! Let her go. She will plead our cause with Rama. She is our only hope.'

Sita stood up. Her storm of grief had passed, leaving her wretched and hopeless. She undid the cords that bound her masses of hair and decided to hang herself. Holding on to a flowering branch she stood, fixing her thoughts on Rama in silent farewell. As she closed her eyes in contemplation she felt her left eye throb, then her left arm and left thigh. These were good omens; she could not ignore them. Rama must be on his way! Her whole body, pulsating with hope, revived, eager to live. Death withdrew defeated, as life came rushing to her rescue.

All this while, Hanuman sat still, studying Sita, missing nothing, noting every expression, every reaction. When the moment came to speak to her, things had to go right, move in the right direction. And he was only too well aware of all the things that could go wrong. For instance, if his speech was too polished and cultivated she might shy away, suspecting treachery. After all, that was how she got here in the first place—Ravana had been a soft-spoken ascetic. Human speech was his only means of communication, but coming from a monkey it might startle her. She might cry out, the demons would rush to attack him, and she might get killed in the process. He could fight them but he would then be too exhausted to fly back. Besides, one never knew in a fight—and he had to return alive. There was no other monkey who could replace him. The whole mission now hung by a single thread, and he was that thread.

There was only one way—to speak of Rama's exploits, to praise him in terms that would win her confidence, her trust. He took the plunge. The moment seemed opportune and such moments had a way of passing, never to return. Delay might be fatal.

He began to tell the story of Rama, bringing it up to date and ended by explaining his presence in Lanka.

Tense and anxious moments followed. Sita's ears pricked up at the very first mention of Rama and she looked round eagerly. Looking up, she discovered the source. Seeing a monkey staring into her face, she swooned. When she revived and saw him still there, she thought she must be dreaming—and monkeys were bad omens. She began to lose heart, to lament, but instantly steadied herself. She had not slept, how could she dream? It was no illusion. Rama and Lakshmana were well and this monkey had a message for her! Hanuman, watching her face, could almost read her thoughts. He relaxed. He could safely approach her now. He came down and questioned her with folded hands. 'Who are you? Why do you weep? I can see you are a queen or a princess. Are you Sita, abducted by Ravana? Tell me.'

He won her over completely with his straightforward manner and sympathetic tone. She poured out her woes. 'My fate is sealed. In two months, I will be dead, killed by this demon who will not take no for an answer.'

Sita spoke freely to Hanuman but still had some doubts and qualms. Hanuman set about clearing them. He could not proceed till he had her completely on his side. He described Rama and Lakshmana at great length, in the minutest detail. His powers of observation were phenomenal, and he succeeded in convincing her that he was indeed what he seemed—a monkey and minister of Sugriva, entrusted with the difficult mission of finding her.

He told her about the ornaments and garment that she had dropped on Rishyamooka.

When she was totally at ease and trusting, he handed her Rama's signet ring. Sita caressed it as if it were Rama himself, so overwhelmed was she with longing and love for her absent husband.

'Rama did not know where you were,' he said, giving her the reassurance she seemed to need. 'He loves you beyond reason, beyond all imagination. He lives a life of denial and total abstinence, austere, ascetic. He sees you, and only you in everything, be it bird or fruit or flower. I say all this on oath. I swear on the great mountains of the earth—Mandara, Vindhya, Malaya, and all fruits and roots, that he thinks of you every moment, asleep or awake.'

Hanuman assured her once again that Rama would come himself, but if she so wished he, Hanuman, could take her back now. 'I will carry you over the ocean to your lord,' he said.

'That is impossible. You are a little monkey. How can I ride your back?' countered Sita.

For answer Hanuman grew in size, assuming his gigantic form. Sita was impressed and thanked him for the offer but declined.

'I might faint, I might fall. Ravana will drag you back, kill you, kill me. Besides, only one man can touch me—my lord, Rama. Ravana did, but that was quite another matter. He used force.'

These were only excuses. She came out with her true reason. 'Would you deny Rama the glory and the privilege of winning me back? His honour is in question, and mine too.'

Hanuman understood. As he saw it, there was more at stake here than individual honour and happiness. The issues went beyond even Rama and Sita. They were issues of right and wrong, good and evil. Rama and Ravana had to meet and fight it out. Rama was right-in-action against Ravana, the might and power of evil and wrong-doing. Sita, the lustre of truth, its glory, would then be re-united with Rama. The wise Hanuman bowed before the workings of destiny.

Taking a jewel, her hair ornament, as proof of their meeting, he left.

Hanuman had done his job. He had found Sita and delivered Rama's message. But he felt he could do something more. He was no mere messenger. He was an emissary, a representative. He had already learnt from Sita that Ravana had chosen to ignore the counsels of his own people. The demon king seemed bent on following a path of confrontation and war. Under the circumstances, a show of strength, a taste of things to come would be quite in order. A good ambassador thought several steps ahead, weighed all possibilities and even, on occasion, acted on behalf of his masters. And the situation in Lanka called for such action. When the enemy reacted, as he was bound to do, Hanuman would have an opportunity to assess his strength.

An idea struck him as he looked around at the idyllic surroundings of the ashoka grove, the pleasure garden of Ravana's women, its arbours, pools and shady walks. He felt a surge of confidence as his plans began to take shape. He would destroy this very grove, wreak such havoc that the lord of

Lanka would be jolted out of his complacency.

He grew in size and strode about, uprooting trees, demolishing pavilions, crushing rocks, trampling on torn creepers and fallen trees. Just one spot was left untouched, and that was the tree under which Sita stood, watching, beginning to understand the workings of Hanuman's complex and ingenious mind. It was an act of wanton destruction, calculated to provoke Ravana. Hanuman straddled the gates, roused and waiting, fully prepared.

As soon as the demons saw Hanuman on the rampage, they pounced on Sita. 'Who is that monkey? What was he saying to you? Look at him now, huge beyond recognition!' Sita was no longer the frightened, trembling woman they had dealt with so far. She replied quite calmly: 'How do I know? You demons change form at will; do what you please. You should be able to tell—only a serpent can read the trail left by serpents.'

They ran in panic to Ravana. 'A huge monkey is creating havoc . . . he spoke to Sita . . . she is evasive about the whole thing . . . everything in the grove is destroyed, except the tree under which she stands . . . isn't that significant?'

Ravana's red eyes smouldered like a funeral pyre and tears of anger came rolling down like drops of oil from a burning lamp. He sent out an eighty thousand-strong force of demons. They were beaten back by Hanuman whose strength seemed to grow with every attack. News of the great monkey began to spread. Judging it the right moment to come out in the open and declare himself, he proclaimed: 'Victory to Rama! Victory to Lakshmana! Victory to Sugriva, lord of the monkeys! I am Hanuman, son of Vayu, the wind god, and servant of Rama. I can crush a thousand Ravanas.'

Hanuman was bursting with warlike energy. 'The temple pavilion still stands. I must attack that.' He walked in and pulled out one of its gilded pillars. Whirling it round at great speed, he set it alight and then set fire to the temple. The guards rushed out to fight him, but Hanuman, with just a deafening roar, knocked them senseless. Then crying victory to Rama once again, he rose into the sky, looming over Lanka threateningly: 'Sugriva commands hundreds and thousands like me. They lead armies of monkeys, each with the strength of many elephants. They will descend on Lanka in their millions, and attack you tooth and claw. For you and your lord have incurred the wrath of Rama of the Ikshvakus.' The challenge to Ravana was clear and unmistakable.

Ravana was greatly agitated. He knew that matters had taken a serious turn. 'I have seen Vali and Sugriva in battle. They are formidable, but no real match for us. This Hanuman, of whom you speak in such terrifying terms, is no mere monkey. He is masquerading as one. He must be dealt with promptly.'

His bravest warriors went out to crush Hanuman—Jambumali, his five generals one after the other, and seven sons of his ministers, followed by Aksha. Hanuman killed them all, exulting in his own strength that seemed to heighten with combat.

Ravana then sent for his son Indrajita who had proved his valour against

Indra himself. 'You are the best, Indrajita. I know you will succeed where the others have failed. I rely on you to bring this creature to heel.'

It was a well-matched fight. Indrajita concentrated on Hanuman, devising ways of capturing him, for he realized that killing him would not be easy.

'How do I get him to stand still for a moment?' he thought. He decided to use the powerful missile of Brahma that would immobilize him. The weapon struck. Hanuman fell and lay motionless. He, too, had just worked out a strategy. 'Indrajita thinks I am caught. I could easily escape, but won't. This way, I will be in Ravana's presence sooner than I imagined. His curiosity will make him want to see me.'

The demons bound him with ropes, hurled insults at him and struck him. Hanuman gave no sign of life, although the effects of the missile had already worn off. Bound hand and foot, he was brought before Ravana and his assembly of demons. Only Indrajita sensed that Hanuman was not really affected.

Hanuman looked at Ravana, at the splendour of his throne, his crown of gold and pearls, his body decorated with sandal, his whole aura of lustre and power, and paid silent tribute. 'What beauty, what courage, what valour, what lustre! He could have ruled the heavens and Indra himself if only he had not been evil.'

While the monkey pondered on this single tragic flaw that would work against Ravana and in Rama's favour, Ravana sized him up.

'Is he Nandi, Shiva's great bull, I wonder? I mocked him once and he was greatly incensed....'

He ordered Prahasta, his minister, to interrogate him. Prahasta began accusingly: 'You are not what you seem. Why are you here? Who sent you?' Was it Indra, Kubera, Varuna, Yama or Vishnu himself, thought Ravana. 'Why are you here? Tell us the truth and we will set you free. Lie to us, and you will pay with your life,' declared Prahasta.

Hanuman was direct. It suited him to be so. 'I am what I seem, a monkey. I wished to meet Ravana, so I destroyed the grove. I allowed myself to be captured. I am here to further Rama's cause.' Hanuman found himself addressing Ravana.

'I come from Sugriva and speak on his behalf. It is in your interest to listen to me. I have met Sita and talked to her. As a person of learning and merit acquired through rigid penance, you are aware of what is right and what is wrong. It is wrong to take another's wife by force. Therefore, I ask you to restore Sita to Rama. She is like a serpent or a meal of poisoned food that is bound to strike at your vitals and destroy you.

'I know you cannot be killed by gods, celestials or demons, so great is the merit you have earned through your penance. But Sugriva is none of these, and Rama is a mortal. Bear that in mind.

'You have seen what I have already done to your precious grove. I could do much more, but that is Rama's prerogative. He will do the rest. He has vowed to do so.

'Do not play into the hands of fate. Do not subject Lanka to the horrors of war with Rama. His anger will consume you and yours. Rama is no ordinary foe. Do not take him on in your ignorance.'

Hanuman's tone had been calm, his words full of wisdom and common sense. But they fell on ears deaf with arrogance. The complete confidence with which he spoke infuriated Ravana. He ordered: 'Consign him to his fate. Kill him.'

Vibhishana, Ravana's brother, spoke up for the first time. 'This is against the code of courtly conduct. Envoys enjoy a certain immunity. It is against established custom to kill him. You should know; you have spent years studying the law. You are allowing anger to cloud your judgement. Punish, by all means, but assess the situation before you pronounce sentence.'

Ravana argued: 'He is an evil-doer and death is what he deserves.'

Vibhishana persisted. 'Under no circumstance is an envoy to be killed while on duty. This monkey has destroyed much, done us grave injury and deserves to be punished. You may maim, shave, whip him—any, or all three would be permissible. Execution is ruled out.

'He is only the purveyor of a message and a mission. Your wrath should be directed against the master, not the servant.'

Ravana reluctantly gave in to Vibhishana's forceful plea. In a voice full of contempt, he said: 'A monkey's greatest pride is his tail. Set it on fire and let the creature go. He will be a sorry sight when he returns to his kith and kin. That should cut him down to size!'

Ravana was still seething. Adding insult to injury was not enough. A pile, a heap of insults was what this monkey deserved for his presumption.

'Put him on display right here, in Lanka. Take him round with his tail burning.'

His henchmen were prompt in carrying out his orders. They wrapped Hanuman's tail round with rags soaked in oil. He began to grow and they wound more and more cloth, poured more and more oil.

'This is even better than I thought. I can see Lanka by day, taken round by these foolish demons who can't see beyond their monstrous noses. Fate is taking over. Ravana is not only deaf to good counsel but blind to the future—the very near future, at that.'

He swished his tail in triumph as they took him down highways and streets and lanes, blowing conches, beating drums. Hanuman saw the glory of Lanka, the mansions of the rich and the powerful, garden and park and grove. 'Here comes a spy,' they kept announcing, jeering and mocking all the while. He was their giant performing monkey, their special bag of tricks for the day.

Sita, too, had got to hear of Hanuman's humiliation. She prayed with folded hands before the fire: 'If I have been a chaste wife, flare gently, O Lord. If my penance means anything, do not burn him.'

Her prayers did not go unheeded. The fire did indeed burn cool, for the wind, his friend, Hanuman's father, blew with the healing touch of ice.

'The power of Rama, the affection of my father and Sita's great virtue, protect me,' guessed Hanuman, as he walked around, inspecting, assessing, hardly hearing what was going on around him.

And then it happened. Hanuman burst his bonds, killed the city guards and escaped. 'I should destroy this citadel. The fire on the tip of my tail shall

have its due. I shall propitiate Agni, god of fire. The city of Lanka shall be my offering.'

From roof to roof he leapt, setting the city ablaze. Molten streams of gold, bearing precious stones, flowed from mansion and palace. He wrought havoc, burning, killing. Lanka was a bouquet of flames, held by spirals of blue smoke, an offering to the gods and a lesson to the demons. Hanuman had gone far beyond his brief, carried away perhaps by destiny in spate. At last, sated with destruction, he dipped his burning tail in the ocean, snuffing out the flame that had lit the torch of war with Ravana, king of

Lanka.

As Hanuman sat, recovering from his great exertion, he began to doubt, and then to fear. Had he overdone things? He had let anger sway him. Sita might have come to harm, perhaps even burnt to death, through his folly and haste. Nothing seemed to move in the desert of ashes that was Lanka. 'I have really behaved like a monkey,' he reflected, full of remorse.

But how could fire burn fire? Sita was a clear flame of virtue and chastity. Even he had survived the conflagration; how could she be touched? Aerial voices echoed his thoughts. 'Sita is safe, Sita is safe.' Relieved, Hanuman decided to meet Sita before he went back.

He saw her, whole and unharmed. She was apprehensive. How would the others ever get across? Hanuman reassured her and then stationed himself on a mountain, poised for flight. He leapt into the air, wearing garlands of trees like a garment. They seemed to move and toss their heads, humming with happiness as the wind, in a great rush, whistled through them. Hanuman was on his way back in rapid flight. Swimming the skies, he darted fish-like in and out of cloud masses, dragging them like great nets after him.

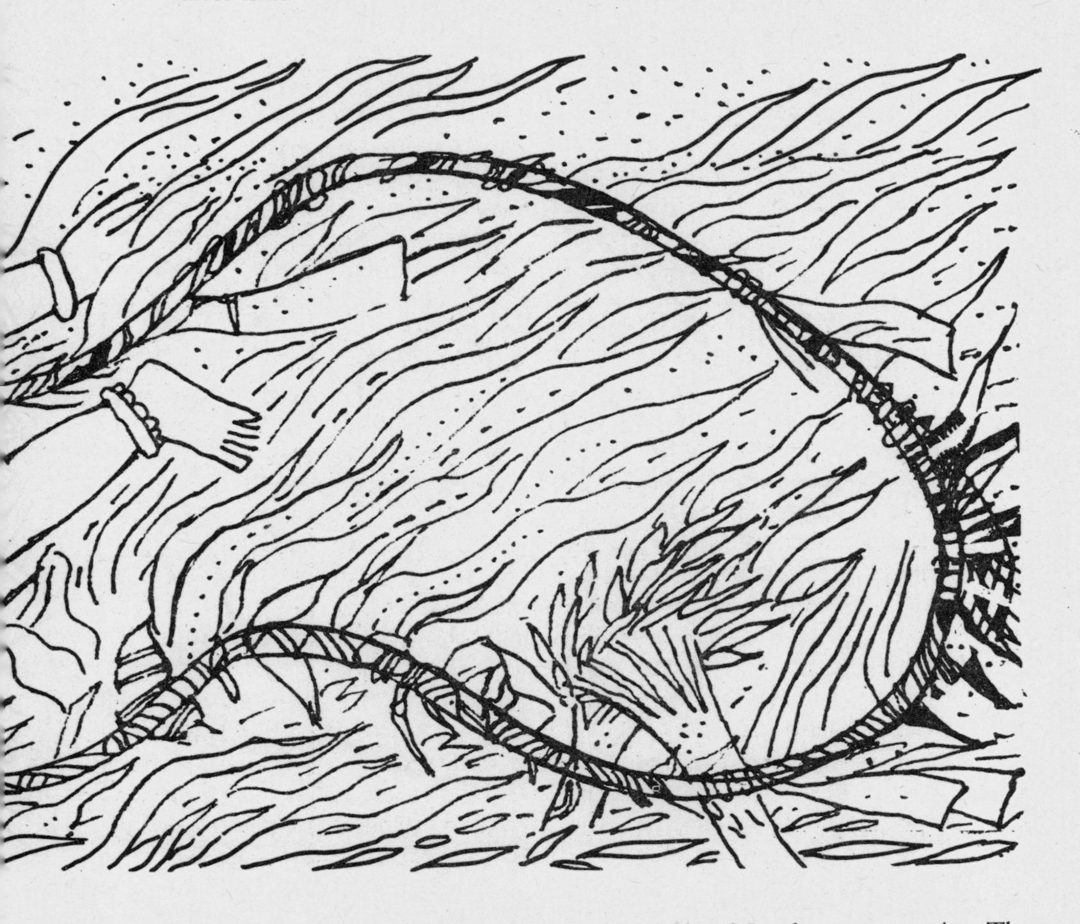

The monkeys saw him descend on the Mandara mountain. They concluded from his shouts of joy that he came bearing good news. 'He has been successful,' said the bear Jambavan as they surged forward, craning their necks to catch a glimpse of him. They greeted him with folded hands, spread out branches for him to sit on, offered fruits and roots and, with suppressed excitement, waited for him to speak.

Hanuman addressed Angada and Jambavan. He was brief and to the point.

'I have seen Sita,' he said. Taking the young Angada's hand, he continued:

'I have seen her in a grove of ashoka trees, waiting, faint with grief.'

Their anticipation gave way to cries of exultation. There was much thumping and lashing of tails as Angada and Hanuman sat on the Mandara mountain, glowing with success and satisfaction. The monkeys wanted to hear everything, down to the last detail, and Hanuman told them the whole story, how he had found Sita, how he had already given Ravana some indication of their power.

Angada was impatient to go ahead. 'Let us get Sita here and surprise Rama. While we are around and capable, why should we trouble others?' Hanuman's success had filled him with enthusiasm and courage. Gone was the old despondency. He could face Sugriva and the future like the prince and heir apparent that he was.

But Jambavan restrained him. 'We were ordered to find Sita, not to bring her back. Rama would not like us to conquer Lanka. He wishes to do that himself. He is the hero of this venture. Let us not do anything to diminish either his glory or his status.'

The monkeys set off to tell Sugriva. Their way lay through Madhuvana, Sugriva's private garden grove, full of rare flowering trees and orchards. They feasted on roots, fruits and honey and in boisterous monkey fashion, celebrated Hanuman's triumph. Running, leaping and swinging from trees, they quaffed great quantities of honey straight from the comb, hurling the empty combs at each other playfully. It was a scene of much merrymaking, of drunken laughter and maudlin tears that was rapidly turning into a stampede.

Sugriva's old uncle, Dadimukha, who was in charge of the park, first sent his guards, then came himself, to quieten them. But they chased away his men and defied him. Angada and Hanuman, drunk with honey and victory, indulged them. Dadimukha ran to Sugriva.

'My lord...' he began, in fear and confusion.

'I hope things are all right with you in Madhuvana. You look troubled...' said Sugriva.

'My lord,' said the old man, plucking up courage, 'things are not well, not well at all. The garden is quite desolate, laid waste....They defied me blatantly and attacked my men. I can't understand it.'

Lakshmana was curious. Sugriva said to him, a smile on his lips: 'That must be Hanuman celebrating. They are out of their minds, obviously, with joy. As far as I am concerned, they are pardoned even the devastation of my prized garden, Madhuvana.'

Dadimukha could not believe his luck. They had got away, and he with them! 'Let them eat and drink and make merry, Dadimukha. Don't worry. Tell them I am waiting to hear from them.'

Dadimukha went back. Wanting to ingratiate himself with Angada, he flattered him. 'I am sorry we tried to obstruct you. After all, you are the crown prince. This garden is yours to do with as you please. Sugriva was far from angry. He seemed to be quite happy to place Madhuvana at your disposal. He wants to see you all, immediately.'

Sugriva was now in a position to comfort and console Rama. 'The long wait is over. I am sure that Hanuman brings good news. They have exceeded

the time limit set by me, yet dared to return. They are taking their own sweet time to report; they have destroyed a valuable piece of ancestral property they never set foot in, normally. All these are signs of heady success. Can't you hear the sounds of jubilation, the chatter and the clamour? Hanuman will not disappoint us, bless him.'

The monkeys came flying. Hanuman touched hand to head in humble salutation and with characteristic brevity let drop the magic words, filling Rama's ears with the sweetness of nectar. 'I have seen the virtuous Sita, safe and unharmed.'

9

War Clouds over Lanka

Things were beginning to move. Lakshmana looked at Sugriva with respect and fond regard. Rama, too, was all admiration for Hanuman who stood there, head lowered and heart open to the feelings of devotion that came pouring in. This prince in exile, grieving for his lovely wife, had stolen his heart.

Rama questioned him about Sita, her state of mind, her health. Hanuman told him everything—what he had seen, what he had heard, what he had done. He told him that Sita had resolved to kill herself at the end of the month. 'Here is her hair ornament,' said Hanuman, handing over the jewel to Rama. Like Sita, he too fondled the piece, and mourned: 'What greater sorrow can there be than to see this jewel without Sita? It was her father's gift to her on her wedding day. What did she say, Hanuman? Tell me again, for her words are like medicine to an ailing man.'

'She talked of an incident at Chitrakuta, how a crow. . . .'

'Yes, yes, I remember. It was bothering her....'

'... and how with a blade of grass and a mantra you destroyed his eye,' said Hanuman.

'How well I remember! I could not bear to see her troubled even by a crow!'

'Exactly,' intercepted Hanuman, determined to pull him out of the sea of sorrow in which he seemed to be drowning. 'Sita was wondering how this same Rama was now so slow in coming to her help. "Remind him of that incident, describe my present humiliation, so that he may come here with the speed of wind and rescue me!" she said.'

Hanuman drove his point home. 'I left reassuring her that we would arrive in Lanka with our forces, that as soon as your exile was over, she would see you crowned king of Ayodhya with her beside you.' And with this reminder to Rama, Hanuman stopped talking and waited.

Rama praised Hanuman in glowing terms. 'There are those who fail in the tasks they set out to do and those who do only what they are asked. But there are also those, Sugriva, like your minister Hanuman, who do more than their appointed task. They are the best. I cannot yet reward him in a fitting manner. All I can do is to embrace him with affection and gratitude.'

Rama grew thoughtful. How would the monkeys perform in the war to come? Could they do what Hanuman had done? 'I have my doubts—and there yet is a vast ocean to be crossed.'

Indeed there was. They were standing on the shore of a sea of troubles—

of that there was no doubt.

Sugriva, unlike Rama, was full of hope and plans of action. 'We must build a bridge. That is the first step,' he said. Rama replied: 'You are right. The only other way is to dry up the ocean, or do penance. We shall decide when the time comes.'

He asked Hanuman to give him a full and clear account of Lanka, its situation, its strengths. Hanuman began: 'The city has four heavily barred gates, each guarded by thousands of well-armed men. Their weapons are highly sophisticated. There are ramparts and moats to protect the city from invasion. There are troops centred in the heart of the city, too. Ravana is alert, always on guard. However, the groundwork is done. I have filled up the moats and levelled the inner ramparts. We have only to cross the sea, and the city is ours for the taking.'

Rama was ready to leave. 'It is midday, Sugriva, a good time to start. My right eye throbs and victory beckons.'

He deployed the forces himself and issued instructions. Nila was to go ahead on an exploratory mission. 'Make sure that your route has a plentiful supply of fruits, roots and water. Get there and occupy the area before the enemy denudes it and starves your troops to death. I myself will be at the very centre with the others, riding on Hanuman's shoulders, and Lakshmana on Angada. Bringing up the rear will be wise old Jambavan with Sushena. The right and left flanks will be guarded by Kesari and Gaja.'

They proceeded, clearing paths, blazing the trail to Lanka and Ravana. A mood of high hope and courage prevailed and Lakshmana echoed their thoughts as he said: 'The wind blows cool, the forests bloom. The season is kindly, and so is fate. Our armies are on the march.'

They made good progress, going past forests, villages, rivers and over mountains. Rama began to see the advantages of having a monkey army. They were fleet and sure of foot, agile and nimble. With the greatest ease they cleared the way of obstructions and scaled mountains to survey and reconnoitre.

The army reached the ocean and the monkey hordes stopped to gaze in wonder at its vastness. 'We shall camp here, in this pleasant forest, in sight of the ocean,' said Rama. 'We need to consult and plan and work out strategies. Let everyone keep to his own division. Good order must be maintained.'

The ocean frothed milk-white in the moonlight, tossing high with waves, murmuring ceaselessly as it churned and leaped and churned again, rolling up, pulling in.

Rama's thoughts went out to Sita. 'O wind, touch her, then touch me. Cool this fire of love and separation that burns me! When will I shed the soiled garment of longing and wrap myself in the joy and warmth of her embrace? Time passes, and youth with it.'

Lanka lay close, yet far and the only frail bridges in sight seemed to be his thoughts, his yearning, his sorrow.

In Lanka, Ravana was in consultation with his cabinet. Hanuman had left them no alternative. It had to be war.

Ravana held forth to his ministers. 'Consultation is the basis of victory. It stems from three sources—first, from those skilled in the field, professionals;

secondly, from friends and well-wishers and thirdly, from your own kith and kin. He who takes all three types of advice is the wisest and the best. Then comes the man who depends only on his own opinions and conclusions, and lastly, there is the type that launches into action unthinkingly, and fails even to follow up what is happening.'

The ministers listened, for none dared intercept or contradict. It was a captive audience. He went on, laying down the law, propounding the theory of counselling and consultation, for he was a learned man who thought he knew it all.

'And, of course, advice is of three types. The best is a unanimous view, based on traditional tenets arrived at after much discussion and consultation. The next best is a reconciliation of varying opinions, involving some compromise, some give and take, but in the end, a clear consensus. The worst of course is much discussion and a total lack of agreement. For in consensus lies the welfare of the state.

'Rama will be here shortly. He has superhuman powers and commands strengths we have only begun to see. So let us sit together, consult and begin to act.'

No one could have taken objection to his learned and sensible discourse. He had argued and presented the case for consultation and consensus admirably. There were those who questioned the need for war at all, but they were, for now at least, silent. The fawning majority would have their say first. They vied with each other in praising Ravana.

'You have conquered the subterranean region, the northern mountains, the guardians of all four quarters, divine and semi-divine beings. These are only monkeys. Indrajita can handle them singly. A human being is no match for you. Hanuman took us unawares. Now, we are prepared. The city has been violated. We will kill mercilessly.'

They came out with hasty, impractical ideas. 'Let us pretend to be Bharata's men, enter the enemy camp and kill them.'

There was much boasting, bluster and bombastic language, much licking of lips at the thought of monkey flesh and the carnage to come.

And then rose the first voice of caution, from Vibhishana, Ravana's brother.

'One attacks when the enemy is vulnerable. They are now on guard. Who can gauge Hanuman's valour? Don't underestimate them. What wrong has Rama done? He punished Khara for doing grievous wrong, for overstepping limits. It was a defensive measure. Sita is a danger to us. She stands for the limits you are crossing, the limits set by dharma, by what is right. Give up this quarrel, for one cannot quarrel with dharma, and that is precisely what you are doing. Return Sita before this city is destroyed together with all its beauty and prosperity. I speak out of love for you. You are my brother.'

There was no response from Ravana to this long appeal. He merely dismissed his assembly and retired to his apartment.

But Vibhishana would not give up. He went to Ravana at daybreak, hoping he had given some thought to what he had said.

'Ever since Sita's arrival, I have noticed evil portents. The sacrifical fire burns less brightly, there are ants crawling in the offerings, serpents haunt the altars, horses neigh helplessly, cows give no milk, vultures screech and jackals howl at the city gates. . . . Give her up, I beg of you!'

Ravana deigned to reply: 'I see no reason at all for fear. Rama will not get Sita. I have defeated the gods themselves. How will Rama escape?'

Ravana was obsessed with Sita. He paid scant attention to anything else, even the impending war. His ministers and friends had to draw his attention to the affairs of state. 'Order the armies to assemble,' he said. 'I will address them.'

Facing the troops, he announced: 'I have courted Sita for a year now, but she persists in thinking only of Rama. War seems to be the only way to win her. Persuasion and patience have failed. I was only waiting for my brother Kumbhakarna to wake from his long sleep of six months. He has done so and is here now. There is nothing more to keep us. I know you will fight to win.'

Kumbhakarna was angry and rebellious and spoke out fearlessly. 'You went into this without consulting us and somewhat hastily, if I may say so. Now that you are in trouble, you expect unquestioning support. You pause to think after the act. It is a weakness that the enemy is bound to detect and make use of, sooner or later.' Ravana was seething inwardly but wisely for once, kept quiet. 'I will fight and fight to kill, while you sit here quaffing wine. You can have your Sita when I have dispatched Rama to the other world,' concluded Kumbhakarna with a sneer.

There were those who could not understand why Ravana hesitated to take Sita by force. His general, Mahaparshva, advised: 'Overpower Sita. Nothing should stand in the way of your pleasures, my lord.'

Ravana was in the mood for confession. 'A long time ago, I waylaid and seduced a heavenly nymph, on her way to Brahma, the creator. When she got to him, he guessed what had happened and cursed me: 'If ever you take a woman by force, your head will burst into a hundred pieces.' That is why I have to wait, mark my time. No one knows about this.'

Vibhishana repeated his warning. 'You harbour a deadly serpent. Its raised hoods are Sita's fingers; its venom, her fear. Return her to Rama.'

Indrajita was angry and rebuked his uncle. 'You are the only one who is afraid. Why do you spread this baseless fear? Even a single demon can finish them. You are naive. You will destroy yourself by giving unwelcome advice.'

Vibhishana felt helpless. He accused them in turn, saying: 'Your lord and benefactor is drowning in the dangerous ocean that is Rama. You should drag him out. Instead, you advise him to plunge headlong into it. Return Sita, I say again, with gifts and gestures of friendship.'

Ravana angrily put an end to their debate. 'Vibhishana, you envy my prosperity and success. Relatives are ever so. They conceal their true feelings and lie in wait, ready to betray. It is part of elephant lore and a well-known fact that one of the herd usually betrays them to the hunter.' He was harsh in in his condemnation of Vibhishana, piling insult upon insult. 'You are like a bee that takes its fill of honey from one flower, then flits to another. The waters of friendship and affection leave you dry and unaffected, just as droplets of moisture roll off a lotus leaf. If anyone else had spoken as you did, he would have been dead by now.'

Vibhishana could bear it no longer. 'Speakers of sweet falsehood are everywhere—speakers of bitter truth, rare. Even rarer are those who are willing to listen to them. I will not stand by and watch you court death and destruction.'

Vibhishana flew straight to Rama and Lakshmana, accompanied by four of his faithful followers. They hovered over the ocean, waiting to alight. Sugriva watched the five demons anxiously. 'They come with intent to kill,' he said. The monkeys pulled up trees and stood ready to attack.

Vibhishana spoke rapidly and directly, loudly enough for all to hear. 'Ravana is wicked. He abducted Sita and now holds her captive against her will. I am his younger brother, Vibhishana. I tried to stop him from leading us all to destruction. But he insulted and humiliated me and so I am here to seek Rama's protection. Inform him of our presence.' They made an impressive spectacle, richly adorned as they were. Vibhishana had all the marks and trappings of royalty.

Sugriva rushed to Rama, greatly agitated. 'He is a spy, sent to sow dissension and assess our weaknesses. We must kill him.'

Rama was calm and collected. 'What do you think?' he asked Sugriva's counsellors.

Angada's approach was less extreme than Sugriva's. 'We must examine him closely before accepting him.'

Jambavan advised: 'It is an unexpected arrival and must be treated with suspicion.'

Hanuman summed up the situation by saying: 'You know best, my lord, but here is my opinion for what it is worth. It is not easy to examine a stranger. An interrogation is likely to yield nothing and may even be resented. One can only draw inferences through conversation. Vibhishana seems too open to be a rogue and he has much to gain from us. He has chosen wisely and decided to change sides for the right reasons, at the right time. He aims to succeed Ravana, I think. He is being practical, and it suits us to accept him.'

Sugriva was still suspicious. 'He is a demon and a deserter. He has let down his brother in his hour of need. How can one ever rely on him?'

Rama defended him. 'There are times when kinsmen can be worse than enemies. He trusts us more than he trusts Ravana. He knows we don't covet his kingdom. He will do no harm. Above all, he has sought my protection. I will not turn him away. Ravana himself will get my protection if he throws himself at my mercy.'

Sugriva came round to his view. Vibhishana was given permission to descend, and granted an audience by Rama.

He fell at Rama's feet. 'Rama, you are the refuge of the world. I abandon my country, my family, my friends. You are my life, my happiness.'

Rama looked at him with his piercing eyes and testing him, said: 'What is the extent of Ravana's strength?'

Vibhishana began by telling him about the boon Ravana had from Brahma, because of which gods, demons and semi-divine creatures could not kill him. 'Younger than Ravana and elder to me is Kumbhakarna, equal to Indra in valour. Prahasta, who fought Shiva's powerful attendants, is his commander-in-chief. Ravana's eldest son, Indrajita, has the power of invisibility. He fights unseen. Mahodara, Mahaparshva and Akampana are his brave generals.'

Rama was satisfied. 'I will return to Ayodhya only when Ravana is killed and you are crowned king of Lanka,' he vowed.

He embraced Vibhishana. Then as proof of his intentions, he ordered Lakshmana: 'Fetch water from the sea. Let Vibhishana's coronation take place here. As far as I am concerned he is already king of Lanka, consecrated by you.'

Vibhishana and his followers were now part of Rama's army. Hanuman and Sugriva included him in their deliberations. 'Think of a way across. That should be our first concern.'

Vibhishana felt that Rama should ask the ocean to make way for the monkey army. 'A dividing of the waters is more than feasible. After all, the ocean was created by King Sagara of the Ikshvakus. He is bound to oblige his illustrious descendant, Rama.'

Everybody jumped at the idea. It had the merit of being a positive step towards action. The monkeys had been getting restive.

Rama was told of their plan. He put it before Sugriva and Lakshmana and asked them to decide. They were prompt in their approval. 'It seems an eminently sensible suggestion. Let us carry it out straightaway. Our troops will be in Lanka before we know it.'

Rama, full of the importance of the moment, walked to the seashore. Part of it was covered with sacred kusha grass. He would seek the help of the ocean, humbly and prayerfully. It was the first step in the long and arduous journey to his beloved Sita. There was much ground to be covered, yet.

In Lanka, Ravana's spy, Shardula, who had gone out to survey the area, reported: 'They seem like a second ocean, those waves of monkeys gathering on the opposite shore, waiting. It is time to send a message, work out strategies.'

Ravana sent Shuka with a message to Sugriva. 'Tell Sugriva he is a brother to me. Why is he getting involved? He should return to Kishkindha. The matter is between me and those two princes. Shuka took the form of a parrot and delivered the message. The monkeys attacked him and brought him down.

'Messengers should not be harmed,' protested Shuka.

'He is no messenger. He is a spy come to gauge our strength, take stock of our numbers. He should be killed.'

As the monkeys fell upon him, plucking at his wings and eyes, Shuka cried out for help. Rama intervened. 'Don't treat him too roughly. He is only acting under orders.'

Sugriva then gave Shuka his message for Ravana. 'Tell Ravana I owe him nothing. He is Rama's enemy and therefore, mine. He is going to be killed and Lanka destroyed. Remind him, too, of Jatayu's death.' Shuka, maimed and bruised, was relieved. He was a trembling mass of feathers, a heap of misery, as he waited for his release.

While the others were busy plotting and planning, Rama lay on his bed of kusha grass, his arm pillowing his head, facing the ocean. It was an arm that

had pillowed Sita, an arm marked by the taut bowstring drawn again and again to release his arrows in battle, a warrior's arm, an arm that protected, long and giving, far-reaching, comforting, powerful.

It was a lonely vigil. Three days and nights had passed and still the king of the oceans did not appear.

Rama's patience was at an end. He fumed: 'Humility does not pay. Good behaviour is mistaken for weakness. It is the arrogant and the aggressive that succeed. Such is the way of the world.

'It is time I shot my arrows into the waters. I will agitate and churn him till he is thrown into confusion and spills over his boundaries, his limits, and I shall dry him up. Both he and I will have crossed the limits of order, into the realm of chaos. There is no other way.' And he drew his bow.

Lakshmana tried to restrain him. 'Calm yourself. Anger is unseemly. It takes away from your powers, your energies. It is self-defeating.' But Rama ignored him, intent on teaching the tardy ocean a lesson.

There was instant chaos, a great din and clamour. Waves rose high as mountains, throwing up aquatic animals breathing fire and smoke in their distress. The winds roared and howled, the earth shook, throwing even the nether regions into confusion. And then the lord of the oceans rose from the waters, towering like a mountain of emerald, streaked with gold and glowing with his own marine wealth of precious gems. On his dark head he wore a crown of flowers. His handmaidens, the rivers of the world, stood round him in humble attendance.

He spoke to Rama in rumbling tones: 'The elements have each their own nature to which they must conform. I am, by nature, deep and difficult to cross. That is my character. I cannot dry up and disappear overnight to please you. You must understand. But I will make it possible for your monkeys to cross. You must calm down.'

Rama, somewhat contrite, said: 'My bow is drawn, an arrow is already in place. I have to aim. You tell me where.'

The ocean guided him. 'There is a tribe that pollutes my waters. They bother me. Use your arrow to destroy them.'

Rama did so. The sea withdrew from that spot, leaving a desert. The arrow also drew out springs and surrounding it, grass and trees began to sprout, and herbs of rare medicinal value. The ocean was pleased. He then advised Rama to have a bridge built.

'The monkey, Nala, is the son of Vishwakarma, the divine architect. He has been blessed by his father with special skills. He will bridge my waters.'

For five days, thousands of monkeys worked under Nala's guidance, using rocks, hills and trees. Nala designed tools and machines that made the job easy. The project was expertly handled. It was a magnificent structure, firm and strong enough to withstand the marching of the vast monkey armies. It streaked the dark and wavy sea, long, thin and glowing, like the parting in a woman's glossy hair.

The troops prepared to cross. Sugriva issued orders. 'Rama will mount Hanuman and Lakshmana will ride Angada.' They were in front, leading, with Sugriva. The rest followed, some marching, some flying, some swimming. It was a tumultous crossing and they roared louder even than the

sea. Reaching Lanka, they set up camp. The gods and celestials, silently and secretly blessed Rama, anointing him with water from the sea.

Rama saw portents that foretold danger to demons and monkeys alike. Stormy winds shook the earth, making it tremble; the clouds rained blood; the moon, beaming black and red, seemed to give out a message of doom.

'Let us not delay, Lakshmana. Let us attack this very day; for the war against unrighteousness brooks no delay. Form battalions, deploy the forces, let the generals take charge and prepare for instant action.'

Rama issued the instructions and selected the different leaders himself. They stood in the *purushavyuha* formation, taking on the lineaments of the human body. 'Angada and Nila, with their divisions, will be the chest. Rishabha will form and guard the right flank, Gandhamadana, the left. Jambavan and his assistants will occupy the belly area, Sugriva the hips. Lakshmana and I will be the head.'

Rama now ordered Shuka to be released. He could inform Ravana of their arrival for all Rama cared. Shaped, ordered and marshalled, the troops were in place and geared fully for battle, ready to face the lord of Lanka and his demon army.

Shuka was in a sorry state when he came back to Ravana and delivered Sugriva's message. 'I was beaten up and badly mauled and tied up, too. Rama is already here. They have built a bridge across the ocean. There is no prospect of peace. Return Sita or prepare for war. They are ready to go into battle immediately.'

Ravana was not in the least put out. 'My arrows will hover over them like bees over flowers in springtime.' He boasted: 'Rama is yet to hear the music that I make with the bow, my vina. He has not heard the groans of my enemies, the melody of death that sounds to the tune of my twanging bowstring. He has a lot to learn. None can conquer me.'

He wanted more details. 'I want to know their exact numbers. The bridge is an impressive feat. I want to know how they did it. Who are their most powerful leaders? Find out and let me know.'

Shuka and Sarana, both went, disguised as monkeys, to investigate. They lost count as they tracked the monkeys down through gorge and ravine, cave and peak. They were everywhere.

Vibhishana spotted them. They were captured and taken to Rama. In fear and trembling, they confessed. 'If you've finished your task of spying, you may leave,' said Rama, smiling, 'and if you've left out something, Vibhishana himself will show you round. Do not fear. Surrender, and you are safe.'

As they were leaving, he gave them his message for Ravana: 'Tomorrow, you shall taste my strength. Summon up the force that you used to carry away Sita, and turn it on me along with your demon armies, for you will see the fall of Lanka, arch, gateway and fort!'

Shuka and Sarana could could not help wishing Rama victory, so carried away were they by his magnanimity, his sense of justice. They returned to Ravana chastened by the thought of war with Rama. 'Rama and Lakshmana, aided by Sugriva and Vibhishana, can dislodge Lanka and establish it where they please, so powerful are they. Rama alone can destroy this city. Give up all thoughts of war, Ravana. Make peace. Return Sita.'

Ravana scoffed: 'It is personal suffering that makes you say this. They have softened you up with rough handling, that's all.'

He ascended the terrace of his mansion to look out on the assembled army, now within sight. 'Point them out, individually—the warriors, the princes and the leaders, Sarana.'

Sarana began: 'That one, roaring, is the chief of them all, the commander, Nila. That one there, lashing his tail, standing tall and red, is Vali's son, Sugriva's heir apparent, Angada. And there is Nala, who built the bridge across the ocean. . . Hanuman. . .Panasa . . . Vinata . . . Kesari, monkeys of all colours and kinds, united under one banner, the banner of Rama and dharma, righteousness.' Ravana's eyes narrowed with concentration as he looked into the distance. 'There is Rama, dark and wide-eyed—scholar, prince and warrior, the hero of Janasthana, come to retrieve his lovely wife.' Sarana's voice broke slightly as he remembered Rama's leniency to him. 'On his right is Lakshmana, Rama's younger brother, a seasoned warrior, accustomed to victory. He, too, has sworn to exterminate you!' Shuka recalled the great strength of Lakshmana waiting to burst its bounds.

'Vibhishana, you can see. Rama has crowned him king of Lanka, in anticipation.' Sarana glanced nervously at Ravana, and looked quickly away as he saw his eyes flash terror.

'Near him is Sugriva. He wears a golden necklace of lotuses in which Lakshmi dwells, guarding his prosperity. It passed from Vali to him, when Rama killed Vali and made Sugriva king of Kishkindha.

'It is an army that runs into millions of monkeys ready to die for Rama, Sugriva and the cause. You will have to defeat them. It is not going to be easy.'

Ravana could see that. The thought depressed him but he reacted angrily when the truth was spoken so plainly.

'You dare stand before me and sing Rama's praises! You are men of little learning who have been taught much by great preceptors. You are poor politicians, indeed, to risk a king's anger—it burns more fiercely than a forest fire. I let you off lightly only because of your past services.' Shuka and Sarana made a hasty salutation and vanished.

Ravana sent out another spy, Shardula. He came back, beaten and bleeding. His information was even more alarming. 'Their lineage is impressive. Sushena, son of Dharma . . . Dadimukha, son of Soma, the moon . . . Nila, son of Agni, lord of fire . . . Hanuman, son of Vayu, the wind god . . . Jyotimukha, son of Surya, the sun god . . . Hemakoota, son of Varuna, lord of the waters . . . and the five sons of Yama, god of death. There is much food for thought here, my lord.'

This time, Ravana did not rail at his informer. He sat in consultation and then entered his palace, preoccupied. Rama had to be tackled with more than just strength. He sent for one of his demons, skilled in creating hallucinations. 'Produce two things immediately. Rama's head and his bow and arrows.'

He went to Sita with these. 'The woman has to be frightened into submission. That should settle matters satisfactorily between

Rama and myself,' he gloated.

With a great shout of joy, he announced: 'Rama has been killed in battle. Now, at least, succumb and be mine, you arrogant, headstrong woman. Do you want to know how he met his end? Listen, then.' There was mockery in his tone. 'They reached here at midnight exhausted, and fell asleep. Prahasta cut off his head in his sleep. The great Rama! He was caught napping. Ha! Ha!'

Sita sat dazed, not responding. 'Vibhishana has been captured, Sugriva and Hanuman killed. Lakshmana is desperate.'

He watched her closely. The words were having an effect. 'They have been routed, utterly.' He called out to his magician. 'Put the head in front of her, bleeding and covered with dust. And his bow and arrow too. Seeing is believing,' he finished, heartlessly.

Sita nearly fainted with shock and grief. She wept and mourned aloud: 'How were you vanquished so easily, my lord? Kaikeyi has had her way. Kill me, Ravana, so that I may join my Rama.'

Ravana left, summoned urgently by Prahasta. Rama's head, his bow and arrows also vanished mysteriously, but Sita was too distraught to notice. One of her guards, Sarama, consoled her, soothing her with sweet words. She had grown quite fond of Sita. Raising her gently, she said: 'How could a man like Rama be killed while asleep? This is a trick of Ravana's. Rama will emerge victorious, believe me.'

Sita looked at her hopefully and Sarama said encouragingly: 'Listen to the roar of the army pouring in, the trumpeting of elephants, the clash of armour. They are flooding the highways of Lanka like a storm-tossed sea.'

Sarama drew a vivid picture of them together, and watched Sita's face soften. 'You will rest your head in Rama's lap, shed tears of joy clasped to his breast as he gathers your trailing tresses in his hands and binds them himself.' Her kindness worked wonders. Sita rallied round.

Sarama offered to take a message to Rama. 'I move swifter than the wind. I would like to give Rama news of you.'

'I would like to first know what is in Ravana's mind, what he intends to do with me,' said Sita.

'He refuses to give you up. Even his mother's pleas have failed. War seems inevitable.'

The two women, one a human, the other a demon, felt a common bond of sympathy as Sita blamed herself for the needless destruction to come. It was her obstinacy, her whim that had led to all this. Her heart went out to Rama and all the others who had been drawn into this whirlpool of circumstance and destiny.

Ravana got his counsellors together for a final consultation. 'You have been praising Rama, overawed by his strength and resources. You are underestimating your own strength.' He had to do something to raise their flagging spirits although he himself was a little shaken.

His great-uncle, Malyavan, spoke first. 'It's a question of time and circumstance. A king should gauge these accurately before attempting war. Peace makes sense to me, at this juncture. The gods themselves are in league with Rama. Let me tell you why.' Malyavan had the privilege of age and seniority, so he went on without interruption from Ravana. 'Through the ages there has been this conflict, the conflict between right and wrong, good and evil. By choosing the path of evil you have alienated the celestials and sages. The smoke of their sacrificial fires clouds your fate.'

Ravana blustered: 'Have you been bribed by the enemy to praise him and defame me? Rama is a mere human, leading a bunch of monkeys for an army. Bridge across the ocean, indeed! He has crossed the bridge of no return, that much I can see, and so should you!'

Malyavan despaired, but as an elder and kinsman, he blessed him and wished him luck.

Consultations were on in Rama's camp, too. Vibhishana had sent his ministers into the city and was giving Rama an idea of Ravana's forces and their deployment. 'We must match our fighting strengths with theirs, pit our best men against their best. Careful planning is called for.'

Using his information, Rama gave the final instructions. 'Let Nila take on Prahasta at the eastern gate; let Angada tackle Mahaparshva; stand Mahodara at the southern end. Hanuman should storm the western entrance and confront Indrajita. The northern gate is the main entrance which Ravana himself handles. I will wait there for him. Sugriva, Jambavan and Vibhishana will occupy the centre and hold it.'

The gravity of war was beginning to cast its shadow on the army. They were tensed to meet the occasion head-on, hoping, each one, to rise gloriously to it.

There was one last strategy. 'Only seven of us will fight in the human form—Lakshmana, Vibhishana, his four ministers and myself. The rest should remain monkeys so that we can spot them easily in the enemy ranks when the battle starts.'

Rama's eyes were great pools of blessing and prayer as he dismissed his troops.

They stationed themselves on Mount Suvela from where they could get a clear view of Lanka. They marvelled at the beauty of that city built on the Trikuta mountain, its golden ramparts topped by a dark ring of demon guards. They spent the night thus, waiting for the dawn and the outbreak of war.

10

Storming the Gates

At break of day, Lanka was etched clearly against the brightening sky. Rama and Sugriva climbed to the very top of Mount Suvela for a better view. They saw Ravana, resplendent, on the terrace of his mansion, under the canopy of royalty, dressed in scarlet robes.

Sugriva, looking at him, suddenly lost control of himself. In one bounding leap he stood before Ravana, heedless of the consequences. 'I am Sugriva, friend of Rama,' he said to the astonished Ravana, as he snatched his crown, flung it to the ground and attacked him savagely.

Ravana picked him up and threw him like a ball, but he bounced back at him. They fought like wild cats. When Ravana showed signs of exhaustion, Sugriva flew up and away, satisfied. It was his first skirmish with the demons and it had not gone too badly. They were both wounded and bleeding, but he had given as much as he had got.

When he returned, Rama rebuked him mildly. 'You rushed off without consulting me. I was worried that something would happen to you. Besides, things must go according to plan. I have to kill Ravana, free Sita and crown Vibhishana. These are my appointed tasks.'

Sugriva was repentant. 'When I saw Ravana basking in all that splendour and glory, I lost control. I am sorry.'

Rama, too, was getting impatient. 'We must attack speedily, especially since the enemy is now on the alert.'

Descending, he gave the signal to advance. They were soon at the gates and took up the positions assigned to them earlier by Rama. The monkeys seemed to settle around that golden city like great clouds of moths round a flame.

It was time that one of their own ambassadors carried a message to Ravana. Rama summoned Angada. 'Tell Ravana he must prepare to receive the rod of punishment that I wield. Tell him to choose a site and get it ready for his funeral rites.'

Angada flew to Ravana's court, delivered the message and threatened the ten-headed demon with dire consequences.

'Kill him,' ordered Ravana. 'He is a nuisance.' Four demons closed in on him, two on either side, and caught hold of his arms. He jerked upright and rose into the air like a bird and they fell to the ground with a mighty thud, as their hold loosened with the force of his ascent. Then, as a parting shot, with Ravana watching, he kicked at the top of his palace, toppling part of its roof.

The monkeys were now in full control. They rushed about pulling up trees, picking up rocks, gnashing their teeth, flailing their arms, lashing their tails. The storm winds of war had begun to blow. Lanka was under heavy siege.

Ravana was getting quite concerned as reports of their activities reached his ears. Battle-cries of victory to Rama, Lakshmana and Sugriva were heard as Ravana's golden trumpets and conches were blown in loud blasts of angry protest. The gates were stormed. The war had started in real earnest. They fought in groups as well as singly. Bodies came floating down rivers of blood like logs, tufts of hair and monkey-fur clinging to them, moss-like.

Rama was attacked by four demons simultaneously. He killed them all at once with four arrows. After that six of them fell upon him and he killed all six together with six arrows aimed straight and fast.

The monkeys used trees, rocks and stones, tooth, nail and claw—tearing, crushing, biting. Sunset reddened the sky. Dusk was followed by the darkness of night. The bloodthirsty demons fought on, though it was difficult to spot the enemy. Rama's arrows flew about, piercing the gloom with their glowing tips like a net of golden fireflies. Angada had singled Indrajita out and they fought a long and bloody duel.

Indrajita's chariot was smashed, his horses killed. He himself felt faint with exhaustion. At that moment, using his god-given powers, he became invisible. Angada and the monkeys rejoiced, thinking he had retreated. But he began to work unseen, attacking Rama and Lakshmana with his magic powers till they were trapped in a mesh of arrows, charged with the serpent spell, and could no longer move.

Rama suspected trickery and quickly sent out monkeys in all directions to look for Indrajita. They flew with the speed of wind but were chased and brought down by missiles that flew even faster.

'Even Indra cannot trace me, now that I am invisible. How can you?' he jeered, as they stood helpless, paralysed by his spell-binding powers. They were bleeding from every pore and fell on a bed of arrows that rained down on them, Rama first and then, Lakshmana.

There was panic amongst the monkeys. They grieved and began to despair, thinking their heroic leaders to be dead, while the demons redoubled their attacks.

Indrajita boasted: 'I have laid low the killers of Khara and Dushana.'

Vibhishana told Sugriva not to lose heart. 'Battles take strange turns and victory is elusive. I assure you the two brothers are not dead. They will regain consciousness. Guard their bodies well; see that no harm comes to them.'

Sugriva was weeping like a child. Vibhishana bathed his eyes, comforted him and advised: 'The army is losing courage. That would be fatal. We must somehow keep their spirits up. You must move about whispering the truth in their ears. I shall also spread the word, counter the rumours that might unnerve and weaken the rank and file.'

Vibhishana pricked up his ears. He could hear the shouts of triumph that rent the air as the demons rejoiced over the death of Rama and Lakshmana. Mingled with their cries of delight were the whispers, moans and groans of the monkeys. 'Quick, Sugriva, before panic grips our troops. Let us move

fast, or they might begin to retreat.'

And they went about swiftly, secretly, getting the monkeys back into fighting fitness, reminding, promising, supporting.

Indrajita went to Ravana with the good news. The young warrior, puffed up with pride, announced triumphantly: 'Rama and Lakshmana are dead. Our work is almost done.'

Ravana embraced his son, and praised him lavishly. His thoughts flew to Sita. He sent for the demon women who were guarding Sita in the royal pleasure gardens. 'Tell her that Rama and Lakshmana are dead, killed by Indrajita. Take her up in my aerial chariot, Pushpaka, and show her their corpses.'

He would have her yet, he thought, with great relish. She would come to him, adorned and glowing, free of fear, liberated from the bonds of marriage that had tied her down to Rama. 'She will come to me in all her loveliness,' he fantasized, as desire quickened his pulse and coursed through his demon veins.

The demons got Pushpaka ready and Sita was paraded round the city by Ravana himself. She saw flags and pennants flying and banners streaming in celebration, for Ravana had already announced the death of Rama and Lakshmana.

Sita was next taken up in Pushpaka to view the ravages of battle. She was alone with Trijata, the female demon who had earlier shown her some kindness and consideration. It was a fearsome sight. There were bloodied corpses everywhere, dismembered bodies were strewn about. Monkeys huddled in groups confused, or ran about in distress. Sita saw Rama and Lakshmana, still and lifeless on their bed of arrows, their beautiful bodies slashed with gaping wounds.

'What is the use of all those predictions of glory for me? Where are the astrologers now? I was to be a queen, or so they said, looking at my feet marked with the lotus. There were no signs of widowhood, they had promised.

'I am blessed from top to toe with auspicious marks, they had declared, after careful scrutiny. My hair is fine, soft and dark, my eyebrows do not meet, my teeth are evenly spaced, my skin pearly and smooth with a touch of soft down and no hair. I am well proportioned, and have the slow, languorous smile of the fortunate . . . or so they said!

'All false,' she lamented, 'everything is false, a bunch of untruths in which I had so much faith, so foolishly.' Sita broke down and sobbed hysterically, inconsolably.

Trijata was staring fixedly at the bodies of Rama and Lakshmana while she tried at the same time to calm Sita. She took Sita in her arms and comforted her. 'Listen to me. Your husband is not dead, nor is your brother-in-law. They are only unconscious. Let me tell you why.

'Look at the play of expression on their faces—anger, eagerness, joy. A dead man's face is blank and expressionless. Secondly, Pushpaka is a divine vehicle and would allow no ill-fated being to ride in it. It will never be shadowed by misery and sorrow. So all must be well with you and Rama. Thirdly, do you see how carefully they are guarding the bodies? There must be signs of life. Who would watch over two corpses like that? And fourthly, I would not lie to you, of all people. Your character and behaviour have impressed me right from the start. You must believe me. I know death when I see it.'

Sita stopped crying though she was deeply disturbed at the sight of Rama and Lakshmana lying pale and wounded. She yearned to tend their wounds, nurse them back to health and give them both the welcome due to heroes.

Rama was the first to regain consciousness. In a daze he looked round and saw Lakshmana. 'As you followed me to the forest, I will follow you to the land of death.' He was heartbroken as he remembered Lakshmana's great love for him, his loyalty and obedience. 'I must say farewell. Sugriva, go back to Kishkindha. I do not want to fight any more.' Vibishana returned just then and he overheard Rama.

'You are letting me down. You promised me the throne of Lanka. I tell you, Lakshmana is alive. These are all tricks.' But Rama had slipped back into unconsciousness.

It was a grave crisis indeed, the gravest they had faced up to then. Sugriva took matters firmly in hand. 'Vibhishana, you shall have your kingdom. Rama and Lakshmana, too, will revive, I have been told, when the eagle Garuda arrives.' He put Sushena, Tara's father, in charge of the monkeys. 'You lead the monkeys back home and take Rama and Lakshmana with you. I will kill Ravana and bring Sita back.'

Sushena had a more practical suggestion. 'I know from past experience that Brihaspati, teacher of the gods, used herbs from a region near the legendary ocean of milk to revive the unconscious. The monkeys can identify those herbs, I know for sure. Let us not waste any more time.'

As they stood thus, debating and uncertain of what to do next, there was a great rush of air. Huge trees leaned over and fell into the ocean. There was a hissing scurry of snakes as they slid past in vast numbers and vanished into the waters. To their amazement, the serpent power that bound the two brothers began to loosen its hold.

Garuda, mighty eagle, dread enemy of snakes, had landed. He came close and stroked their bodies, caressed their faces, and they were free of their bonds, their wounds healed, their skin glowing and golden once more, their power and energy revived.

'Who are you?' said Rama as Garuda embraced him.

'I am your friend. Perhaps I am more than that, your very life-breath. Those were serpents turned to bonds through incantations. They would have squeezed the life out of you. I came the moment I heard.'

His eagle eyes glowed with love and reverence. 'You will return victorious with Sita and then you will know more about me and my feeling for you. For now, I wish you well.' Garuda rose, and taking the aerial path reserved for eagles, flew away.

With their leadership restored, the monkeys went into a flurry of activity. They chattered, squealed and roared with delight, resuming their positions, returning to the attack. Where all had been quiet and subdued before, there was a rising tide of revelry.

The sounds reached Ravana. He could sense the jubilation even at that

distance. 'Rama is powerless, virtually dead. In fact, they think he is dead. What are they celebrating then?' he thought uneasily.

He told his minister to find out. And there, like apparitions of hope, were the two brothers, wholly revived and ready to take on the demons. The messengers ran back to tell Ravana. 'If they can free themselves of those serpent fetters, charged with deadly magic, then Lanka is truly in danger.' His face paled with the first hint of fear. He sent for his general, Dhumraksha. 'The war is on. Kill Rama . . . .'

Rama stood surveying the demon ranks, watching each warrior fall and getting to know the greatness of each from Vibhishana—Akampana, Indrajita, Atikaya . . . Nikumbha, Narantaka . . . .

Dhumraksha set out in his golden chariot confident of victory but bad omens clouded his hopes. A headless body dripping blood came tumbling down to earth, and vultures perched on his banner and chariot.

Dhumraksha had to deal with Hanuman who attacked him, rock in hand. His chariot lay shattered and Hanuman then broke his skull, crushing it with a mountain peak. One by one, the strongest demons were sent forth. Each one was met by his equal in valour, and each one, after a bloody duel, succumbed. First Vajradanshtra, slain by Angada; then, Akampana who slew the monkeys in hundreds and threw the whole army into confusion. He was killed by Hanuman. Then came Prahasta's turn. Rama killed four stalwarts in a row; this maddened Prahasta and he fought with a fury that turned out to be his death. For the great monkey snatched up a rock and hurled it to crush him. It found its mark. With the death of Prahasta, the demon army had sustained a major loss. Ravana acknowledging the seriousness of the situation, decided to enter the fray.

'Guard the city, keep careful watch over its point of entry, its highways, and the palace. They will push their advantage, make inroads, knowing I am no longer within the gates. I have to take them on myself now, before they break your spirit and your strength. Many of our bravest have already fallen.'

Rama spotted Ravana as he rose into view like a mountain of fury. His royal white canopy shaded his ten heads, his earrings swung golden against his expansive cheeks as he rode into battle, regal and overbearing. Rama witnessed fear rippling, then spreading and deepening into great currents, agitating the sea of battling monkeys. Tidal waves of panic threatened to swamp them as his dazzling presence blinded and took them by storm.

'What splendour strides here,' thought Rama. 'He is the rising sun of destruction, blinding, scorching.'

And then the sorrow and the anger of the past months welled up, flooding his heart and hardening it. He too felt within him the rise of terror and destruction to come. It washed over him in waves of grim determination.

'He comes to slake my thirst for revenge, to ease my throat, parched with longing for Sita. I shall wipe out the wrong of her abduction even as I wipe him off the face of this earth, the wretch. He is doomed.'

The first one to confront Ravana was Sugriva, who rushed at him with a mountain peak covered with giant trees. He hurled it with great force but Ravana's shower of golden arrows splintered it into fragments. Greatly incensed, Ravana chose a serpent arrow and aimed it at Sugriva, wounding him.

Lakshmana next undertook to fight Ravana. 'Give me permission to finish him.' Rama asked him to go ahead, blessing him. 'May your valour be more than his. Look out for his weak points and be careful to hide your own. You need your eyes as much as your weapons when you face an opponent as formidable as Ravana. Go!'

In the meantime, Hanuman and Nila began to attack Ravana. After an initial skirmish or two, Nila became quite small and jumped on to Ravana's banner. From there he leapt across to his bow and then on to his diadem. Ravana visibly flinched at this impertinence. Back and forth, up and down Nila went,throwing the demon king into a state of confusion and irritation, while the monkeys stood around, laughing and jeering.

It was a funny sight. The great warrior was reduced to a scrambling figure of fun as his twenty arms thrashed out, trying to catch hold of the agile little monkey who eluded his grasp every time.

When Nila finally fell, struck by an arrow, Ravana turned to find Lakshmana challenging him to a fight. 'Good sense deserts those about to die, else you would not challenge me,' said Ravana.

'Stop bragging and fight,' retorted Lakshmana, 'I am waiting.'

Ravana's reply was prompt. Seven plumed arrows flew at Lakshmana who brought them down expertly. It was an equal fight. Ravana fainted once, but recovered and hurled his deadliest weapon at Lakshmana who tried to ward it off. It wounded him in the chest and he swooned.

Hanuman, who was standing by, threw himself on Ravana and struck him a mighty blow on the chest. 'Out with your ugly soul, I say. It has lodged too long in your body.'

The demon lost his balance and fell, blood spouting from all his mouths, ears and eyes. He went rolling in the dust and lay under his own chariot, unconscious. Hanuman lifted Lakshmana gently and took him to Rama.

At the sight of his brother, Rama was spurred to instant action. By his side, unfailing, burning with love and devotion, was Hanuman, eager to serve. The moment was now at hand when Ravana would face his destiny. Hanuman and Lakshmana had only prepared the way.

'Mount my shoulders,' said Hanuman, bending low in a gesture of surrender to his hero, Rama. Ravana, regaining consciousness, staggered to a standing position, bloodied, dreadful and ready to fight once again.

'Don't run away. You must face the man who destroyed fourteen thousand of your tribe in Janasthana.' Before Ravana could say a word, Rama shattered, one after the other, his chariot, his arrows, his bow, his glittering crown.

As Ravana stood there, head bare, and humbled, Rama said: 'I will not attack you now, evil as you are. You are exhausted with the day's fighting. Go home, rest, recover your normal vigour and strength and come back, fully armed, riding a chariot. I will fight you then.'

Time and circumstance were gathering speed, racing inexorably towards their appointed moment. The great patterns of destiny were being drawn, directed by Rama. All things out of place or missing would soon be in position, and dharma would once again be intact, in working order.

Ravana turned back without a word. Gladness spread in the heavens, for

the tide of events was turning too. Ravana was beginning to sense, if not defeat, at least the uncertainty of victory.

It was a sad king who addressed his court that day. 'All my penance, even Brahma's boon, is of no use to me. I am not immune to human or animal attack. In my arrogance, I did not see the chinks in my armour.

'But don't lose heart. You have only to be extra watchful, fight extra hard. Victory will be ours yet. Wake Kumbhakarna up. That brother of mine sleeps for months at a stretch. He has just gone to sleep nine days ago, after our last meeting. He is our only hope.'

The demons went to the cave where Kumbhakarna slept, dead to the world. They took offerings of food, flowers and incense. The whole place reeked of blood and marrow, for Kumbhakarna consumed mountains of flesh when he was awake. It was not going to be easy. His breath blew them right out, as soon as they entered. It was quite a struggle to fight their way in, to keep their feet on the ground.

They first spread out the food they had brought—huge pitchers of blood, heaps of deers, buffaloes and boars. Then they smeared him with sandal paste, watching his crowned head in terror as his nostrils flared out with every breath. After that they pounded him with pestles, maces and rocks to the incessant blowing of conches and beating of gongs and drums.

There was not a stir out of him. His breath played havoc with them, throwing them about till they were worn out with the effort of staying upright. Ten thousand demons roared, animals were beaten and goaded into howling and groaning aloud. The whole of Lanka woke up with the noise but Kumbhakarna slept on.

They hit him with huge logs. They pulled his ears, poured pots of water

into them, tugged at his hair, bit him, lashed and whipped him.

Kumbhakarna still slept on.

They were beginning to despair. What could they do? What would they tell Ravana? He had said it was imperative to have him awake and battling for Lanka.

They stepped up their efforts. A thousand elephants went trampling over him. And he moved, ever so slightly, as if something had brushed against him lightly.

'He stirs, he stirs,' they cried, as a gaping yawn set off a minor cyclone in the cave.

Kumbhakarna sat up and looked hungrily at the food, which vanished in seconds as he gobbled it all up. He glowered at them: 'Why have you disturbed me? I hope the king is well... he couldn't be, otherwise he would have let me sleep in peace,' he grumbled.

They spoke all at once: 'Fear stalks Lanka, fear of a human being. Lanka is besieged and beleaguered by his monkeys.'

There was a moment's silence as they waited for Kumbhakarna to absorb this unpleasant news; for worse to follow. 'Rama has struck Ravana and let him off, asking him to return armed!'

Kumbhakarna was wide awake now. 'The dead demons will have gory libations and I myself will drink quantities of Rama's blood,' he roared, ready to go.

Drinking a thousand pitchers of wine to quench his thirst, Kumbhakarna went towards Ravana's palace for clear instructions before proceeding to the battlefield.

The monkeys outside the gates, scanning the city from treetop and hillside, scattered in fear as they saw him stride along the highway. Rama questioned Vibhishana. 'Who is scaring the monkeys so?'

Vibhishana looked into the distance. 'I can't see him yet, but it must be my brother Kumbhakarna.' And he told Rama about his brother's great strength and his one handicap.

He had been a problem child. Even as an infant he was terrible. He used to swallow everyone in sight and was cursed with an insatiable appetite. Indra was worried and went complaining to Brahma.

'If Kumbhakarna is allowed to go on like this the world will soon be depopulated and desolate.' Then, mounting his elephant, Airavata, he attacked him. But Kumbhakarna plucked out Airavata's tusk and struck Indra on the chest with it.

Brahma cursed the demon child: 'From today he will sleep like one dead. Your subjects will be safe, Indra!'

Ravana intervened and pleaded. 'He is your grandson. You must use less extreme measures of control. Let him have a few waking hours.'

Brahma thought for a minute. 'Well, then, he will sleep for six months or so at a stretch and wake for just one day before he falls asleep for another long stretch. But in that one day, he will go about eating ravenously and indiscriminately, like a raging fire.'

Vibhishana advised Rama: 'Let the monkeys be told he is a machine and that they should all gather at the gates ready to counter this deadly device.'

'Yes,' agreed Rama. 'If the mere sight of him at a distance is terrifying to them, what will happen to them when he actually starts fighting? I dread to think.' And the monkeys gathered, confused and frightened, ready to attack this mechanical being, armed with rocks and stones and uprooted trees.

Kumbhakarna reached Ravana's palace and was granted audience in the throne room. 'What is it that you fear?' he demanded to know.

'I fear a man, Rama, son of Dasharatha. He and his ocean of monkeys have overrun the woods and groves of Lanka. My dear brother, you must save us!'

Kumbhakarna mocked! 'You act first and repent later. You are reaping the fruit of your misdeeds. No advice was good enough for you—not your wife's, not Vibhishana's.'

Ravana reacted angrily, 'I am your elder brother. I should command the respect due to a father and a guru. Instead, you preach to me! This is a time when you should go without question, extend support without conditions.'

But Ravana was a changed person. In an unprecedented gesture of humility, he confessed: 'Perhaps I was deluded by blind desire into this folly, but can't you use your strength to retrieve my losses, save my skin and my honour? Is that asking too much? You are a brother and a friend. Act like one!'

Kumbhakarna thought it expedient to humour him. He changed his tune. 'Calm yourself. Rama will be killed and his head will be brought to you. I shall destroy the monkeys and save the demons, never fear!'

Mahodara, a wise and experienced demon, rebuked Kumbhakarna. 'You prate like a foolish creature. And you overestimate your valour. How can you, single handed, kill Rama, destroyer of Janasthana!'

He suggested to Ravana that five of them should attack Rama simultaneously. 'If we succeed, well and good. If we fail, we can pretend we have won and celebrate. Sita will yield. Straight fighting will get you nowhere in my opinion. We must resort to tricks.'

It was an eloquent plea, but Kumbhakarna's conceit and Ravana's folly won the day. Ravana decked him in finery from top to toe and wishing him well, sent him off with an armed escort. Kumbhakarna loomed against the sky, gigantic, terrifying, his great nostrils twitching at the scent of blood, his valour rising at the thought of battle.

There was panic in the monkey ranks and even talk of flight and retreat.

'Your wives will laugh at you. . . after all your boasting. . . . 'Angada reminded them.

The monkeys were past caring. Dignity seemed a poor exchange for life. 'We don't want to die yet,' they said.

Angada somehow managed to bring them round to his way of thinking and they steeled themselves to the battle ahead. It was a day of death and much loss to the simian armies. Kumbhakarna destroyed them in thousands. He picked them up in clusters and devoured them. The smaller ones, whom he swallowed whole, escaped and came spilling out of his nose and ears. It was a grim and amusing sight.

The monkeys attacked him with no effect. Even Hanuman only managed to break his spear. That did not deter Kumbhakarna. He knocked Sugriva unconscious and lifting him up, walked towards Lanka, triumphant. 'I have got their king. They will now disperse and retreat,' he thought as he walked on, accepting the cheers and the welcoming showers of blossom. The city was celebrating. The gloom had lifted.

Hanuman was in a quandary. 'I could rescue Sugriva but that will hurt his pride. He is only unconscious. He would prefer to save himself. Let me not risk his displeasure.'

The flowers, the fresh air and the shouts revived Sugriva. Quickly and with no warning he attacked Kumbhakarna, tearing at his nose, his ears.

Kumbhakarna dashed him to the ground in a fit of fury and Sugriva, bouncing up, flew straight back to Rama.

The monkeys looked at Kumbhakarna in fear and disgust. He was so intoxicated with the sight and smell of blood that he grabbed monkeys and demons alike, swallowing, biting, crunching.

The end was near. Rama stood before him. 'I have come to kill you.' The huge form of Kumbhakarna shook and swayed with laughter.

But not for long. He brandished his mace at Rama only to have his arm chopped off with an arrow. He plucked up a tree with his other hand. Rama sliced that hand off too. As Kumbhakarna rushed at him, Rama cut off both his feet with a crescent-shaped arrow. The demon opened his mouth wide in a roar of pain and anger, only to have it stopped with arrows. As he stumbled closer, Rama chose a final weapon and aiming it carefully, cut off Kumbhakarna's head.

It was a gigantic head. It went spinning over Lanka, toppling many a high mansion before it came to rest. The headless, limbless body keeled over and fell into the sea with a loud splash.

Kumbhakarna, high hope of Lanka, was dead.

The news of Kumbhakarna's death broke Ravana's spirit. He had pinned all his hopes on him.

'Life is now empty of joy, of hope. Lanka, even Sita, is of no consequence.' Self-pity took over, and vain regret. 'I am paying for my sins. I should have listened to Vibhishana,' he sighed.

But all was not lost. He still had a cordon of strength round him in his sons, his remaining brothers and his uncles. For Ravana had four sons besides Indrajita, two brothers other than Vibhishana and Kumbhakarna, and two valiant uncles. They encircled him like a halo of light and hope for the future. He could still bask in their glory, for they were all blessed by the gods, all tried and proven in past battles, emerging invincible, victorious. When he sat amongst them his hopes rose and confidence came flooding back into his battered heart, giving him courage.

As it turned out, he was clutching at straws. In a few fierce bouts of single combat with Angada, Hanuman and Lakshmana, they all perished. It was a battle of wits, fought with strange ammunition full of divine powers. Both sides brought out their secret weapons to startle and surprise the enemy. Warrior matched warrior, strategy countered strategy, but the demons were showing signs of strain.

Ravana sat chanting the names of the brave dead like a litany of despair. He wept for his sons and was beginning, finally, to get the true measure of the enemy. 'Rama must be powerful indeed, and tireless. Our strengths are failing. . . .' Orders were given for increased vigilance at all times. He could feel the enemy pressing in.

Indrajita was still alive. He watched his father's hopes falling, his courage failing. 'You don't have to worry, father. Rama will surrender to me before the day is done.'

He performed special rites for the use of Brahma's missile; chanting mantras over his bow, his arrows, his chariot. The sacrificial fire flared, smokeless, auguring victory. The sun, the moon, the stars could feel the vibrations of the powers that Indrajita was drawing towards him, and trembled. The session of prayers and meditation over, he rose into the air in his chariot and donned the magic mantle of invisibility. And the slaughter of the monkeys began. Nila, Angada, Sugriva, Hanuman, as well as old Jambavan, were severely wounded.

Rama sensed his presence. 'That must be Indrajita, moving unseen. And now he is using the weapon of Brahma. When it strikes us, do not panic,' he told Lakshmana. 'Just give in to its power. Thinking us dead, Indrajita will leave for the city, rejoicing. Ravana will relax his guard and then we will get our opportunity.'

And so it happened. Rama and Lakshmana were struck down and fell unconscious. The monkeys began to disperse in confusion and Indrajita turned back to give his anxious father the glad gidings. The monkey leaders stood around unwilling to take any action. Their guiding force had been withdrawn and they felt powerless.

Vibhishana had to reassure them. 'They are not dead. They have received the Brahma missile as a mark of respect to the Creator, I am convinced.'

Hanuman was the first to respond. 'Let us go round and comfort the others before they leave the field, and attend to those who are bleeding and maimed.' They went through the sea of wounded monkeys. Hanuman was looking for Jambavan. Vibhishana saw him, weakened by loss of blood and breath.

'Vibhishana, you are still alive! I am glad. Is Hanuman all right?'

Vibhishana was curious. 'You don't ask after Rama, Lakshmana, Angada or even Sugriva. You are concerned only about Hanuman. Why is that?'

Jambavan answered in a voice soft with love. 'I ask after him for he is all in all. On him hinges everything. If he lives, we survive. If he dies, we are lost.' Just then Hanuman appeared. There was a touching bond of affection and mutual admiration that linked the two, the powerful son of Vayu and the wise old bear. There was faith, too, and great respect. 'Listen, Hanuman. Fly over sea and land to the far Himalayas, keeping a look-out for the golden peak of Mount Rishabha, and Kailasa.' Jambavan's voice was getting fainter. 'Between those two landmarks, splendid and shining, stands a mountain of medicinal herbs.' Hanuman bent low. 'You must look for four glowing plants, so bright that you cannot miss them. Gather those, for they will revive Rama and Lakshmana.'

Hanuman barely waited for him to finish. He grew in size and raced across the skies, his eyes scanning the earth below. He passed the houses of the gods, the centre of the earth and the hallowed spot where all creation began. He spotted the mountain of herbs, but the plants, knowing he had come to gather them, stopped glowing and went into hiding.

Hanuman could not wait. He tore off the whole peak and holding it aloft, started his return flight, following the sun which lit up the peak with its shining minerals and glowing herbs and bathed Hanuman in a fiery wash of colours. It was as if, blessed by the sun god, a jewelled orb fashioned in his own image, fired sky and earth and poured liquid gold over the sea.

When Hanuman landed, the fragrance of the aromatic herbs spread, healing the monkeys, wounded as well as dead. They began to move and

stretch and glory in life renewed, as they took deep, reviving breaths. Rama and Lakshmana too opened their eyes to the welcome sight of a whole army back in action. And Hanuman got ready to fly back with the mountain of magic herbs.

As for the dead demons, they had been flung into the sea and were therefore denied the healing draughts of medicated air. Fortune did seem to frown on Ravana.

Sugriva consulted with Hanuman and they decided that Ravana would be in no mood to fight. His armies had taken a severe beating and four of his brave sons were dead. Now was the time to attack Lanka. 'We should order the armies to storm the fortifications.'

The monkeys rushed and the demons fled leaping from turret to terrace to tower, trying to escape from their vicious attacks.

The city was set on fire. The few remaining leaders were killed—Kumbha by Angada; Nikumbha, his brother, by Hanuman. Khara's son, wanting to avenge his father's death, challenged Rama and was instantly killed.

The war was now right in the enemy's camp. Ravana sent for Indrajita who went readily into battle again. He fought veiled in smoke, using every weapon, every strategy at his command, killing monkeys by the hundreds, shooting arrows at Rama and Lakshmana till they were pierced and bleeding all over.

Lakshmana wanted to use the terrible weapon of Brahma and exterminate everybody. But Rama was against indiscriminate killing. 'Use the serpent arrows. They are deadly enough. Indrajita is bound to fall, sooner or later.'

Meanwhile, Indrajita, too, was reviewing his plans. Mere strategy, however ingenious, he realized, would not do. He resorted to trickery.

It was a cruel trick to play. He created an illusory Sita, sat her in his chariot and drove out to confront them. Hanuman saw Sita first. How did Indrajita bring her out of the ashoka grove? If he had done so with Ravana's permission, why? Surely he would not expose her thus and risking losing her, after all that had happened. A host of questions arose in his busy monkey brain. As Indrajita came closer, the monkeys, led by Hanuman, hurled themselves at him.

It was time for the great scene. Indrajita dragged Sita by the hair, as she shouted piteously for help.

Hanuman was outraged. 'You dare to lay a finger on her hair, you villain. It is the touch of death, you fool!'

'She has caused enough trouble. Watch me kill her,' Indrajita shouted back. 'After that I will kill Rama, Lakshmana, you, Sugriva and Vibhishana.' And with that, he cut off Sita's head.

Rama was about to send Jambavan to Hanuman's help when he got news of Sita's death. Rama fainted and Lakshmana raved and ranted at him: 'Your dharma should protect you. It is a poor thing, a weakling, else Ravana should have been in hell by now. So much for your principles.

'Dharma is your guiding light,' he said to Rama who was moaning as he came back to consciousness. 'But it has actually misguided and misled you. We live in a topsy-turvy world. Only the wicked seem to prosper.'

He could not stop the accusations that came pouring out of him. 'It is a matter of might, not right, and wealth is the foundation of all worldly success. By accepting exile, you have impoverished yourself. You are good and you are poor. You are, therefore, among the failures of the world.' He blamed him now as much as he had praised him earlier. 'Your dharma has brought this calamity upon us.'

Vibhishana arrived and, as usual, put them wise to Indrajita's trickery. 'I know Ravana only too well. He will not harm Sita. This is sheer delusion.' There was urgency in his voice. 'Let us act fast. I happen to know that Indrajita is praying to his patron goddess, performing a sacrifice that will bring him invincibility when he completes it. We must disrupt it. These are all tricks to distract us.' Ordering the monkeys to attack with all their might, Vibhishana went with Lakshmana to look for Indrajita.

In a grove, dark with old trees, stood a lustrous banyan tree. 'This is the grove where the goddess Nikumbhila resides, and it is here that Indrajita offers sacrifices to acquire invisibility and invincibility. If he completes the rites, we are done for.'

But Indrajita had already emerged, clad in shining armour. He had left the sacrifice midway, hearing of fresh attacks. Vibhishana whispered to Lakshmana: 'Look, Lakshmana, there comes Indrajita, visible, vulnerable. We are safe.'

Indrajita saw Vibhishana and said bitterly: 'You are my father's brother, my uncle. You grew up with us. Do family ties mean nothing to you?' He was harsh and unrelenting in his condemnation. 'You are a slave, running errands for strangers, a deserter with no love or loyalty.'

Uncle and nephew faced each other with pain and sorrow in their hearts. Vibhishana was ready with his defence. His voice was heavy with regret. 'Grant me the respect due to an uncle and an elder, even if you do not understand or accept my motives. I am a demon with human values and qualities. I value right above might. How could I continue to support Ravana who uses might to overcome right? The unrighteous should be abandoned as one runs away from a burning house!'

He warned the boy: 'Your neck is already in the noose, you stare death in the face, Indrajita. For Rama is death, death to the evil-doer.'

Lakshmana, who had been standing by waiting for the exchange between uncle and nephew to be over, now took up his bow. Indrajita shouted out: 'I knocked you unconscious not long ago, Lakshmana. Have you forgotten?'

Lakshmana, a true man of action, called back: 'Do rather than say. Boasting won't take you far. Fight.' And he let loose his arrow.

Indrajita was taken by surprise. 'You have a short memory. I bound you down early in the battle, both you and Rama. Have you forgotten?'

And they fought, each trying to tire the other out, to break his spirit. Lakshmana destroyed Indrajita's chariot and killed his horse.

Indrajita asked the demons to keep fighting, while under cover of darkness he went back to Lanka to get a chariot and fresh weapons. But he could not continue to bear for long the fury of Lakshmana's attack, nor his valour. Without his defensive armour of invisibility, he was at a loss. He fell, his head cut off.

Hanuman and Vibhishana congratulated Lakshmana. Rama greeted him

affectionately. 'By killing Indrajita, you have virtually killed Ravana. Sita is now within reach, Lakshmana.' With Indrajita gone, Ravana would have to appear. Evil would have to face the power of good. Rama was waiting. The cause of dharma called for patience.

11

Rama confronts Ravana

Indrajita's death affected Ravana very deeply. He could not understand it. After all, the boy had pitted and proved his strength even against Indra, which was how he had earned his name, Indrajita, 'conqueror of Indra'.

'The sages of the world will sleep peacefully, now that Indrajita their arch enemy is dead,' he mumbled, as he paced up and down, mourning, lamenting the death of his bravest son.

The thought roused him to fresh anger and he shook off his apathy. He revelled once more in his virtue and his prowess. 'My penance was long and arduous and my boon from Brahma is protection enough. Who will dare challenge me?'

Ravana squared his shoulders and roared: 'Let the drumbeats announce my arrival on the field of battle. Get the chariot ready. Place my bow in it.' He had worked himself up into a frenzy. A demoniac urge to destroy gripped him. 'Firstly, I must kill Sita, Indrajita only played at killing her. I will do the real thing.'

He ran, drunk with the thought of wanton destruction, and entered the ashoka grove, brandishing his sword, slicing the air in sweeping strokes, glaring at Sita. Sita paled. 'He is frustrated enough to kill me,' she thought. 'Perhaps, I deserve to die.' She heard shouts of triumph, sounds of celebration. 'Has he killed Rama and Lakshmana?' And then, with great regret, 'I should have gone with Hanuman. I should have been sitting safe in Rama's lap.' Her eyes filled with tears and she shrank into herself, waiting for the end.

Ravana's counsellor stopped him. 'You should know better than to kill a woman. The scriptures forbid it, and you are a learned man. Vent your wrath on Rama. Your quarrel is with him, not with his weak and helpless wife.'

He withdrew reluctantly and the counsellor breathed a sigh of relief.

Ravana summoned his assembly and prepared for war. He ordered the leaders of his army to fight as they had never fought before. 'Go out with only one object—to kill. And remember, attack Rama savagely. Wound him, but leave him alive. I would like to kill him myself.'

The demons went immediately into action. Casualties were heavy on both sides, running into thousands, till Rama appeared and tilted the balance in favour of the monkeys. He went through the enemy ranks like a hurricane which is perceived only in the destruction it trails.

He was everywhere at once, and nowhere, so fast did he move, defying

time, defying space. There were a thousand Ramas playing havoc with demon lives, and yet not one to lay hold of. Omnipresent, intangible, his golden bow flashed past, circling like a blazing torch, setting fire to their eyes and their dazed minds.

'There he is . . . . and there . . . . Where? Not here . . . . Yes, he was. . . . and there, too, look . . . .'

Rama spun them on the wheel of time in dizzy rounds of death, driven by justice and revenge. Battered, bruised and exhausted, they straggled home to Lanka.

The gods were delighted and the heavens echoed to their applause. For the vast army of Ravana—horses, elephants, chariots and men—had been routed by Rama, in a display of unequalled valour and courage, presaging doom to come.

There was weeping and wailing among the demon women and much casting back of thoughts on past events.

'Why did Shurpanakha have to fall in love with Rama of all people? That is what started it off. If Ravana had listened to Vibhishana, Lanka would not have been turned into one big burial ground.' 'Even the death of Indrajita hasn't brought him to his senses.' 'Sita will devour us.' And so they wept, complained and accused.

Their cries pierced Ravana's ears till he could bear it no longer. A blind fury possessed him and he vowed: 'Today all deaths shall be avenged, all women consoled. The ground will be covered so thickly with monkey corpses that no bit of earth will show through!'

His left eye twitched, his left arm throbbed. But these bad omens did not deter Ravana. He felt invincible. Mounting his splendid chariot, he sped away through the gates where Rama and Lakshmana had camped. His three generals Virupaksha, Mahodara and Mahaparshva followed him. The monkeys were subjected to another wave of attack and slaughter. But in no time at all Ravana's three generals were killed by Sugriva and Angada.

Ravana raged: 'The spreading tree that is Rama will be cut down today and I will have its sweet fruit, Sita.'

Rama and Ravana fought with extraordinary weapons full of the world's powers and energies. Fire and wrath and hellish darkness played on their tips like the dance of destruction.

Lakshmana tore down Ravana's banner and struck at his chariot. Vibhishana killed his horses. In retaliation, Ravana aimed a weapon of sheer energy at Lakshmana hitting him. Rama tried to reduce its impact with a prayer and blessings but Lakshmana fell. Rama, saddened but roused, attacked Ravana again.

'Guard Lakshmana's body,' he said to the monkeys, continuing to fight. Like a true warrior, he was spurred on to fresh heights of valour by this setback. 'You will see the world rid of either Rama or Ravana,' he cried. 'Watch us fight, see my true spirit rise to destroy the evil that is Ravana.' There was a lull in the fighting and Rama let sorrow and dejection take hold of him. 'Of what use is life without my brother beside me? I feel my strength and power ebb.'

Sushena consoled him, and then asked Hanuman to fly to the Himalayas to fetch him herbs. 'You know the place. You've been there once before.' Hanuman flew off and was back once again with the whole peak. Sushena selected and crushed the herbs and put a few drops into Lakshmana's nose, and he rose full of life and wholly healed.

'You return from death to revive me, dying of sorrow for you, Lakshmana,' Rama cried.

'On with the fight,' was Lakshmana's joyous reply.

The gods who are witnesses to everything, and who were specially interested in the battle between Ravana and Rama, felt that Rama needed a chariot. 'He fights on foot, while the demon rides,' they said to Indra, who then offered not only his chariot but his charioteer, Matali, as well. Matali appeared before Rama with folded hands, offering his services. Rama ascended the golden chariot of Indra and the fight was resumed.

As Rama and Ravana met, Rama faced him with his wicked deeds. His tone was ironic. 'You stole my wife like a common thief. How brave of you.' Ravana flinched at Rama's direct assault on his character. 'You crossed the limits of virtue and good conduct, and for that there is no forgiveness. I shall feed you to the jackals.'

Ravana could feel the scorching effect of his inglorious past as Rama faced him with it, his voice low and menacing.

It was a war of nerves and Ravana was losing. Good, in the ascendant, was pressing down on evil. Ravana visibly waned as Rama waxed strong and eloquent. 'Enjoy the bitter fruit of your actions,' he warned. Ravana's charioteer could see his master weaken and lose courage. He moved away swiftly, unobtrusively, giving him time to revive.

Ravana snapped out of his apathy and rebuked his charioteer. 'Do you think me weak, lacklustre, cowardly, impotent?' he spluttered. 'You dare take the initiative and withdraw?' The charioteer thought it best to keep quiet while Ravana gave vent to his annoyance. 'Has the enemy bribed you?' he went on. 'Take me back before Rama leaves and I am branded as a coward who retreats in the face of danger!'

The charioteer replied, choosing his words carefully. 'I was only shielding your fair name and reputation. You are exhausted, the horses are tired and sweating. I was playing for time. Besides, there are bad omens, which I don't think you should ignore.'

He proceeded to defend his move. 'A good charioteer is sensitive to the winds of battle, knows when to advance, retreat or mark time. He anticipates his master. You must trust me,' he finished gently.

Ravana had calmed down. 'Take me to Rama,' he said quietly, and rewarded the faithful charioteer with an ornament.

Rama saw Ravana return. The gods had already intervened and it was now Agastya's turn to strengthen his hands with spiritual fire.

'Receive this ancient treasure, hoary with tradition, from me. It is the *Aditya-Hridaya,* the hymn to the sun. Let your thoughts reach out to the light, the power, the glory that is Surya. Recite it thrice and victory will be yours. Bless you!'

Rama drew his thoughts in and let the sound of prayer fill his head with the light of knowledge, the brightness of the sun. It was the fuel that his fire needed to blaze out and destroy the darkness that was Ravana. He felt fully prepared and utterly tranquil. Body, mind and spirit were now one and functioning smoothly.

'Turn the chariot round and face Ravana,' he ordered. 'Quick, Matali, speed up, you are Indra's charioteer,' he said, eager to get on. The chariot drove up, covering Ravana with a cloud of dust.

As Rama and Ravana met and clashed, the troops of both sides froze with fear. Rama cut off Ravana's head only to see another sprout in its place. In this way a hundred heads had already sprung up, replacing the ones that fell. Days and nights passed and the end seemed nowhere in sight. Matali then said to Rama: 'This is a futile exercise. It is time to use Brahma's missile. How well I know that weapon! It was made by Brahma for Indra, then given to Agastya and now, you have it. I am familiar with its powers. Take my word for it. It will be a timely use of the deadliest weapon in your armoury.'

It was a very special weapon, capable of breaking down all barriers, reaching all targets, fashioned by the gods in divine unison from the essence of all the five elements. Winged by the wind, tipped by fire and sun, its haft was made of space, bearing the weight of the world's high mountains. Strung with the lustre of creation, it twanged when in use, giving out the notes of death, releasing the energy of righteous and timely destruction. Guided by the hand of dharma, it never missed its target. It had drawn blood unfailingly. It rested now in Rama's quiver, waiting to fly at Ravana, bearing its gift of death.

Rama recited the Vedas, drew his bow and aimed at Ravana's chest. The arrow pierced his heart, hit the earth and returned to its quiver, drenched in demon blood. It had done its work.

Ravana fell from his chariot. His vital breath sought its way out. His great bow came clattering down as his grip on life and weapon loosened. The pomp and circumstance of royalty, the fear and trembling and fuss that surround a warrior-king came to a swift, silent stop.

Vibhishana was heartbroken. 'The glory of Lanka dies with you. Why were you so heedless, my brother? You were a great tree rooted in fame, blooming with valour. In you rose the sap of ascetic merits. Today you lie sprawled, struck down by the raging tempest that is Rama.'

Memories of childhood and youth, ties of blood and companionship tugged at his heartstrings, and he mourned a brother, a protector, a king.

Rama comforted him. 'He fell without yielding. One does not mourn a warrior who dies fighting. As for winning and losing, these depend on the fortunes of war.'

Vibhishana was touched by Rama's sympathy. He realized that his own feelings for Ravana, older than his differences with him, went very deep. 'He was braver than most, perhaps than all but you, Rama. But his power shattered at your touch like waves that break on the seashore.'

Vibhishana paid homage to his brother in words that Rama acknowledged with the grace of a true monarch. 'Ravana was pious and learned and a true hero. He lived a full life, giving much, receiving much, enjoying and

experiencing much too. With your permission. I would like to perform his last rites.'

Ravana's wives came to the gates, wailing. They fell over him and wept, placing his heads on their laps. Some rolled on the ground and groaned, some fainted, some moaned softly. Mandodari's lament was the most piteous. She chided him in death as if he were alive and listening. 'You who made the three worlds tremble have been killed by a mortal. But then, he was no ordinary mortal. You should have realized that when Khara was killed.' She reproached him bitterly. 'Your passion for Sita distorted your sense of reality. You were destroyed by the fires of enraged chastity, for she was pure and chaste and outraged by your persistent attentions.

'You had women more beautiful than her. In many ways I myself am superior to her. But you were blind with passion; you were infatuated. Death comes to all, but you went courting it. Sita signalled your death. We could all see it coming—death for you, followed by destruction for us.'

Her eyes misted over with love as she reminisced: 'I ranged the mountains of the world in your aerial chariot with you by my side. And now . . . ?' She recalled his light flirtations, his sense of fun, his beauty. 'Your face shone with the lustre of the sun, the moon and the lotus, dazzling, gentle and tranquil by turns. I think of your drunken, roving glances and weep for the days and hours that are past, never to return.'

She was led away and Vibhishana entered Lanka to arrange for the royal funeral.

Ravana lay in state in a golden palanquin, dressed in silken garments, adorned with jewels. They bore him, facing south, with banners flying high, singing and beating drums. Priests and mourners, holding firebrands, walked ahead. The womenfolk followed. They placed him on a funeral pyre of sandal and other fragrant woods, and covered him with the skin of the black antelope to the chanting of Vedic mantras. The various ritual articles were put in place: at his feet, a cart; on his thighs, a mortar; round him wooden vessels, and sticks of fragrant wood. Curds and clarified butter were poured over his shoulders and the sacrificial goat killed. Clothed in a wet garment and scattering parched rice, Vibhishana lit the fire. Following this, oblations of water and sesamum were offered. Ravana's mortal remains had been prepared, according to custom, to cross over from the realms of life into the regions of the dead.

The demons wept and Rama rejoiced. It was the death of one more enemy, signifying the triumph of the good and the right.

With the need for anger and violence gone, Rama laid down arms and assumed, once more, his benign and smiling cast of countenance, his gentle ways. He returned Indra's chariot to the heavens and dispensed with Matali's services, thanking him for everything.

Rama had not forgotten his promise to Vibhishana. Immediately after the funeral, he summoned Lakshmana and said: 'Lanka is waiting for its new king and we have the privilege of presiding over the coronation. Arrange for the ceremony to be performed, Lakshmana.' Lakshmana sent for water from the oceans. Pouring some out of a golden pitcher, he consecrated

Vibhishana, and with that simple ceremony, amidst friends and fellow warriors, formally installed him king of Lanka. He was joyfully accepted by ministers and subjects alike. The tarnished glory of Lanka would shine out afresh, they hoped, under Vibhishana.

12

The Return to Ayodhya

It was only after these duties had been performed that Rama thought of his own reunion with Sita. Hanuman was waiting, head bowed and hands folded, for he knew there would be a message for him to convey. He had already learned to think and feel with Rama.

'With King Vibhishana's permission, enter Lanka, give Sita all the news, see what she has to say and report back to me.' It was a brief message but Hanuman could read between the lines. He went straight to the ashoka grove and found Sita sitting under a tree, drooping with sorrow, surrounded by demon guards.

She barely looked up. Hanuman started to speak. 'Rama is well and so are Sugriva and Lakshmana . . . . ' She stared at him tongue-tied, her eyes widening with joy and wonder. Colour came flooding back into her lovely face. She sat so till Hanuman had finished giving her all the news and asked: 'What are you thinking of, my lady? You haven't said a word.'

Her voice broke as she answered: 'I was speechless with happiness. I don't know what to give you in return for the good news you bring. Nothing on earth or heaven will be reward enough.'

Hanuman was overwhelmed: 'Your sweet words of affection are my reward. I want nothing more.'

He then looked round at the demon women and said: 'Do you want me to deal with these misshapen monsters who have spent all their time harassing you?' He bared his teeth at them, offering to kill or torture them. 'You have only to say the word,' he told Sita.

Sita was forgiving in her attitude to them. 'Why blame them? They were only carrying out orders. It is not their fault. It is my fate. One must not be vindictive.' She cast them a reassuring glance. 'We must be merciful and tolerant, for who is perfect?' Hanuman asked Sita if she had a message for Rama. 'I wish to see my lord,' she said. He hurried back with the message. Rama was visibly moved and turned to Vibhishana: 'Let her bathe, perfume and adorn herself. Then bring her to me.' Vibhishana hastened to obey him. Sita wanted to set out as she was, so impatient was she to meet her lord. Vibhishana dissuaded her: 'Do as he says. He is your husband.'

She arrived in a palanquin carried by demons, with a large escort. They stopped a little way off, expecting Rama to go to her. Instead, he asked for her to come closer.

Both demons and monkeys had gathered, eager to catch a glimpse of Sita. Vibhishana ordered them to disperse. Guards armed with sticks began to clear a path for her. Rama was annoyed. 'Let them be. She can descend and come to me on foot. They have my permission to look at her unveiled. A woman's protection is her virtue, not walls or curtains.' It was clearly a test.

Vibhishana escorted her through the crowd. Lakshmana, Sugriva and Hanuman looked on unhappily as Sita walked with slow, uncertain steps, shrinking from the public gaze, her face clouded with doubt and confusion. But when she looked up and saw Rama, her fears vanished. Her countenance cleared to reveal the beauty and the lustre that had ravished Rama, prince of Ayodhya, and held him captive all these years. She stood close to Rama, waiting for some word of greeting or endearment.

Rama's tone as he began to speak was serious and matter-of-fact. 'I have won you back. I have wiped out both insult and enemy. I have avenged the wrong done to you.' It was a public declaration of honour restored. An acknowledgement of the help and support extended to him by strangers followed. 'Hanuman, Sugriva and Vibhishana were with me throughout. I am grateful, and have rewarded them suitably.'

Sita barely noticed the uncomfortable pause that followed, the slight shift in Rama's tone of voice and expression—she was so happy just to be with him. 'Doubts have been cast on your character and that hurts and irks me. I cannot ignore them either.'

Was she hearing right? Rama suspected her of infidelity! 'I will have nothing more to do with you. You are free to leave me. Go where you wish, with whom you wish. The ties that bind us stand dissolved.'

So he was rejecting her! She was shocked by his lack of trust and shamed by the slur he was casting on her virtue. The accusation that followed was categorical and the judgement final. He was giving her no opportunity to defend or explain herself.

'What man of honour would take back a woman who has lived in another man's house? With your beauty, and given Ravana's character, it is almost certain that you have been defiled. It cannot be otherwise.'

Sita wept. She had waited for some word of love and had got instead this blast of condemnation. She wiped her tears and faced him. 'When you sent for me, you could have conveyed this message. I could have killed myself. I would have been spared this humiliating rejection.' She was not going to spare him, either. 'Your speech is surprisingly coarse. You speak like a man of the street to a common woman. You use a general yardstick to measure a woman like me—one whose character is above question.' Her defence was eloquent. 'If I have been touched by Ravana, it was an accident of situation. It was not the result of any desire on my part. I was abducted. My heart is yours and that remains untouched.'

She spoke with righteous indignation. 'Your anger makes you mean and small minded. I may be Janaka's daughter but I claim lineage from the earth, Prithivi, my mother. You who know everything, obviously don't know me.' Her eyes began to fill. 'You took my hand in marriage. You choose to disregard that fact. And disregard, too, my devotion to you.'

Talking and crying at the same time, she said through her tears to Lakshmana: 'Prepare the fire. It is the only way out of this hateful situation. I do not wish to live, falsely charged and discarded by my husband. Let the fire, supreme witness of the world, bear testimony to my virtue.' Her words

were met with the silence of consent.

Lakshmana looked angrily at Rama but did not dare to raise an objection. Sita went round the fire, prayed to the gods and invoking Agni, god of fire, pleaded: 'Guardian of all three worlds and their supreme witness, protect me! As my thoughts have not turned from Rama, protect me! As I am pure, though he thinks me sullied, protect me!' And she walked fearlessly into the flames.

The gods arrived in a body and protested. Brahma spoke for all of them. 'How could you let her do this? How could you suspect Sita of infidelity? You should be aware of your origins. You are divine, and chief among gods.'

Rama answered humbly: 'As far as I know I am a man, born of Dasharatha. You tell me who I am.' He seemed strangely calm.

'You are Narayana, you are existence itself. . . .You are the Himalayas, the essence of the Vedas, you are the sacred syllable, Om . You lie on the waters of life, resting on the coiled serpent that is the world. . . .You have taken incarnations as Varaha, the Boar and Vamana, the Dwarf, and you are born as Rama to rid the earth of Ravana. You are dharma, you are universal Man, you are Vishnu, and Sita is Lakshmi.'

Their praise was like a ritual of installation, and Rama had shoulders broad enough to receive the mantle of universal responsibility.

He looked towards the fire into which Sita had disappeared. Out of it rose Agni himself, bearing Sita. Clad in red, wearing ornaments of gold, she shone like the early morning sun. The supreme witness himself bore testimony to her innocence: 'She is sinless. She has not betrayed you by thought, word or wayward glance. She was not touched. Accept her, I order you to. Let there be no more argument.'

Rama sat lost in thought for a moment, then let the joy he had held back flood his whole being. 'Her public ordeal by fire was necessary. Otherwise, tongues would have wagged and fingers pointed. I know she is pure. I need no proof. She is as much part of me as my glory. I would hate to give her up.' And he welcomed her back into his heart and soul.

Shiva blessed him: 'Go back to Ayodhya, and your family. Perform the horse sacrifice and consolidate the Ikshvaku dynasty.'

Dasharatha's spirit appeared and looking fondly at his beloved Rama, declared: 'Even the heavens are joyless without you. Kaikeyi's cruelty still stings. Get back to Bharata.'

It was Indra's turn to bless Rama and grant him a boon. Rama asked for the dead monkeys to be brought back to life. 'And wherever they may be, in season, out of season, there must be abundance of flowers and fruits, full and flowing rivers.' Indra smiled indulgently. 'That is not going to be easy, but I shall see that it is done.'

The gods left with a benediction. 'Return to Ayodhya and your brothers. Be the reigning king of Kosala.'

Vibhishana wanted Rama to stay on for at least a day, but Rama was eager to get back and see Bharata. 'The Pushpaka will reach you there in a day,' said Vibhishana, referring to Ravana's special aerial chariot. But Rama would not postpone his return journey.

All was set for their immediate departure. The Pushpaka was got ready.

Vibhishana distributed gifts and money to the monkeys at Rama's request. He rewarded them generously for their services. Vibhishana and Sugriva had one last request. 'Let us come with you to Ayodhya, pay our respects to your mother and attend your coronation.'

Rama was only too happy to take them with him. Sugriva, Vibhishana and their ministers and counsellors climbed in excitedly. They were a happy and intimate group. They had seen and done much together. It had brought them close—monkeys and demons and men.

Rama pointed out important landmarks to Sita as they flew over familiar territory, retracing their steps, their thoughts and memories. Lanka and the battlefields. . . Rishyamooka. 'Let us stop here and take the monkey wives with us,' suggested Sita. So Tara and others from Sugriva's palace joined in. And finally, Ayodhya. After fourteen years and miles of journeying over hill and valley and sea.

They stopped at Bharadwaja's hermitage, a short way out from the city. Rama made his first enquiries here. He was apprehensive. 'Is the city free of epidemics? Has Bharata ruled well? Are the queens still living?'

Bharadwaja answered all his questions. 'My students bring news from the city whenever they go. I keep myself well informed.' He insisted that they stay for a day with him and arranged that the trees were laden with flowers and fruit and the combs oozed floods of honey. The monkeys made themselves at home and ate and drank their fill.

Ayodhya weighed on Rama's mind, and even more, Bharata. An envoy had to be sent ahead so that he could have some idea of what was happening. He had the ideal person on hand—Hanuman. 'Rush to Ayodhya, then go to Guha for the latest news. Tell him about us, too.'

The most delicate part of the mission was the visit to Bharata. 'Tell him that I return victorious with powerful allies. Watch his reaction, study his expression minutely.' Rama had his own reasons for such circumspection 'Who would not covet a kingdom he has ruled for fourteen years? If Bharata is in the least bit reluctant to give up power, I will let him continue. But I must be certain in my mind. Come back quickly, Hanuman.' Hanuman assumed a human form and set off for Ayodhya. At Nandigrama, he recognized Bharata, clad in bark and antelope skin. He was emaciated, his body covered with dust, his hair tangled and matted. He had his ministers, his priests, his army chiefs and prominent citizens with him.

Hanuman sprang the message on him without warning, giving him no time to dissemble. 'Rama enquires after your welfare. He is back, victorious, with Sita and Lakshmana. . . .' Bharata fainted with the shock of sudden joy. When he came back to consciousness, he embraced Hanuman, shedding tears of happiness. 'How can I reward you enough?' he said and got together gifts for him. He gave him a hundred thousand cows, a hundred flourishing villages and sixteen young maidens, rich and beautiful, and belonging to good families.

Hanuman left, assuring him that Rama would be there the next day.

Bharata ordered Shatrughna to get Ayodhya ready to receive Rama with music, dancing, garlands, banners, and pennants. The streets were lined with soldiers and kept clear for his entry. An army of labourers levelled and smoothed the highways. Armed escorts, cavalcades of elephants, horses and chariots, along with the three queens of Dasharatha, got ready to receive Rama. And all this royal pageantry moved to Nandigrama where Bharata waited, Rama's pair of sandals on his head. The canopy of power shaded them and they were fanned with yak-tail whisks.

Bharata said to Hanuman anxiously: 'Is this one of your monkey tricks? I don't see any signs of Rama.'

'Don't you?' said Hanuman, grinning. 'Look at those trees; they bear flowers out of season. Bharadwaja arranged that for his monkey guests. Notice the trampled groves—my compatriots at their usual game of wanton destruction. And do you see that heap of sheer raidance in the sky? That is Pushpaka, Ravana's divine chariot, made by Vishwakarma for Kubera, god of wealth. It belongs to Rama now.'

Bharata watched with rapt attention, palms together in respectful salutation. Pushpaka landed and Rama emerged. Greetings were exchanged all round. The monkeys had all turned human for the occasion. Bharata declared: 'We are four brothers and now you are the fifth, Sugriva.'

He bent down and reverently placed Rama's feet in the sandals that had symbolically reigned in his stead. 'I return the kingdom put in my charge, the responsibilities entrusted to me. I desire to see you king of Ayodhya. Inspect your treasury, your storehouses, and your armies. By your grace they have increased ten-fold.'

Rama embraced Bharata and took him on to his lap like a loving father. Bharata felt secure and protected.

The procession moved to Bharata's hermitage. There, Rama stepped out of Pushpaka and through wish and thought, directed the chariot back to Kubera, its rightful and original owner.

Rama sat apart, his spiritual preceptor by his side. Bharata tried to convey the trying time he had had, governing Kosala. 'As long as the wheel of time turns, so long may you rule, Rama! How can a donkey outpace a horse, or a crow fly better than a swan? That was my situation. Thrones are made for such as you.'

Bharata was worn out with the pain of long separation, feelings of guilt and the hardships of ruling a kingdom as vast and unwieldy as Kosala. 'Keeping the frontiers intact is like keeping a dam in good repair. One has to be ever alert. Leaks have to be plugged and weak points strengthened.'

The party, exhausted with the strain of travel and the excitement of reunion, prepared to bathe, refresh and adorn themselves. Sita gave herself up to the luxury of royal toiletry after years. She was assisted by the senior queens. The monkey wives bathed and beautified themselves, helped by Kausalya who attended on them personally, out of sheer gratitude and love for her son.

Rama was robed and adorned by Bharata, Lakshmana and Shatrughna. They assembled, ready to enter the city, spectacular in their fresh clothes and finery. Sumantra arrived with a magnificent chariot and Rama mounted it. Bharata held the reins, Shatrughna held the royal canopy, Lakshmana and Vibhishana swirled the yak-tail whisks. Sugriva rode the royal elephant Shatrunjaya, and the monkeys followed on nine thousand elephants. It was a

solemn and impressive procession. On the way, Rama spoke of his alliance with Sugriva, Hanuman's valour, the strength of the demons, the exploits of the monkeys. The people of Ayodhya wondered at his friendship with the simian tribes and their love for him.

In Ayodhya, the ministers and counsellors, with the spiritual guidance of Vasishtha had already decided on Rama's coronation ceremonies and celebrations. Sugriva was also consulted. As lord of the monkeys he had a key role to play. He gave the monkey leaders four golden jars encrusted with jewels for water from the four oceans and five hundred rivers. 'Be ready with these by dawn,' he said, and they flew off in all four directions to carry out his orders.

On the coronation day, Rama ascended the jewelled throne of Ayodhya with Sita by his side. Vasishtha, the chief priest, and the counsellors consecrated them with pure and fragrant water. The celestials assembled to anoint them with the juices of all the sacred herbs.

Jewellery and gifts were given and received. Vayu, the wind god, gave Rama a necklace of gold, Indra gave him a necklace of pearls. Rama in turn lavished money and gifts on those present. Sugriva received a crown, Angada a pair of bracelets. To Sita he gave a necklace of priceless pearls with the lustre of moonbeams.

Sita wished to give Hanuman something as a mark of her special favour. She unclasped her necklace of pearls and looked at Rama with a glance full of meaning. Rama understood and smiling, said aloud: 'You may give that to whom you please.' Sita turned to Hanuman and held it out. Wearing the necklace, the valiant Hanuman sat like a high mountain on whom a white cloud had come beautifully to rest.

13

In the Name of Dharma

Rama took leave of the kings who had assembled for the coronation, over three hundred of them. Bharata, Lakshmana and Shatrughna escorted them back to their homes. They talked of the war they had not witnessed, and the opportunities they had missed to serve Rama, and sent the princes back loaded with gifts and tribute.

Another month passed in gracious hospitality before Rama bade farewell to the monkeys and Vibhishana. He advised Vibhishana: 'Rule with righteousness ever in mind. Deviate from dharma and you will come to grief. And think of me with love and affection.'

Hanuman declared his allegiance in memorable terms. 'As long as your story is told in this world, so long do I wish to live—no longer. The nectar of your deeds shall dispel my fears and anxieties, be my very life-breath.'

Tenderly embracing Hanuman, Rama assured him: 'So shall it be. My story will live, and you, with it. And in my heart will live the fond remembrance of every deed, however small, that you have done for me.' And he removed from his person a necklace of great value and placed it lovingly round Hanuman's neck.

It was a tearful parting. They had been campaigners together in an extraordinary war under extraordinary circumstances. It had changed them all and bound them in bonds of everlasting love, loyalty and devotion.

Life resumed its normal course in court and city. Rama rejoiced in his kingdom, his brothers, his mothers, his lovely wife. The reign of Rama, *Rama rajya,* was marked by happy events and the absence of calamity.

There was no disease, no death of infant or youth; no woman was ever widowed; for there were no violent or untimely deaths.

The winds blew mild and balmy, good rains nourished the earth, trees bore flowers and fruit in joyous abundance.

People were contented, immersed in the fulfilment of their own individual duties and destinies. Envy, jealousy and enmity ended before they began, for Rama's benevolent glance spread friendship and sweet amity.

Rama and Sita were happy in their respective duties, he as king and courtier, she as royal householder and guardian of domestic harmony. He took wise counsel and performed the daily functions of state with due attention and care. She prayed, worshipped and went through her morning chores and, adorning herself, joined her husband for quiet hours of happy communion.

The palace groves were their special delight. Still pools bearing clusters of lily and lotus soothed their senses, the contented hum of bees lulled them into a state of tranquillity. Flowering trees and arbours green with shade sheltered them in a private world of love and longing. He would offer her honey-wine and they would partake of choice foods while music and dance entertained them.

One day, Rama looked at Sita with special pride. She was glowing with the beauty born of approaching motherhood. He wanted her cup of happiness to be full to the very brim, and said: 'You bear our child, Sita. What fresh excursions of pleasure can I arrange for you?' Sita smiled and replied: 'I would like to visit the sages who live on the banks of the Ganga, to spend just one night in their hermitage and seek their blessings.' Rama was charmed by the simplicity of his wife, by her humility and her devotion. 'That is easy, my love. You shall go tomorrow,' he promised, as he left to join a group of his companions, courtiers and jesters. It was a merry gathering, with everyone in high good humour. Quips were exchanged and much pleasant banter flew about. All were intent on amusing and entertaining the king.

Rama, ever mindful of his responsibilities, picked out a stray reference to matters of state and asked one of the jesters in serious tones: 'Tell me, Bhadra, what do people in town and country say of me, my brothers, Sita? And of my government? Kings are always targets of criticism. It is good to keep a hand on the pulse of our subjects, and never miss a beat.'

Bhadra replied: 'All is well, my lord. They praise your invasion of Lanka and the defeat of Ravana. The crossing of the oceans astounds them each time they mention it and they speak of your life with Sita. . . .'

'Why do you pause?' asked Rama, quick to detect the slight hesitation. 'Tell me all, good and bad, for it is thus that rulers should sense the mood of the times. Do not fear.'

'Well then, my lord,' said Bhadra. 'They wonder what joy Sita could give you, having sat in Ravana's lap when he carried her away by force. They wonder, too, that you are not revolted by the fact that she stayed so long in the house of a *rakshasa* like Ravana.'

'Go on,' said Rama, bracing himself for worse to come. 'You need not fear my wrath.'

'They say more, my lord. They are afraid that you have established a dangerous precedent. Women will go astray, and men will treat such matters lightly, for what the king does today, the subjects will do tomorrow. That is what they say, my lord,' he said, shocked at his own temerity.

'Is this true?' he asked the assembly of well-wishers. With bent heads and with the utmost reverence, they answered as one man: 'Yes, my lord, he speaks the truth.'

Rama sat, lost in deep thought, trying to absorb the hurt, his face mirroring the pain. Sita was innocent, he knew beyond all doubt. She had even gone through the ordeal of fire in Lanka. But the people of Ayodhya questioned the propriety of her reinstatement. They judged her wrongly, but the voice of the people must be heard. They were right. A king sets the pace and must therefore be exemplary. That was the prime need. All else was secondary.

Rama controlled his reeling senses and sent for the guard. 'Hurry and ask Lakshmana to come, and Bharata and Shatrughna too. There is urgent business of state. It can't wait.'

The brothers came at once. They could see his turmoil as he looked at them, his eyes moist with tears of sorrow. He clasped them to his breast as if seeking reassurance in their touch. 'You are my wealth, my life, the very basis of my power. I rule because of you.' They waited for him to come to the point. What was he going to spring on them, they wondered. Rama plunged into the matter without further ado. 'Be most attentive, my brothers. Listen to what my subjects have to say of Sita.'

The words came spilling out. The hideous truth stared them in the face. 'I have had to clear her character once before, though I knew she was innocent. She went through the ordeal of fire, she, daughter of Janaka! The problem has arisen again. Sita's fair name and my reputation as an effective ruler are both being questioned and found wanting.'

'There is only one way out—she and I must go our separate ways!' It was Rama, ruler by right rather than might, speaking. The princes were silent, helpless in the face of this stark tragedy.

Rama turned to Lakshmana, his brother and companion in distress over the long years of exile. 'Take her away, beyond my borders.'

Lakshmana wished he could blot out the royal order and the harsh details that followed. 'Take her close to Valmiki's hermitage by the river Ganga. I will have no discussion on the matter. Any resistance will incur my displeasure.'

As the brothers gaped in awe and wonderment at the strange and cruel ways of just governance, Rama turned once again to Lakshmana, his voice breaking with sobs: 'She told me yesterday she wished to visit those sacred retreats. Now, go!'

The next morning, Lakshmana ordered Sumantra to harness the swiftest horses to the royal chariot. 'Prepare a soft and luxurious seat, for the queen will ride to the forest today.'

Lakshmana then went in to Sita. 'You wish to visit the ascetics near the river Ganga. I will conduct you there myself. The chariot is waiting.'

Sita got ready, taking with her heaps of costly clothes and finery. 'I will distribute these to the women,' she explained. She was excited at the prospect of visiting a hermitage, and her mind was filled with pleasurable thoughts. A few bad omens worried her, and she anxiously enquired if all was well with palace and court. Lakshmana assured her that nothing was wrong, and with a heavy heart sat back, thinking of the parting to come.

They halted for the night on the banks of the Gomati, setting out again the following morning. Lakshmana was weeping openly as they got down from the carriage and stood on the banks of the Ganga.

Sita was puzzled. 'Are you crying because you cannot stay away from Rama for two days? That is childish. I am eager to get back, too, Lakshmana. As soon as we have met the sages, we will be on our way. Take heart.'

They boarded a boat that was to take them across the river, while Sumantra dismounted and led the horses away for the night. He would wait to take them back.

They reached the opposite bank. Lakshmana's anguish could no longer be hidden. With folded hands he spoke to Sita, his great body wracked by sobs. 'Only death could save me from grave calumny. The world will condemn this mission of mine and yet, God knows, I am innocent of this offensive deed.'

Sita was alarmed. 'He speaks of a fate worse than death, of innocence and guilt! What can this mean?' Aloud, she said: 'Lakshmana, I fail to understand. You speak in riddles and seem greatly agitated. What is the reason for this distress?'

'What can I say? Once more, the people have chosen to break Rama's heart. They question your virtue and blame Rama for taking you back. He is compelled to reject you. I have been ordered by Rama to leave you here, away from Ayodhya, away from him!'

Sita listened in stunned silence and Lakshmana stood, head bowed, not daring to move.

'The sage Valmiki is a friend of our father, Dasharatha. You will be safe. Think of Rama, have faith in him and you will be blessed.'

Sita was in a daze. It took her a while to respond, even with tears. 'Surely my body is a heap of misfortunes. I think it was created solely for the purpose of grieving. Am I to live alone, abandoned and condemned by one as compassionate as Rama? Condemned without reason, too!' She sounded desperate as she said: 'I cannot end my life, either, for with it would end the royal line. I happen to bear the seed of the lkshvakus.'

Her message to Rama was heart-rending. 'Tell Rama I love him and that I am pure and unsullied. He knows it too, but chooses to sacrifice me to satisfy his subjects. I could have been spared this. But I will endure it like the dutiful wife that I am. A husband is a god and a preceptor and lays down the law. Wives are expected only to follow.'

There was a note of proud defiance in her final remarks. It was a parting shot that went straight home. 'Repeat my words to Rama and mind, take note, bear witness to the fact that I came here already far advanced in pregnancy.' There was no mistaking the barb, the sting. 'Let no doubts be cast on that at least,' she seemed to imply.

Lakshmana could only say: 'How can you ask me to do such a thing? You know I have never raised my eyes above your feet!'

And he left, turning back again and again to look at Sita, who was now sobbing loudly and uncontrollably.

It was so that some boys from Valmiki's hermitage found her. They went running to the sage. 'There is a lady here who must be from a wealthy family, the wife of some great man. She is weeping her heart out.'

Valmiki, who knew everything through his ascetic insights, went to her. 'Do not weep, dear lady. I know who you are and why you are here. I also know you are blameless. Take comfort from that knowledge.'

Sita stopped crying and Valmiki spoke sweet words of solace. 'Not far from here are some female ascetics. They will care for you. You have a home. Do not despair.' He led her to the women, walking a little ahead. They greeted him warmly.

'What can we do for you? It is so long since you visited us.' Valmiki

introduced Sita and left her in their charge. 'She is Dasharatha's daughter-in-law. Her husband has rejected her though she is innocent. She needs all the care and affection we can give her, and she is fully worthy of it. I vouch for that. Treat her with all due respect and honour.'

Valmiki had done well. Sita was in good hands.

On the way back, Sumantra consoled Lakshmana. 'Rama is destined to suffer much, sorrow much. Separation from those whom he loves has been foretold. One must bow to destiny, Lakshmana. You must accept this and learn to bear it.'

Sumantra's wise and mature attitude helped Lakshmana to bend before the cruel and inevitable ways of fate. Rama, too, informed by Lakshmana of his predestined lot, calmed down considerably and immersed himself in matters of government, paying attention to every aspect, applying his mind, heart and soul to the welfare of his kingdom.

One day, while Rama sat discussing matters of state, a group of ascetics were announced. They had come with their usual problem. 'We live across the Yamuna river. A demon, Lavana, wielding a powerful weapon, a trident given to his father by Shiva himself, is creating havoc. He has attacked and killed many of us.'

Bharata offered to go but Shatrughna put in his claim. 'Bharata has already had his share of service to you. I have not. Let me go; this is my opportunity.'

'Very well,' said Rama, 'In that case you must prepare to take over the territory once you get rid of the demon. So go through a coronation ceremony here, before you set out.' Shatrughna protested, saying he was quite happy where he was, helping Rama. He had no personal ambitions. 'I want no kingdom to rule.' But Rama insisted. It was time, he felt, that his brothers began to lead their own lives, have their own separate areas of responsibility.

'Take care,' he said. 'Attack Lavana while he is out prowling for prey. He leaves his trident behind at such times. It is only so you will manage to kill him.'

Shatrughna set out with a large army and many words of advice from Rama. 'Keep the soldiers happy. Pay them well and in time, and win them over with sweet speech. Take a troupe of dancers and musicians with you to keep them entertained.'

It was Shatrughna's first independent venture and he listened carefully. 'When you enter Madhuvana, the woods where Lavana lives, enter alone and armed and challenge him to single combat. This whole expedition should take you through summer and into the rainy season. Go with my blessings,' said Rama.

Shatrughna's first stop after a month was Valmiki's hermitage. He halted his armies some distance away and entered the holy precincts alone. He was welcomed by the sage and asked to spend the night there.

On that very night, Sita gave birth to twins. Valmiki was given the news and he went at once to bless and congratulate her. With a handful of kusha

grass the sage warded off the evil that hovers over all beings at birth. He ordered the women to pass the blades of grass over the elder boy and named him Kusha. The second boy was also blessed with the lower segments of kusha and was therefore named Lava, meaning 'bit' or 'piece'.

Shatrughna, too, heard the news, and was deeply moved. He ventured near the hut and uttered a heartfelt blessing, wishing Sita all happiness. He could hear Rama's praises being sung and the children's names being taken. He was a proud brother and uncle. He stood a long time in the drip and rustle of a rain-drenched night, churning the silence with thoughts of Rama, miles away, denied the simple joy of fatherhood.

Shatrughna left in the morning and after seven days reached the banks of the Yamuna. The sage Chyavana told him of the defeat of Mandhata of Ayodhya, an Ikshvaku, at the hands of Lavana. He described the rout of the king and his armies. 'It was a total massacre. Lavana's trident is deadly. But if you wait till tomorrow and catch him when he is out scouting for food, your victory is assured.'

Shatrughna crossed the Yamuna at dawn and stood ready, armed with his bow, at the gates of the city, hoping to catch Lavana as he returned, fed and fully satisfied.

They met. Lavana laughed and said: 'There's room for more. I'm not full yet. I've eaten thousands like you. What are you going to do with that bow? You are walking into my open mouth, you fool!'

Shatrughna shouted back: 'Get ready to die!' Lavana sneered: 'Rama slew my uncle and his family. You will be swept away like straws in the wind. Let me get my weapon.'

Shatrughna was too quick for him. 'Do you think I will let you go? I am not a fool. I will attack, and attack now!' It was a tough fight, but without his trident, Lavana was no match for the valiant Shatrughna.

The gods rejoiced and blessed him. Shatrughna entered the city and occupied the throne. He ruled for twelve years, improving the place and increasing its prosperity. But his thoughts turned ceaselessly to Rama and Ayodhya. He decided to visit the city of his boyhood days and re-establish contact with his own people.

Shatrughna started for Ayodhya with a small escort of soldiers and servants and once again halted at Valmiki's hermitage. The sage, who had watched his fight with Lavana from the heavens congratulated him, touching his nose to Shatrughna's head in the traditional gesture of affection.

As they rested, duly fed and refreshed, sounds of stringed instruments grew into a steady strum of sweetness, and with it, a rising chant of words rang out, clear as a bell in the forest stillness. And then it broke over them in great waves, the story of Rama, soul-stirring with its heroic exploits, heart-rending in its pathos, its tragedy. Shatrughna wept, reliving the past and his companions listened transfixed, heads bowed in reverent obeisance. They were soon agog with curiosity and full of questions. Puzzled and confused, they turned to their king: 'Ask Valmiki, my lord, about this. Were we dreaming. . . ? ' Shatrughna only said: 'It is not proper to question a person like him. This is a place where miracles are the order of the day. That should satisfy us.'

He had discouraged his men from prying, but he himself slept little. The ballad of Rama had only sharpened his sense of loss and separation, and he started off for Ayodhya at daybreak.

He entered the city, rode the familiar streets and was soon standing before Rama. As he feasted his eyes on the splendour of his radiant presence he confessed: 'I have been twelve long years away from you and feel like a calf separated from its mother. Let me return.'

Rama hugged him and scolded gently, lovingly: 'You are a king, and kings do not desert their kingdoms for foreign lands. Yes, Ayodhya is that to you, now. Visit me from time to time, but go back you must. You have a responsibility to your subjects.' Shatrughna bowed to the inevitable. Rama was right. It was in the fitness of things that he should return. At the end of a happy week, he left, escorted to the borders by Lakshmana and Bharata. It had been like old times for the four of them, so closely bound in the ties of brotherly love.

Rama now considered performing the Rajasuya sacrifice to establish his supremacy and consulted Lakshmana and Bharata whose opinions he valued greatly. Bharata spoke out freely, voicing his doubts. 'You are the support of the world, the protector of the universe, the salvation of all beings. Therefore, I think it inappropriate for you to perform the Rajasuya. It will mean the ruin of many royal houses, the death of countless brave warriors. It will unleash a great deal of violence and bloodshed, and that would do you no credit.'

Rama was dissuaded. Bharata was a skilled debater and knew how to argue and press home a point. 'I think you are right. You have an old head on young shoulders, Bharata.' Lakshmana came up with an alternative to the Rajasuya. 'The horse sacrifice, the Ashwamedha, is one that exalts and purifies. There is divine precedent for its good effects. Even Indra resorted to it when he wanted to cleanse himself of the sin of murder.' Rama agreed. And preparations were made for performing the Ashwamedha in Ayodhya.

Rama put Lakshmana in charge and instructed him to invite sages who were skilled in the performance of sacrifices, particularly the Ashwamedha—Vasishtha, Vamadeva, Jabali, Kashyapa. He asked for elaborate arrangements to be made. Invitations were issued to Sugriva and the monkey chiefs, Vibhishana and other prominent *rakshasas* from Lanka, as well as learned men, ascetics and neighbouring kings.

The sacrificial site was announced. 'I would like it to be located on the banks of the Gomati, in the Naimisha forest,' ordered Rama.

Provisions of high quality were ordered in vast quantities—rice, sesamum, lentils, salt and cooking oils; aromatic oils, incense and sandalwood.

A whole township made up of cooks, maids, dancing girls and musicians, actors and jesters sprang up overnight, for the palace women and queens were expected to take up residence on site. Special tents and pavilions were erected to accommodate visiting monarchs and dignitaries, their families, retinues and regalia. With a note of poignant regret, Rama ordered the golden statue of his absent consort to be installed, indicating her symbolic presence at the ceremonies. It was with this image by his side that Rama had

conducted many a sacrifice during his long and successful reign. It was a reminder to him of the golden years they had spent together, years filled with the living warmth of flesh and blood.

When the site and sacrificial platform were fully set up, Rama arrived with his army. He was more than pleased with what he saw and signalled the start of the sacrifice. With due pomp and ceremony, the dark sacrificial horse, chosen with care and according to ritual specification, was let loose to wander at will. Lakshmana, assisted by a band of priests and soldiers, followed the animal around, carefully watching its movements, on the alert for any challenge to Rama's overlordship. The horse would be led back after a year, unless it was caught and bound as a gesture of open hostility.

Meanwhile, the ceremonies, and celebrations continued. There was generous giving of alms, gold, silver and gems. 'Let all wants be satisfied, all wishes granted, all desires fulfilled', was the royal injunction. Gifts and money flowed as never before in any sacrifice within living memory.

Valmiki and his disciples were there, too. They built themselves a cluster of huts in a charming grove, and stocked their camp with the necessary provisions—fruit and roots, the humble fare of ascetics.

The sage had a very special presentation to make. Kusha and Lava, Rama's sons, had been trained to sing the Ramayana, the poem that he had composed out of the resounding elements of a heroic life. It was a rich and well-ordered musical presentation, planned in careful stages, an act of faith which had been a long time in the making.

'Sing your song of praise to Rama before sages and scholars, princes and priests, on the highways and in the streets. Let the music charm all those gathered here on this great occasion.' The boys bowed assent. They were confident and full of enthusiasm. 'I have fruit from the mountains, specially gathered. It will sustain you through the long hours of strenuous singing,' said Valmiki. He was about to see his vision of poetry come to life, the essence of heroic verse take audiences by storm and draw them into worship of Rama of Ayodhya. He knew, too, that the moment was ripe for a fated reunion and that he, Valmiki, had been chosen to conduct the proceedings. 'Sing, above all, at the entrance to Rama's pavilion; follow his wishes and orders. And sing twenty cantos at a time.' As the boys waited, devout and attentive, their faces shining with the ardour of youth, he reminded them: 'Do not expect or accept any reward; for what use is gold to us ascetics?'

It was his final instruction. In the morning, they would go out into the world as gifted wandering minstrels with a special repertoire of epic song. They spent the night in eager anticipation of a golden inaugural dawn.

The two young voices rose with the sun, taking wing on notes of mellow devotion. The beat, the metre, the cadence, the flow of both music and words was irresistible. Rama heard and was intrigued. He made immediate enquiries.

During an interval of rest he sent for them. He also got together experts in music, dance, poetry, rhythm and metrics; men learned in astronomy and astrology, men skilled in the performance of sacrificial rites; connoisseurs of the arts, aesthetes, dancers and musicians. It was an impressive gathering.

The boys began to sing. They sang like twin celestials, drowning their listeners in a sea of memorable song. People sat spellbound, drinking in with their eyes and ears the sight, the sound of Kusha and Lava.

The resemblance of the young boys to Rama did not go unnoticed. It was remarked upon openly. 'Take away their robes of bark and they are like little replicas of Rama.'

As planned, they sang twenty cantos and stopped. As the applause died down, Rama ordered eighteen thousand gold pieces to be given to them and other gifts besides. He was taken aback when they refused. 'What can we do with gold and rich gifts? We are hermits who live in the forest.'

Rama enquired: 'Who is the author of this poem? Where does he live?'

'The ascetic, Valmiki, composed this poem. He is here, attending the sacrifice. The epic about your life is made up of twenty-four thousand verses and contains a hundred narrative episodes. It is divided into six parts, with a seventh concluding one. You could hear most of it, with breaks, if you can spare the time, my lord.'

Rama spent many hours listening to the epic ballad. He realized soon enough that the young musicians were his sons. It was time that he got Sita back, he thought.

He sent a message to Valmiki asking him to bring Sita into his presence for a public demonstration of her innocence. The gathering, the occasion, seemed right. Valmiki assented and the trial, all over again, of the blameless Sita, consort of Rama, was fixed for the morrow.

Curiosity had reached fever pitch. Rumour and speculation had been rife and the citizens of Ayodhya, as well as the vast number of guests at the Ashwamedha, waited for the appointed moment of judgement and revelation. Rama, upholder of dharma, would put Sita to the test, and remove all doubt and suspicion from the minds of his beloved subjects forever. They would not miss the spectacle for anything.

Sita arrived, clad in ochre, pacing slowly, head bent, hands folded. She wept, thinking of Rama. Her mind, till now full of his absence, was filled with his presence.

The crowds stirred. Some cried 'Victory to Sita,' others, 'Victory to Rama.' There were many who sympathized with her and they sighed, 'Alas, poor Sita.'

Valmiki looked straight at Rama. 'You rejected her for fear of public censure, but she will prove her innocence yet. These two boys are her sons, your sons. May all my penance prove fruitless if Sita is found guilty. I fearlessly declare her pure and chaste.'

Rama replied: 'I never doubted her. But even after the ordeal of fire in Lanka, my subjects questioned her virtue. I was compelled to abandon her by the constraints of my dharma, my royal responsibilities.'

Rama looked fondly at the young boys. 'I acknowledge my sons, Kusha and Lava, and know that Sita will prove to the satisfaction of all those assembled here that she is utterly innocent.'

The gods, too, arrived to witness this ceremonial of righteous judgement, stringent and cruel in its demands, and difficult to administer.

Sita stood still with palms joined in salutation, eyes lowered and riveted to

the ground as if she would cleave it with all her will. Then she phrased her declaration of innocence with simple clarity.

'If I have not thought, even in passing, of any man but Rama, goddess of the earth, Madhavi, make way for me. If in thought, word and deed only Rama exists for me, let me come to you, O Madhavi. If it be true that I have known no other except Rama, open your arms to receive me, O Madhavi!'

The earth opened up and from it rose a jewelled throne borne by four hooded serpents, their bodies gleaming with the treasures of the underworld, their domain. Seated on the throne was the goddess Madhavi herself, queen of the earth. She drew Sita into her arms and sat her down beside her. A rain of flowers showered the pair with colour and fragrance and the skies resounded with the blessings of the gods and celestials.

The throne began to descend under the astonished eyes of the multitudes who had gathered there. The riven earth closed over it and over the earthly life of Sita, queen of Ayodhya.

The world and all its creatures stood still for a moment in silent tribute to injured innocence.

14

The Realms of Brahma

Rama was shattered. Leaning on a sacrificial staff, he seemed bent and old and beaten as he stood weeping over his lost wife.Then he raged. He ranted and raved and shouted: 'Return Sita to me or take me with you. I know you well, you are my mother-in-law. You yielded Sita up to Janaka when he turned the earth with his plough. If I can cross the ocean and retrieve her from Lanka and the demons, I can rip you and get to her wherever she may be.'

He threatened: 'The earth shall cease to be, for I will flood you out of existence!' The assembly was stunned by the violence of his reaction. Brahma restrained him. 'Remember you are Vishnu the Preserver. This anger does not become you. You will join her in good time. Control yourself.'

Rama calmed down and heard Brahma say: 'Your future is clearly foretold in the concluding part of Valmiki's epic. Tomorrow, with a select band of sages, listen to it and you will know all, you who are the supreme ascetic.'

Rama then retired to Valmiki's hut and passed the night mourning for Sita. In the morning he summoned Kusha and Lava and asked them to sing the rest of the epic, so that he might come to know the workings of his destiny on earth.

After they had sung the concluding portion, Rama took leave of them all and returned to Ayodhya. He had to live out the rest of his life, which was now a stretch of emptiness. The desert of his days was watered only by the duties of ruling Kosala and the performance of sacrifices. This he did with fervour and devotion, the golden image of Sita ever by his side.

The queen mothers grew old and died, Kausalya first, then Sumitra, then Kaikeyi. The years rolled by and took their toll of life, of happiness. Rama reigned in all for eleven thousand years, years of growth and prosperity for the fortunate inhabitants of Ayodhya and Kosala.

There was a whole new generation of Raghus and their affairs had to be settled. Bharata's two sons, Taksha and Pushkala, were ready to shoulder responsibilities. Yudhajita, Kaikeyi's brother, sent news of a kingdom by the sea, inhabited by celestials. Rama asked Bharata to march with his young sons and annex the territory. The campaign was successful and Bharata established Taksha in Takshashila and Pushkala in Pushkalavata, two splendid capital cities. The expedition had taken him five years.

Lakshmana's sons came next, Angada and Chandraketu. Rama advised

him to look for a pleasant and peaceful region with little danger from hostile neighbours and rebellious subjects. With Bharata's help and Rama's the two were soon installed in two fortified cities—Angada in Angadiya, and Chandraketu in Chandrakanta. Having completed his task, Lakshmana returned to Ayodhya. Bharata stayed on for a year, till Chandraketu was firmly established and then, he too returned.

Bharata and Lakshmana served Rama through his entire reign. The three brothers glowed like steady sacrificial flames, bright with fame and glory and goodness.

Rama's days on earth were numbered. The spirit of Time, its ripeness, Death in the form of an ascetic, soon stood at the gates of his palace.

It was Lakshmana who received him. 'Tell Rama I come with a message from an all-powerful sage, the lord of them all.'

Lakshmana went in to announce him. 'There is a hermit who waits at the gates, a messenger who seeks audience with you. Radiance falls about him like the light of the sun.' 'Usher him in,' said Rama, sensing the importance of the moment, its grave significance. The ascetic came in, bringing light into a room already bright with Rama's presence.

Rama enquired politely: 'What message do you bring from your master? You come as an envoy I understand.' The sage hesitated. 'We must meet alone. An interruption will lead to dire consequences, for you yourself will have to kill the one who disturbs us, whoever he may be. My master demands the utmost secrecy, complete and inviolate.' Rama turned to Lakshmana. 'Dismiss the guard and stand at the door yourself. See that we are left undisturbed.'

The visitor watched Lakshmana leave and swung round to face Rama. 'I come from Brahma. I am Time or Death, call me what you will. The Creator has the following message for you:

'"Rama your task is done, your purpose accomplished. It is time to revert to your original form. Become once again Narayana of the Waters, resting on Ananta, the coiled and endless serpent that is the world. In that form you created me, Brahma, on the lotus that sprang from your navel as you reclined in the sleep of creation.

'"Your time on earth is over. You have ruled eleven thousand years. Now return to us."'

Death said: 'You may ignore the message and stay on a while if you wish.'

Rama faced Death readily and with confidence. 'I am glad you came. I would like to leave. Brahma is right. There is no reason to delay.'

As the two stood talking, the sage Durvasa arrived at the gates of Rama's palace seeking immediate audience. Lakshmana explained that Rama was busy and not to be disturbed. He was extremely polite and tactful, because everybody knew that Durvasa had a quick temper. It was no use. Durvasa flared up. 'I must see him at once, or else, I shall curse you, Rama, Bharata, the kingdom and your whole clan.' Lakshmana had no alternative. 'If I interrupt, only I perish. If I don't, all is lost.' He went in.

Rama hurried out to Durvasa. 'O Rama, I am famished,' said the sage. I have fasted for a thousand years. You must feed me straightaway.' Rama

presided over the meal himself. As the sage thanked and blessed him, Rama remembered what Death had said. Lakshmana would have to die and Rama would have to kill him!

Lakshmana was fully prepared. 'Do not grieve, Rama. You must honour your promise. It is the way of dharma.'

Rama called his council of priests and ministers. Vasishtha found a way out. 'Banish Lakshmana. It is as good as killing him. That is the best we can do. You cannot cheat Death. His word is law.'

Lakshmana left hurriedly, weeping at the thought of exile and separation from Rama. He did not even go home for a formal leave-taking. He walked towards the Sarayu, river of their childhood, and reining in his senses with his mind, he sat in meditation, his whole being directed inwards. He held his breath and waited till he grew invisible and was transported bodily to heaven. All that marked the departure of that great soul was a heap of flowers that rained on him in final benediction. He had joined the gods in heaven.

Rama's heart was broken and his spirit too. He had no further desire to live. 'I shall make Bharata king and leave for the forest. I shall follow Lakshmana.' But Bharata would not agree. 'Install your sons—Kusha in southern Kosala and Lava in the north. Send word quickly to Shatrughna. I too will leave with you.' He thought of his lonely vigil at Nandigrama and had no intention of going though another such ordeal.

The people of Ayodhya and his allies in the Lanka war, monkeys, bears and demons, also wanted to follow Rama. Events were moving to their destined end.

Two capital cities, Kushavati for Kusha and Shravasti for Lava, were planned and constructed with the utmost haste. Shatrughna had been informed and he made arrangements for his two sons to take his kingdom. His son Subahu ruled in Madhura and Shatrughati in Vaidisha. And then, with a single chariot, and no panoply, Shatrughna left for Ayodhya.

All of Ayodhya and most of the guests who had come for the Ashwamedha decided to leave with Rama. He did not try to stop them, and only made a few exceptions. 'Vibhishana, as long as my name endures, your empire will flourish. You must go back to Lanka.'

He had, as always, a special word for Hanuman. 'Whenever my story is told, gladness will fill your heart. Then think of me, my friend.' 'I will live, Rama, since you wish it, and to thy lasting glory.'

There was just one more fond farewell—to Jambavan, the ancient bear and veteran campaigner. 'You must live till the Kali Yuga, the fourth and final age of the current cycle of Time. We are now only in the second. That is thousands and thousands of years yet, my aged friend.'

At dawn Rama conferred with Vasishtha. 'Let the sacrificial fire, burning bright and pure, go before us, and the sacrificial awning too. You will lead the way.' Vasishtha busied himself making all the arrangements for the rites of departure.

Rama, clad in fine silk, reciting the Vedas, holding the sacred kusha grass in his hands, walked barefoot down the path that led to the Sarayu. On his right was Shri or Lakshmi, on his left, Bhudevi, Mother Earth.

His weapons came to life, assuming human form, and joined the procession. The sacred mantric syllables and incantations were with them too, vibrant, resonating on the tongues of the devout following of ascetics and learned men. It was a happy procession, a march of joy. No one wept or mourned, for they were with Rama, led by him to their destinies.

Not a leaf, not a creature stirred in Ayodhya. It was as if the city never was. The riverside wore a festive look. Aerial chariots and the heavenly hosts hovered over its banks, celestial music filled the air, a divine radiance flooded the skies and the breeze blew cool and fragrant.

Rama walked into the Sarayu and was welcomed by Brahma, and absorbed into his original form and substance, the lustre of Vishnu. He asked for a place for his multitudes of followers and devotees, and Brahma assigned them a celestial region, Santanaka, very near his own world, Brahmaloka. Sugriva, head held high, prepared to merge with the sun, his beginning, his element.

They all walked into the sacred river Sarayu, and stripped clean of their mortal bodies, were borne to worlds beyond our reach.

The Principal Characters in the Ramayana

Agastya: A sage associated with southern India who gave Rama weapons, prayers and blessings at crucial moments in his life.
Agni: The god of fire.
Ahalya: Wife of the sage Gautama, cursed by her husband for infidelity. Rama releases her from the curse.
Aja: Father of Dasharatha, king of Kosala.
Akampana: A demon messenger of Ravana.
Ananta: The serpent on whom Vishnu, the Preserver in the Hindu triad of gods, reclines.
Angada: Son and heir apparent of the monkey king Vali of Kishkindha.
Angada: Son of Lakshmana.
Anshuman: Grandson of King Sagara, ancestor of Rama who went in search of his 60,000 uncles.
Bhagiratha: Son of Dilipa, ancestor of Rama. He found the remains of the 60,000 sons of Sagara, and then managed to bring the river Ganga down from the heavens to sanctify their remains.
Bhagirathi: Another name for Ganga, after Bhagiratha had brought her down to earth.
Bharadwaja: A sage who lived close to Ayodhya.
Bharata: Son of Dasharatha and Kaikeyi and brother of Rama, who reluctantly accepted the crown and ruled for 14 years during Rama's exile.
Bhudevi: Goddess of earth.
Brahma: The Creator in the Hindu triad of gods.
Chandraketu: Son of Lakshmana.
Dadimukha: Uncle of Sugriva, and guardian of Madhuvana, Sugriva's pleasure garden.
Dashagriva: Literally, 'the ten-necked one' — another name for Ravana the demon King of Lanka.
Devarata: An ancestor of Janaka, from whom he inherited the great bow of Shiva, later strung and broken by Rama. This feat won him his bride, Sita.
Dhumraksha: A prominent demon of Lanka.
Dilipa: Son of Anshuman, father of Bhagiratha, ancestor of Rama.
Dundubhi: A buffalo-demon, enemy of Vali.
Durvasa: A sage, known for his impatience and quick temper.
Dushana: Ravana's brother.
Gadhi: Father of Vishwamitra.
Gaja; Gavaksha: Prominent monkeys in Sugriva's camp.
Ganga: A heavenly river who came down to earth and the nether regions as a result of King Bhagiratha's penance.
Garuda: Vishnu's mount; a giant, fabled eagle.
Gautama: A sage, and husband of Ahalya.
Guha: King of the Nishadas, a feudatory tribe of Kosala, and a friend of Rama's. He helped Rama, Sita and Lakshmana to cross the Ganga.
Hanuman: Minister of Sugriva.
Heti: One of the two first rakshasas or demons created by Brahma.
Himavan: King of the Himalaya mountains and father of Ganga and Uma.
Ikshvaku: Illustrious ancestor of Rama. He was the son of Manu, the lawgiver. The dynasty is referred to as the Ikshvaku dynasty after him.
Indra: Chief of the gods.
Indrajita: Literally, 'conqueror of Indra'. He was Ravana's eldest son.
Jahnu: A sage who swallowed Ganga.
Jahnavi: Another name for Ganga when, after being swallowed by Jahnu, she was released through his ears.
Jamadagni: A sage and father of Parashurama, who questioned Rama and questioned his valour.
Jambavan: A wise and ancient bear, born of Brahma's yawn.
Janaka: King of Videha, and father of Sita.
Jatayu: A giant vulture and friend of Dasharatha.
Kusha: Son of Rama.
Kushadhwaja: Brother of King Janaka.
Lakshmana: Son of Dasharatha and Sumitra, brother and inseparable companion of Rama.
Lava: Son of Rama. Kusha and Lava were twins.
Lavana: A demon destroyed by Shatrughna during Rama's reign as king of Ayodhya.
Madhavi: Earth goddess, also known as Prithivi and Bhudevi.
Mahadeva: Literally, 'the great god'—another name for Shiva, the Destroyer in the Hindu triad of gods.
Mahodara; Mahaparshva: Ministers and generals in

Ravana's army.
Mandavi: Wife of Bharata, daughter of King Kushadhwaja.
Mandodari: Wife of Ravana.
Manthara: Kaikeyi's scheming handmaiden.
Manu: The lawgiver and first ancestor of Rama.
Maricha: Ravana's uncle. As a golden deer he was the fatal attraction that led to Sita's abduction by Ravana.
Matali: Indra's charioteer, lent to Rama in his fight against Ravana.
Nala: Engineer of the gods who helped build the bridge across the ocean to Lanka.
Narada: The wandering musician-sage who by his description of Rama, inspired Valmiki to compose the Ramayana.
Narayana: A name for Vishnu in his aspect as 'lord of the waters'.
Nikumbhila: Patron goddess of the demons of Lanka.
Nishadas: A feudatory tribe of Kosala.
Nriga: A king who was turned into a chameleon because of his habit of procrastinating.
Parashurama: Son of Jamadagni. He was a hater of warriors and kings and circled the earth 21 times, exterminating the warrior clans.
Prajapati(s): 'Mind-born' sons of Brahma. There were 12 of them. Not to be confused with Brahma who is also referred to as Prajapati.
Prahasta: Minister, commander-in-chief of Ravana's armies.
Pulastya: Son of Brahma and grandfather of Ravana—one of the Prajapatis.
Pushpaka: Aerial chariot made for Kubera by Vishwakarma; later acquired by Ravana.
Raghu: An illustrious ancestor of Rama. The dynasty is referred to as the Raghu dynasty after him, and his descendants as the Raghus.
Rama: Son of Dasharatha and Kausalya, his chief queen.
Rambha: Heavenly nymph on whom Ravana forced his attentions.
Ravana: Ten-headed demon-king of Lanka.
Ruma: Wife of Sugriva.
Sagara: Ancestor of Rama whose 60,000 sons were destroyed by the sage Kapila.
Sampati: Elder brother of Jatayu, the vulture. He provided the first clue in the search for Sita.
Sarama: Wife of Vibhishana, one of Sita's guards.
Shabari: An aged female ascetic who found salvation when Rama visited her hermitage.
Sharabhanga: One of the ascetics whom Rama visited.
Shardula: A spy sent by Ravana to Rama's camp.
Shatabali: A prominent monkey leader.
Shatananda: Janaka's family priest; son of Gautama and Ahalya.
Shatrughna: Son of Dasharatha and Sumitra, twin brother of Lakshmana.
Shatrunjaya: Rama's personal elephant.
Shrutakirti: Wife of Shatrughna and daughter of Kushadhwaja.
Shuka: Spy of Ravana.
Shurpanakha: Sister of Ravana.
Singhika: A demoness who waylaid Hanuman.
Skanda: Son of Shiva, also known as Kumara and Kartikeya.
Soma: The moon god.
Subahu: Son of Tataka, brother of Maricha.
Sudarshana: Vishnu's discus.
Sugriva: Younger brother of Vali.
Sumali: Ravana's grandfather.
Sumantra: Minister and charioteer of Dasharatha.
Sumati: Sister of Garuda and mother of Sagara's 60,000 sons.
Sumitra: Wife of Dasharatha and mother of Lakshmana and Shatrughna.
Surasa: Demoness who obstructed Hanuman on his way to Lanka.
Surya: The sun god.
Sushena: A monkey leader and father of Tara, Vali's (and later Sugriva's) wife.
Sutikshna: An ascetic whom Rama visited.
Taksha: Son of Bharata.
Tara: Wife of Vali and then of Sugriva.
Trijata: A demoness who guarded Sita in Lanka.
Tripathaga: Literally 'one who travels three paths' another name for Ganga.
Uma: Wife of Shiva.
Urmila: Wife of Lakshmana.
Vajra: Indra's thunderbolt.
Valmiki: Sage and composer of the Ramayana.
Vamadeva: Sage and counsellor in Dasharatha's court.
Vamana & Varaha: The dwarf and boar incarnations of Vishnu respectively.
Varuna: God of waters. In Vedic times god of justice and morality.
Vasishtha: A sage and chief priest and counsellor in Dasharatha's court.
Vayu: God of wind.
Vedavati: Sita, in a previous incarnation.
Vibhishana: Brother of Ravana.
Vinata: Mother of Garuda and wife of the sage Kashyapa.
Viradha: A demon killed by Rama.
Virupaksha: A prominent demon of Lanka.
Viryashulka: An appellation of Sita, meaning 'prize for valour'.
Vishnu: The Preserver in the Hindu triad of gods.
Vishravas: Father of Kubera and Ravana.
Vishwakarma: Architect of the Gods.
Vishwamitra: An ascetic who sought Rama's help in ridding his hermitage, Siddhashrama, of demons.

Notes on the Colour Plates

No. 1 (facing page 2): *Valmiki and the Heron*
The sage, Valmiki, grieves over the bird killed by the hunter's arrow. A symbolic representation of the origin of the verse form in which the Sanskrit Ramayana is composed.

No. 2 (facing page 10): *The Slaying of Tataka*
Rama's slaying of the demoness is his first encounter with the forces of evil. In their natural form these forces are normally represented as hideous and of disproportionate dimensions.

No. 3 (facing page 20): *Rama Bends the Bow of Shiva*
The bending of the bow is not just a trial of strength but serves to reveal the divinity in Rama, a divinity also hinted at in the colour of his skin—the blue of the god Vishnu—and in the prayerful attitudes of King Janaka and the sage Vishwamitra.

Sita dressed in bridal red waits with the marriage garland.

No. 4 (facing page 30): *Kaikeyi, Manthara and the King*
In the Hindu tradition a wife greets her husband fully adorned. Kaikeyi's dishevelled appearance in this picture and her scattered jewels are therefore a forceful message to her husband, the king.

Note also the drab creeping figure of the envious Manthara whose attention seems, significantly, fixed on the jewels.

No. 5 (facing page 38): *Dasharatha kills Shravana*
The calm and verdant green of the landscape, and the peaceful attitude of the young ascetic by the river, underscore the randomness and senselessness of the killing. Dasharatha's clothes intrude an arrogant and martial note into the tranquillity, as he shoots the arrow towards the sound.

No. 6 (facing page 50): *Bharat Enthrones Rama's Sandals*
Although the traditional symbols of kingship are shown around the throne: the *chhatri* (the umbrella-like shade held above royalty) and the lion-faced pedestals, Bharata's feelings of worship are reflected in the lamp and the heaped offering of flowers which are more appropriate to a shrine.

No. 7 (facing page 66): *Ravana Deceives Sita*
This is an example of the Indian tradition of narrative painting; the story of the three-fold deception is told within one frame. Thus we see, simultaneously, Rama's hunting of the false deer, Lakshmana's response to the cry imitating Rama; and Ravana's appearance in disguise.

The sombre colours of the foliage show the reaction of nature to the presence of evil; the deer's deceptive sparkle is shown in lighter tones.

No. 8 (facing page 76): *The Princes go to Sugriva*
This painting brings out the heroic personality of Hanuman as well as his semi-divine attributes. Red, the colour Hanuman's body, symbolizes his towering strength and valour. In the Hindu convention, idols of Hanuman are smeared with vermilion and oil.

No. 9 (facing page 86): *The Gathering of the Monkeys*
The bright, fresh colours and lively movement in this painting reflect the childlike exuberance and innocent playfulness of the monkey clan as they gather with offerings for their king, Sugriva.

No. 10 (facing page 102): *Ravana Torments Sita*
Sita's posture of complete withdrawal contrasts here with the arrogance of Ravana's stance as he makes overtures to her. Note Sita's unbound hair and drab clothing—appropriate for a virtuous wife separated from her husband.

No. 11 (facing page 120): *Rama Storms the Ocean*
This painting depicts the only moment in the epic when Rama departs from his noted control and moderation. Hence the chaotic motion of the waves which reflects the turbulence and violence of his mood.

No. 12 (facing page 144): *The Defeat of Ravana*
The contrasts, in this painting, of bright and dark colours, Rama's upright stance and Ravana's toppling heads, spell out the theme of good triumphing over evil, and the ultimate supremacy of divine powers over demoniac forces. Note the depiction of the *brahmastra*—fashioned from wind, fire, sun and space—that is a moral force as much as a warrior's weapon. Note also the emphasis on circles which have multiple and powerful cultural connotations: the wheels of karma and dharma and the God Vishnu's weapon, the discus.

No. 13 (facing page 150): *Agni Vindicates Sita*
Agni, the god of fire, is the supreme witness to all solemnities, as well as the great purifier. Here he bears witness to the purity of Sita—herself the embodiment of virtue.

No. 14 (facing page 154): *The Coronation*
More than the crowning of a mortal this painting reveals the divine consorts enthroned in glory. Rama has returned to his original divinity as the god Vishnu with Sita as the goddess Lakshmi. This concept is reinforced by the bright halo and the prayerful attitudes of the worshippers.

No. 15 (facing page 160): *Sita and her Sons*
The twin princes in their cradle show their divine antecedents in the colour of their skin: the blue of the god Vishnu. The sage Valmiki holds a handful of the sacred Kusha grass from which the princes' names originate. A festoon of flowers and mango leaves is hung to celebrate their birth.

No. 16 (facing page 168): *The Messenger of Brahma*
This picture is conceived as a visual hymn of Rama's return to the ultimate effulgence of his cosmic form.

NOTE

The small black and white picture that runs through the book is of Narada, the divine messenger, and the sage Valmiki, the composer of the epic.